P9-CFF-683

Grand Passions
and
Broken Hearts

Grand Passions and Broken Hearts

Lives and Lusts
of the Great Composers

Basil Howitt

 Robson Books

First published in Great Britain in 1998 by Robson Books Ltd, Bolsover House, 5–6 Clipstone Street, London W1P 8LE

Copyright © 1998 Basil Howitt

The right of Basil Howitt to be identified as author of this work has been asserted by him in accordance with the Copyright, Designs and Patents Act 1988

British Library Cataloguing in Publication Data
A catalogue record for this title is available from the British Library

ISBN 1 86105 158 1

All rights reserved. No part of this publication may be reproduced, stored in a retrieval system, or transmitted in any form or by any means, electronic, mechanical, photocopying, recording or otherwise, without the prior permission in writing of the publishers.

Phototypeset by Intype London Ltd
Printed in Great Britain by
Creative Print and Design Wales, Ebbw Vale

CONTENTS

To fellow musicians everywhere,
especially those who are struggling
to pay their way in such difficult times

Overture

Libidos Anonymous, Sexual Recovery Anonymous, Sexaholics Anonymous, Sex and Love Addicts Anonymous, Recovering Couples Anonymous . . . Four men in this volume – Paganini, Tchaikovsky, Sir Arthur Sullivan and Puccini – would, if they were alive today, be eminently suitable candidates for treatment at one or more of these astonishing New Wave clinics for sex addicts across the pond. So would countless other composers. Suffice it to mention, purely at random, Sibelius, who was described by a fellow student in Vienna as 'the worst skirt-chaser of us all'; Bizet, who as a young man kept a diary 'containing little about music or people – other than prostitutes'; Glinka, who in the early 1840s moved about from one European city to another 'pursuing women as though they were an endangered species'; and Schubert, who seems to have developed an addiction to transvestite Viennese rent boys.

High libidos are now believed often to correlate with high work rates, and the aforementioned quartet of composers in this volume certainly substantiate the claim. These men also enjoyed in their own day the idolisation or status now accorded to pop stars, and in varying degrees also testify to the undeniable potency of success and fame as aphrodisiacs and openings for seduction.

As we shall see, Arthur Jacobs has shown that the scrupulously and graphically logged orgasm counts of Queen Victoria's blue-eyed boy Sir Arthur Sullivan coincided spectacularly with the intensity of his work rate as a composer and mover-and-shaker in Victorian musical circles. Although researches in the cases of Paganini, Tchaikovsky and Puccini have not been so precisely correlated, readers will later be in no doubt that Tchaikovsky's addiction to what he called his 'damned pederasty' or 'natural compulsions' was at times insatiable. Especially when abroad, he was forever searching out adolescent prey in bordellos, bathhouses and other gathering places for promiscuous gays. As for Paganini, his goatish behaviour, be it with prostitutes or princesses, dwarfs the legendary libidos we read about of promiscuous pop idols, cradle-snatching business tycoons, certain notorious politicians (including a good many presidents of the United States), and countless monarchs over the centuries, not least our own Edward VII. In similar vein, Puccini, the only composer in this cluster of six who married, picked up 'chorus girls, waitresses and other readily available admirers . . . with as little emotion as the wildfowl on Lake Massaciúccoli'.

Many great creators in genres other than music seem to have been sexually very active in their preferred ways: at random, Shelley, Balzac, Tolstoy, Bertolt Brecht, Picasso, Bertrand Russell, Jean-Paul Sartre and Kenneth Tynan immediately spring to mind. So does Albert Camus, who once reportedly set up four different dates with four different mistresses in as many days when he was about to return to Paris from Loumarin in December 1959, having spent the summer there with his wife and children.

Creative drives can also replace rather than stimulate the libido, however. It appears that Mahler, in Edward Seckerson's words, 'sublimated through music alone, and that no-one, but no-one, could serve a higher purpose in his life than to act as an inspiration, a sounding board and a support for his creative tasks'. His wife Alma, a woman drawn compulsively to men of artistic genius, undoubtedly fulfilled this role. But as a beautiful, sexually active woman much younger than her husband who had notched up several lovers before her marriage, she inevitably eventually sought satisfaction elsewhere during it. (She insisted in her memoirs that Mahler was a virgin before their union.) Her affair with the aptly named architect Walter Gropius, whom she later married after Mahler's death, caused the composer intense pain during his last year.

Although Brahms seems to have been a frequenter of brothels, he was certainly no libertine. His life story, marked by much 'unhappiness, frustration, shyness, loneliness, self-doubt and lack of emotional fulfilment', reinforces one of my ever-strengthening impressions: that the most sublime music comes most often from men deeply unhappy in love. Certainly not *always*, though; Bach and Richard Strauss being two remarkable exceptions at opposite ends of the emotional spectrum. It seems that Brahms only really made love to womankind between the sheets of his scores in such

2

works as his 'sumptuously amorous' Double Violin Concerto. Beethoven's story, which has many similarities to that of Brahms except that he never doubted his own greatness, is perhaps the supreme example of suffering in love linked to sublime art. And although Haydn was sustained by an uncomplicated religious faith and enjoyed two substantial extra-marital liaisons which were creatively productive, the prevailing view of his later life was that '[his] rather unhappy and childless marriage is the reason he composed so much'. Such at least was the reminiscence of the Swedish musician J.F. Berwald who called at his home in Vienna in 1799. Taking just one more composer at random, the violinist Tasmin Little is in no doubt that the 'bitter-sweet beauties' of Delius's music were built on the tragedy of his early love life. In 1897, in the company of his wife of only a few months Jelka Rosen, he returned to Florida in an unsuccessful search for his love-child Frederick William whom he had fathered at the age of 22 by Chloë Baker, then a seventeen-year-old negro employee on his father's orange plantation. 'Knowing that he had a child and would never see it again must have been unbearable,' comments Ms Little. 'I'm sure the emotional crux of his music stems from this experience of lost love and lost offspring.'

And who knows? This prevailing alliance of unhappiness with great art may also be true of men and women – highly sexed or otherwise – who have painted, sculpted, or written novels, plays and poetry. Unrequited love certainly fuelled the creative fires of Dante, Petrarch, Shakespeare and Goethe.

There are, it is true, some very successful practitioners at the lighter, populist end of the arts business who lived or now live in conjugal bliss. Three who spring to mind in three different genres are that consummate purveyor of erotic light opera, Franz Lehár, the detective novelist Raymond Chandler and the painter Anthony Green. Lehár embarked on a long and happy marriage in his late twenties which must surely have stimulated the flow of so many irresistible tunes from his pen. Chandler replied to letters of condolence on the death of his wife Cissy (twenty years older than himself), that

> for 30 years, ten months and four days, she was the light of my life, my whole ambition. Anything I did was just the fire for her to warm her hands at. That is all there is to say. She was the music heard faintly on the edge of sound.

I cannot so far think of any great composer who quite matches the 'red-hot nuclear love' which the renowned painter Anthony Green professes and celebrates endlessly in his work for his 'darling Mary' and their children. 'Without her, I doubt I would ever paint another picture,' he said of Mary in a 1997 edition of BBC 1's *Omnibus*.

Mendelssohn was certainly happily married, although it is very doubtful whether his wife Cécile ever really supplanted his near-incestuous affections for his beloved sister Fanny, whose cruelly premature death so undeniably precipitated his own. It is in any case arguable that he peaked as a composer at the age of just sixteen with his String Octet and, shortly afterwards, with the Overture to *A Midsummer Night's Dream*. And indeed, there are those who have seriously argued that for all its ineffable tenderness, vitality and iridescence, his music would have gained in depth of feeling from his exposure to an ecstatic and angsty liaison, or to the torments of unrequited passion.

Wagner had a disastrous first marriage, and although he vowed to his second wife Cosima that 'everything is yours before I write it', their marriage was most definitely on his terms; it didn't stop him determinedly pursuing 'on the side' his ego-boosting muses, notably Judith Gautier and, right into his seventieth and final year, Carrie Pringle. Even the Mozarts' half-dozen or so years of evident conjugal passion seem to have disintegrated into infidelity on both sides in the last two years of their marriage. In any case, Mozart was, according to some leading scholars, a manic-depressive and his wife, Constanze, was very much second choice to her elder sister Aloisia who had ditched him.

Richard Strauss, however, perhaps busts my theory. Arguably the composer of the world's most powerfully erotic and, at times, near-pornographic scores, he lived in life-long monogamous adoration of his wife, the fabulous singer Pauline de Ahna, in spite of her sharp temper and scolding tongue. The love he expresses for her in the music of his wedding present, the *Four Songs* Op. 27 (does a more rapturous, melting song than 'Morgen' exist?) is undimmed, for instance, thirty years later in his opera *Intermezzo* (Op. 72) in which she appears thinly disguised as Christine, and he as Robert Storch. Strauss is said to enshrine Pauline's very soul in this opera, in an A flat major Interlude of surpassing beauty.

Notwithstanding these observations, the subtle and complex connections between life and creativity remain elusive. 'What is the relationship between a composer and his music?' asks Jim Samson in the preface to his recent *Chopin* in the Master Musicians series.

> In other words, how do we draw the process of composition into the centre of biography, where it surely belongs? Or to put it the other way round, how can a composer's life explain his music? . . . Too little is yet known about the mental processes involved in composition to allow any but the most obvious connections to be made. Primary causes remain stubbornly elusive.

Alexander Poznansky has similar thoughts in his enthralling psycho-sexual biography of Tchaikovsky:

> A work of art nearly always obscures and transcends the experience that gives impetus to its composition. Still, from the point of view of creative psychology, the two realms must necessarily be connected, however mysteriously or unpredictably.

The related and vexed, although endlessly fascinating aesthetic question of what music 'means' and whether it is an 'abstract' or 'programmatic' art is outside the scope of this overture. But in all this, one thing is certain. Some composers have made it clear that their music is spiritual autobiography; that in it they are revealing their deepest feelings about their relationships with particular women or men, about their love lives in general, and about their view of the human condition.

Berlioz is perhaps the most obvious of all cases. Some time after temporarily exorcising his demonic obsession with the Irish actress Harriet Simpson in his *Symphonie Fantastique* (which came with an explanatory programme), he wrote on the title page these lines from a poem of Victor Hugo:

> My heart's book inscribed on every page . . .
> All I have suffered, all I have attempted . . .
> The loves, the labours, the bereavements of my youth.

So much of Brahms's music also bears, in Eric Sams's words, 'the unmistakable undertone of autobiographical fantasy', albeit more covertly. To take one less obvious example, Clara Schumann is embedded, in what is known as the Clara-motif, in the very engine-room of the First Symphony. Initially, the motif appears in an inner part played by the bassoons and cellos, but later it becomes crucially important at the climactic point in the movement. Brahms was not seriously exaggerating when he attributed all of his inspiration to this remarkable woman with whom he had such a complex and almost certainly unconsummated relationship over nearly 43 years.

> By rights, [he once wrote to her] I should have to inscribe all my best melodies, 'Really by Clara Schumann'. If I just think of myself, nothing clever or beautiful occurs to me. I have you to thank for more melodies than all the passages and such things you take from me.'

Tchaikovsky was equally emphatic that his music was the key to his love life. In an answer to his patron Mme von Meck as to whether he had ever been in what he identified as 'non-platonic' love, he replied that he answered that question first and foremost in his music; that he had 'repeatedly tried to express in my music the torments and bliss of love'. (He certainly experienced much more of the former than the latter.)

On a lower plane (so some would say), that Czech composer of hypnotic schmaltz Zdeněk Fibich (1850–1900) poured out his passion for the writer Anezka Schulzová in his piano pieces *Moods, Impressions and Reminiscences* and his symphonic idyll *In Twilight* (which includes the famous Poème). Fibich left his wife and children for Schulzová in his early forties.

One could go on and on, but there is no further need to make the point that Orsino's famous opening words in *Twelfth Night* apply in reverse – that Love is very much the Food of Music.

It is a pleasure for me to express my thanks to a few of my friends who in one way or another were midwives at the birth of this book. Valerie Langfield generously read through the entire manuscript and made countless corrections and suggestions, most of which I adopted without hesitation. Henriette Harnische and Clare Gallaway responded with unfailing patience to e-mailed requests for translations. And throughout the book's gestation, my clarinettist friend Philip Jones has been an untiring supplier of spicy snippets and lender of countless CDs. The latter enabled me to explore repertoire less familiar to me as a cellist who has done most of his professional playing in chamber and ballet orchestras rather than in large symphony bands.

I must acknowledge especially my deep indebtedness to the Tchaikovsky scholar Alexander Poznansky for his encouragement and help with my own chapter on the composer. What started as a simple request to Mr Poznansky for permission to quote from his *Tchaikovsky: The Quest for the Inner Man* led me to another of his books, *Tchaikovsky's Last Days*, which toppled, at the eleventh hour, my long-held view on the death-by-cholera vs suicide issue.

No writer of a book like this can work without heavy dependency on *Grove's Dictionary of Music and Musicians*. Its value in offering concise summaries of often very complex sequences of events and situations is inestimable. The same remark applies also to James Anderson's indispensable (and more affordable) crib, *Dictionary of Opera and Operetta*.

℘AGANINI

Baron and Knight of the First Class of the Order of St Stanislas

... a public life of super-stardom, a private life of loneliness and lechery, including entanglements with a Nymphomaniac, a Whore, a Harridan, a Minx and a Broken-Hearted Baroness ...

Born: Genoa, 27 October 1782
Died: Nice, 27 May 1840

I see that you've received the quartets ... Play them patiently and you won't find them bad. In Turin you will have suffered from the cold but not from boredom. There are lots of prostitutes there.
Paganini to his close friend Luigi Germi, 31 January 1820

Princess Elise did not always attend or else did not remain all through the concert, because my music placed too great a strain on her nerves.
Paganini to his friend and biographer Schottky

After having heard, seen, and spoken to me, she [Baroness Helene von Dobeneck] fell so much in love with me that she no longer knows any peace of mind and will die if she doesn't eventually get me. I've had the pleasure of knowing her nine months now.
Paganini to Germi, 30 August 1830

a person given to promising credulous girls to marry them with the object of accomplishing his libidinous aims, though he never had the slightest intention of honouring his promises ...
Lawsuit, Civic Archives, Genoa

Wherever he appeared he was at once encircled by a flying squadron of infatuated women.
Vienna correspondent of the *Harmonicon*, 1828

It is curious to hear people, especially women, talk about it [Paganini's playing]. Without any hesitation they give utterance to what are in fact confessions.
Goethe in a letter to Karl Zelter, 1829

The chisel was introduced between the table and the rib; a slight cracking noise–Paganini bounded from his chair. Every movement of the tool brought fresh beads of perspiration to the brow of the tortured man who loved this fiddle more than he cared for any other inanimate thing in the world. He said 'it was as if the chisel were entering his own flesh.'
Louis Vidal, quoted in de Courcy

More than in any other chapter, I am indebted here to a single source for information: G.I.C. de Courcy's monumental two-volume biography, Paganini the Genoese, which is universally acknowledged as the definitive work in English on this phenomenal maestro. Most of the unacknowledged quotations are taken from her book. I have also found very useful information in Alan Kendall's Paganini: A Biography.

Arguably the world's greatest-ever supervirtuoso of the violin, Niccolò Paganini is certainly the most hyperactive libertine to appear in these chapters. During his goatish late adolescence he rutted his way through a stream of slatterns and strumpets impossible to quantify. He continued in like fashion, and also vastly extended his social field of play, until at least his early forties, when for about four years he was cornered by an 'iniquitous beast' who bore him a son and, not unreasonably, made sure she emptied his wallet before releasing him from her clutches. His encounters and liaisons overall could well have exceeded the 130 or so of the legendary Giacomo Casanova, who was obviously capable of considerable finesse with his amours when so disposed. Whereas Casanova was a gourmet of love, Paganini, like Don Juan, was a priapic gourmand.

It was probably during Paganini's late adolescence that those beckoning, raddled, street-corner Annetas, Cecilias, Carolinas, Marias, Paulinas and all the others, who did such good business in an era when nice daughters didn't, or weren't supposed to, passed on to him (and his comrades) the *morbo gallico* or 'French disease' that was to wreak such havoc in 'the long Calvary of his later years'. One wonders what he (in common with so many other composers) made of the tell-tale lentil-sized pink marks on his mouth or penis when they first surfaced, turning quickly as they would have done so into the size of sharply defined small coins, drab red; or of his swollen glands and the non-itchy rashes that almost certainly erupted a few weeks later on his face, palms and soles. Probably very little. (The Italian association of syphilis with France derives from its importation thence by soldiers of Charles VIII at the end of the 15th century.)

Throwing off parental constraints at the age of eighteen in

1801, Paganini first based himself in Lucca, where he made a stunning impact at the Festival of Santa Croce, playing a concerto lasting 28 minutes at the end of the Kyrie during Pontifical Mass. He then settled into a life of composing, teaching, leading the new national orchestra, solo concertising – and heady debauchery, or 'heaping pleasure upon pleasure', as he himself described it, heavy gambling included. Certainly temptation in Italy was everywhere, according to the French writer Henri Beyle (Stendhal) who noted 'the inviting and easy manners of the women, openly flaunting their lovers like their arms and breasts in the modish Roman costumes that revealed all their physical charms'.

Paganini's 'delicious moments', as he once called them, came to encompass the entire social spectrum: princesses, ladies-in-waiting, baronesses, gentlefolk, singers, seamstresses, *demi-mondaines*, doxies – they all, according to location, either stripped off, or adjusted their paraphernalia of hoops and petticoats, and whipped off their drawers for him – perhaps for a quick gavotte, even, as his coach trundled homewards after a gig. The only difference sometimes was who paid whom. It is generally assumed that Napoleon's sister, the slender, short, black-eyed nymphomaniac Princess Elise Baciocchi, installed by her brother in the Palazzo Provinciale as ruler of Lucca in 1805 when she was 25, gave the maestro a priceless Florentine mosaic and a diamond ring for services 'off the record', as well as for his sensationally successful *Napoleon Sonata for the G string* dedicated to her in 1807. Paganini was in her service initially as the Court's Concert Master, and also became a Captain of the Royal Gendarmerie and member of the Princess's bodyguard, attired in appropriate resplendent uniforms.

The mutual admiration society later turned sour and, feeling underused and inclined to cock a snook at court etiquette, Paganini quit her service in 1809 to take up a career as a 'free artist'. De Courcy has effectively scotched the story that they later got together again for old times' sake when they were both in Trieste in 1816.

At the other extreme, when he was in Paris as he entered his fifties, Paganini himself stumped up no less than 16,000 francs for a diamond solitaire of $34\frac{1}{8}$ grammes, 'mounted in gold setting', possibly for a baroness he had ditched, or for a certain Charlotte Watson, of whom more later. Certainly this eighteen-year-old hussy was also the proven recipient of various inducements to join him in an abduction pathetically disguised as an elopement-of-mercy from London in 1834: a diamond ring reset in solid gold setting, a diamond cross weighing 12 carats, earrings weighing 8½ carats, another article weighing 4½ carats, all totalling £367 17s . . .

Although capable of extreme generosity – invariably to all members of his family, and notably to the struggling and demoralised Berlioz with a gift of 20,000 francs (then two years' decent income) after hearing his *Symphonie Fantastique* and *Harold in Italy* in 1838 – Paganini the multi-millionaire could certainly be mercenary and tight-fisted. It is easy to picture him during his exhausting years on the road – what he called his endless 'wanderings of Ulysses' through Europe between 1828 and 1834 – driving a hard bargain with the pock-marked ladies of the night in the murky red-light zones of Vienna, Hamburg, Berlin, Munich, Warsaw, Prague, Paris, London . . .

Perhaps the convenient availability of the whores as much as his parsimony determined his well-known preference for grotty digs over grand hotels. We read in de Courcy that he would spend most of the day before a gig resting up in a darkened room, or, in later years, 'sitting in the twilight in a trancelike absorption, lost in melancholy broodings over his rapidly declining health and the brief time still before him'. According to his reliable secretary-manager George Harrys who joined him for a month in 1830, Paganini was a lone wolf with a genius for solitude, which is just as well because he never had a satisfying, enduring relationship with any woman. His uncontrollable lechery did, however, drive him into prolonged and scandalous scrapes and entanglements at various times in his life with a whore, a harridan and a minx. Only once in his youth does he seem to have had a genuinely reciprocal love affair, which came to nothing, with a devoted young dressmaker named Eleanora.

According to a certain Dr Julius Siber, writing in 1914 in the *Jahrbuch für Sexuelle Zwischenstufen* (Annual for Variations in Sexual Behaviour), our hero was also attracted to men, though how he could possibly have found time or energy for them defies all conjecture. Dr Siber cites, not altogether convincingly, the following characteristics of Paganini as bearing the indisputable hallmarks of the homosexual: 'hysteria, tendency to tears, irritability, carelessness in dress, vanity, femininity, the mania of posing as sick in order to arouse the sympathy of others, and his negative reaction to women'. Certainly Paganini's closest friend for some 30 years Luigi Germi, a professional lawyer and amateur musician, seems to have meant more to him than any of the women he bedded. The warmth of his letters to Germi – I love you with all my heart' (1820); 'I adore you' (1824); 'I feel a void in my heart. If you were near me I should be happier' (1825) – is matched nowhere in his rafts of letters to Germi about his *amourettes* and affairs. Feelings of similar intensity were reserved only for his mother, who seems often to have told him of her dream that an angel had prophesied a meteoric career for her little Niccolò, and for his son Achilles, born on the wrong side of the blanket but legitimised in 1837 and ever 'an unspeakable comfort' to his father. Of the latter Paganini said to his first biographer Schottky, 'I love him very dearly and am almost jealous of him. If I should lose him, I should be lost myself, for I can't bear to be parted from him. And when I wake at night my first thought is of him'.

Paganini's personal claim to greatness as a composer rests primarily on his miraculous one-off masterpiece, the *Twenty-four Capricci for violin alone* (Op. 1), though there are those who feel that the bravura variations *Le Streghe* (Witches' Dance, Op. 8) are also a remarkable creative achievement. Otherwise, his compositions are essentially 'skeletal frameworks upon which to hang his personal brand of virtuosity'. Nevertheless they are invariably seductive in their easy-listening mix of dazzling bravura and luscious streams of melody.

The glittering *Capricci*, inspired by Locatelli's *L'arte del violino* (1733) which also contains the same number of solo caprices, are technically imaginative and audacious to the point where virtuosity and creative inspiration are inseparable. One-off they may be, thanks to Paganini's congenital mental indolence, but their effect on so many other composers has been truly remarkable. The *Capricci* have sparked off important works by Chopin, Schumann (who was especially overwhelmed by Paganini), Liszt (perhaps his pianistic counterpart), Brahms, Rachmaninov and Lutoslawski. Countless lesser mortals (depending on your point of view, of course) have also been inspired by them, including Andrew Lloyd Webber (*Variations for Cello and Rock Band*), John Dankworth and Benny Goodman.

His unique contribution to the expansion of dazzling violin technique is, of course, beyond any doubt. The Frankfurt orchestral director Carl Guhr made a close study of Paganini's armoury and mentioned especially such innovations as ricochet bowing (any number of notes in one thrown and bouncing down-bow or up-bow), double-stopped harmonics, the use of left hand pizzicato, very individual fingerings, and the revival of *scordatura* (retuning the strings for special effects). Totally at variance with today's practices, Paganini manipulated the bow exclusively with his forearm and wrist, holding his upper arm close to his body.

The extraordinary flexibility in his left hand 'spider fingers', enabling him to execute near-impossible double trills up to the octave, and the laxness in the wrist of his right side enabling such prodigious bowing feats, may have been due to a rare condition known as Marfan's Syndrome. At least, that's according to Dr Myron R. Schoenfeld, writing in the *Journal of the American Medical Association* of January 1978.

Given the appalling syphilitic consequences of his lechery, not to mention his other severe illnesses, it is amazing that Paganini lived out a lifespan of nearly 58 years. His tough constitution and his grim, limpet-like grip on life somehow enabled him to endure more than twenty years on a wrack of ever-intensifying torture – though it is hardly surprising to discover that he appears to have contemplated suicide. He took a prescription 'for shortening one's life' with him to Vienna in 1828, at the start of his six years of gruelling European schedules that were to shatter his health completely.

Besides syphilis in all its stages (well advanced by his late thirties), his toll of other diseases included pulmonary tuberculosis (originating probably from childhood) and laryngeal tuberculosis. From 1838 he suffered bouts of aphonia, or complete loss of voice, which in any case was said to sound like a 'cracked pot'.

As was so often the case in those days, the incapacitating treatments for his syphilis, including bleeding, doses of opium, mercury, the Roob cure (a powerful fruit syrup laxative) and the then notoriously shattering Leroy's Cure of drastic purgatives and emetics, achieved little beyond harrowing side-effects. The core of the Leroy philosophy was to reject bleeding, the use of leeches, mercury, quinine and dieting, in favour of the

> only one effective medicine: the purge – loosen, remove, refine, rarify, expel, clean, purify, eject the material that irritates and aggravates.

The most random sample of Paganini's sufferings and symptoms over the years is horrifying: severe diarrhoea; bloated stomach; acute, agonising coughs and suffocation attacks when 'one could hear him inhale a block away'; a cadaverous complexion retained after an illness in 1822; jaundice; mouth infections (arising from the mercury treatment), including foul ulcers, excruciating abscesses, sloughing of the jawbone, and loose teeth 'literally hanging by a thread', just enough to enable him to masticate; halitosis 'that would fell a hippo'; intestinal disorders from the age of twenty, probably nervously induced . . . the list goes on! All these were aggravated by his many emotional crises and highly strung temperament and could stop him treading the boards for months at a time.

Let two graphically detailed extracts of Paganini's dire medical history taken from letters that he sent to Germi serve for scores more in similar vein:

[Prague, 1828] I started the cure with the waters [at Carlsbad] but was seized with a fearful inflammation of the salivary glands caused by the ulcerated root of a left molar, the pus having destroyed the bone internally. Forty-eight poultices day and night for a month and a half were of no avail in reducing the inflammation. Meanwhile, I can never describe my suffering to you . . . I placed myself in a chair, rigid as a statue, and they operated on me, armed with a huge needle, scalpels, and scissors. My intrepidity surprised the professors.

[31 Jan 1837] For the moment I'm taking certain powders that tend to diminish the tenesmus [continual tendency to evacuate bowels or bladder] and I'm introducing graduated tin catheters into the bladder to draw off the urine. I'm now at No. 3. As soon as I reach No. 6, he will introduce a medicament at the neck of the bladder so as to enable me to draw off the urine without an instrument, that is so that I can void urine naturally and freely.

Why did the Women Go Gaga?

He threw me into hysterics. I delight in him more than I can express – his wild ethereal figure, rapt look – and the sounds he draws from his violin are all superhuman.
Mary Shelley, author of *Frankenstein*

It seems at first surprising that a man with such leprous symptoms in the close-up zone should have been so irresistible to so many women. However, our own obsessions with personal freshness were surely unknown in that perfumed, painted, powdered and pomaded insanitary world where running hot water and daily showers were unknown. Smelly breath, unsavoury armpits and sniffy private places must have been par for the course in both sexes, and especially perhaps among troupes and artistes travelling endlessly in boiling hot summer weather! Perhaps the heavy use of perfumes by both sexes was then as much to smother bodily odours as to enhance personal attractiveness.

Be that as it may, power and wealth have forever been the most potent aphrodisiacs. The mere fact of his being the greatest star of his time – achieved by market-driven tactics like generally doubling normal ticket prices wherever he went, and insisting on a 60 per cent box office take – was enough to secure Paganini a constant stream of women. In January 1829, for example, he predicted he would net about two million lira in total (perhaps £750,000 in today's money) from his planned European travels (over six years), and he earned £10,000 *then* from just eighteen concerts in London in 1831. By the end of his life he had not only racked up fabulous sums of money in the bank, but also acquired a collection of 22 priceless instruments, including twelve Strads and two Amatis, and a vast iconography of jewels, ornaments, portraits, manuscripts and all the rest.

'The German beauties . . . are head and ears in love with me,' he wrote, quite believably, to Germi in 1830 from Baden-Baden. Some two years earlier the Vienna correspondent of the *Harmonicon* wrote that 'Wherever he appeared he was at once encircled by a flying squadron of infatuated women', reporting also the mania for Paganini memorabilia satisfied in every conceivable form of merchandise, from lithographs, china cups, gloves, fans, walking sticks, hats, loaves, and snuff boxes, to sonnets and cheap and cheerful *objets d'art*. There were even hairdos 'à la Paganini'.

There was far more to his woman-appeal than his mere billions of lire. Any Tom, Dick or Harry with enough money can pull women enough – but not necessarily princesses and baronesses as well as gold-diggers and rough trade. We must look also to the mysterious chemistry between this 'emaciated black puppet' (as Schubert and his circle thought of him in his standard garb of shabby black frock coat and long trousers, with a coloured waistcoat), and his fiddle – a chemistry essentially unfathomable, it seems, like love itself, in spite of the oceans of ink consumed in the effort to pin it down. A chemistry he perhaps slowly divined during his endless hours of practice in childhood, when he was even deprived by his father of food if he failed to maintain the punishing regime imposed on him.

As soon as his infinitely precious Guarneri del Gesù was under his chin Paganini became a magician, a necromancer, a 'weaver of spells and enchantments' – over men as well as women, of course, but crucially over the latter. 'But to tell you the truth, there emanates from my playing a certain magic that I can't describe to you,' Paganini wrote without false modesty to Germi from Bologna in July 1818. And from London in 1832: 'I regret that there is a general opinion among all classes that I'm in collusion with the Devil' – a point made many times, of course, by many people, including a Dominican monk in Venice whose bishop banned Paganini from profaning the cemetery on the Lido with his free performances there. In Harold Schonberg's words, 'he did everything except come wrapped in a blue flame'.

With any musician the sound is the man, is the soul of the man – if he has one. Every single player lays himself bare every time he scrapes, blows or bangs his instrument. Was it perhaps the soul, the spirit, the very essence of Paganini – demonic or otherwise – streaming through his violin with such incandescent intensity that seared so many female hearts and dissolved them into puddles? In Paganini's own typically prosaic words to Germi in a letter of 3 August 1830, 'when they hear the language of my music, the lilting cadence of my notes makes them weep'.

Perhaps, also, for women there was something very attractive about a man who was so completely self-assured and devil-may-care about what he was doing; someone who was utterly in control, in the sense of having his audiences in the palm of his hand. And for those women who became attached to him, however temporarily, the reflected limelight would also have been irresistible.

As an ardent lover himself of many women, Germany's greatest ever poet, Goethe, understood the maestro's effect on them. Here he is writing to the Leipzig musical guru Carl Zelter in 1829, after hearing Paganini in Weimar:

For this pillar of flame and cloud, I lacked a base for what one calls enjoyment, which for me always hovers somewhere between the sensuous and the intellectual. I only heard something meteoric and then couldn't account for it. Yet it is curious to hear people, especially women, talk about it. Without any hesitation they give utterance to what are in fact confessions.

The poet Heinrich Heine, so often breathtakingly poignant, whose lyrics were the favourite choice of many composers from Schubert (in his late works) to Richard Strauss, waxed beautifully about 'this man whose music evoked thoughts of love; this mysterious conjuror who

> looked as though he had risen from the underworld ... Is that a living being who wishes to delight the audience at the moment of his dissolution, or is it a corpse that has arisen from the grave, a vampire who sucks, if not the blood from our hearts, at any rate the money from our pockets?
> ... All doubts and mystification ceased as soon as the wonderful master raised his violin and drew the bow across the strings – such music as the ear has never heard – such music as the heart alone can dream when one rests at night in the arms of the beloved ...'

As if he needed further assets as a lady-killer, Paganini was also a keen and practised dancer!

Off duty, Paganini, like many brilliant practising musicians, was essentially a very ordinary man, happiest (his lust duly sated) when talking shop in the company of other players. He had no wider cultural aspirations. He was the sort of man who would nowadays while away some of his free time doing the crossword in the evening paper, or manoeuvring model trains or toy soldiers, with a packet of Woodbines to hand.

On Stage

'It is enough to make you lose your mind!'

Paganini's smash-hit appearances in Berlin in 1829 were the high point of his German tour which spanned two years. In fact they were probably the zenith of his entire career. Many vivid eyewitness reports help to sharpen our sense of these occasions and of the enigmatic genius at the centre of them. Here is an account from one of the cultural doyennes of Berlin high society, Mme Rahel Varnhagen von Ense, whose illustrious salon was one of the intellectual centres of the capital. She pinpoints neatly the maestro's baffling mix of the pantomimic, the preternatural and the sublime:

I heard Paganini on Wednesday . . . he plays far better on a single string than on all four. More correctly, surer, cleaner, more Italian, more audaciously and therefore with more *élan* and dramatic accent . . . He really doesn't play the violin – he doesn't have the tone (or tones) of Rode, of Durand, of Haack, of Giornovichi – but he actually talks; he whimpers, imitates a thunderstorm, the stillness of the night, birds that descend from heaven but do not soar towards heaven – in short, poetry. In the prayer from Rossini's *Moïse*, he plays the different voices as they enter one after the other, and then all together . . . I swear to you that I was forced to repeat again and again the words of the harpist – '*Wer nie sein Brot mit Tränen ass*' [*Who never watered his bread with tears*, from Goethe's *Song of the Harpist*] – to shudder, to weep. It was the very embodiment of the poem. But enough of that. The stalls were *not* inclined to applaud him, *but they simply had to*! I saw persons in front of me break out into applause who had hissed when he was welcomed. The court, the whole audience clapped. Everyone has to admire him even though it maybe only astonishment. He looks old, worried, starved, and good-natured. The bows with which he acknowledges the applause date from the dark ages! Everybody laughed – he too. Pantomime along with it – but modest on the whole.

In Berlin, Paganini bewitched even the most stiff-necked, po-faced critics A.B. Marx and Heinrich Ludwig Rellstab, never men remotely to be swayed by popular opinion. Here is a snippet from Marx's review in the *Berliner Musikalische Zeitung* of the same concert, which was given before the king and all the royal family, and 'about eighty titled ladies and a large contingent from Leipzig':

The man appeared to be bewitched and had a bewitching effect; not alone on me, or on this or that person – *but on everybody*. He came out on the stage and plunged at once into the *Ritornelle*, in which he conducted the orchestra and shot the orchestral texture with dispersed sparks of tone like shafts of lightening – then to pass into the most melting and daring melody ever heard from a violin. He sails nonchalantly, unconsciously, over all technical difficulties, interspersed with the most audacious flashes of satirically destructive humour till his eyes take on the glow of a deeper, darker passion, the tones become more penetrating and onrushing so that it seems as though he were lashing the instrument . . . Then he stamps his foot and the orchestra rushes in and fades away in the thunder of the unparalleled enthusiasm of the audience, which he scarcely notes, or acknowledges with a contemptuous glance or a smile in which his lips part in a strange way and show his teeth. He seems to be saying you *must* applaud me, whoever or whatever I am, or whatever mood comes over me in my pain or with whatever fetters my feet may have been burdened, which have lamed the happy, dauntless step of youth . . . This was not violin playing, this was not music – it was witchcraft – and yet *still* it was music only not the kind to which we are accustomed.

And here is Rellstab in the *Vossiche Zeitung*.

Never in my whole life have I heard an instrument weep like this . . . I never knew that music contains such sounds! He spoke, he wept, he sang! . . . After the concluding trill, a wild ovation broke loose . . . the ladies leaned over the balustrade of the balcony to show they were applauding; men stood on the seats the better to see him and call out to him. I have never seen the Berliners in such a state! And this was the effect of a simple melody!

Next, a report which highlights the knockabout music-hall clowning that Paganini 'descended' to in his late twenties, driving his more downmarket Italian audiences wild, and surely making the women go weak at the knees. It comes from the pen of the writer and archaeologist Jacques Boucher de Perthes, in a letter to his father from Leghorn on 9 February 1810:

I've told you of an Italian with whom I made music at Prince Baciocchi's. He's just been giving some concerts here which have been a *succès fou*. He's a Genoese by the name of Paganini and is self-taught; therefore, he plays like nobody else. But he spoils his playing by *pantalonnades* unworthy of the art and his fine talent. I've heard him add a *point d'orgue* [a cadenza in this context] to a concerto of Viotti's in which he imitates a donkey, a dog, a rooster, etc. Sometimes, at the beginning of a number, one of the strings breaks. You think he's going to stop but he goes right on playing on three strings. Then he plays variations on the G string. Where he excels is in his arpeggios, multiple stopping, and a pizzicato that he produces with the left hand. He then performs a *mélange* of all these things. It is enough to make you lose your mind! The Italians – who love these *tours de force* – applaud him like mad and, when he leaves the theatre, three hundred people follow him to his hotel . . .

And then sometimes, we can be sure, his chosen belle followed him to his bedroom.

Finally, here are two portraits, notably sober and precise, of the man on- and off-stage by the chief magistrate of Raguse (Dalmatia) Matthäus de Ghetaldi. Ghetaldi is describing his meetings with Paganini on a visit to Venice in 1824 when the maestro was almost 42:

[2 October] After the concert we chatted for a long time with Paganini, who was very exhausted. Probably because when he plays, he uses his whole body; and he is physically very weak. While playing he gave the beat continually with his left foot, which was very disturbing. Then he would bend the upper part of his body, and straighten up, again. Twice he waved his bow in the air and made fearful grimaces. I think he's a charlatan even though he's very accomplished. His style of playing pleases the people enormously. In the evening he showed his left hand to Dr Martecchini (who had just arrived from Trieste). It's astounding what he can do with it; he can move the joints laterally and can bend the thumb back till it touches the little finger. He moves his hand as flexibly as though it were without muscles or bones. When Dr Martecchini remarked that this must be the result of his mad passion for practice, he flatly contradicted him. Yet every child knows that he still practices seven hours a day, only his vanity won't let him admit it. However, Dr Martecchini stuck to his guns whereupon Paganini began to rage and shout, calling the doctor a thief and a robber. It was very unpleasant but we had to laugh . . . How he can have such a demonic effect in the concert hall is beyond me. When he tore round the room swearing, he looked very ridiculous. Later, he quieted when Mme Bianchi [Paganini's mistress] arrived round ten o' clock. He then showed us some astounding tricks on his violin. For instance, he plays a melody with two fingers while he plucks an accompaniment with the three first fingers. It often sounded as though three people were playing. His passages in double stops are dazzling, and I've never heard anyone run over the strings so fast . . . Then he imitated a donkey, a parrot, and a thrush – all wonderfully natural. This annoyed Messier Naldi, who whispered to me that that was something for the village fair but not for the concert hall. Later, Dr Martecchini tried to play on his violin and found, to his astonishment, that it was completely out of tune. Whereupon Paganini simply doubled up with laughter, and said that he always played on a mistuned violin.

Ghetaldi continues, crucially, in a later letter, to reveal Paganini's out and out mercenariness at its worst:

> As a man he is incredibly disagreeable, impolite and impertinent. He showed Dr Martecchini some little tricks on the violin and then charged him a high fee for this lesson, though he was Dr Martecchini's guest for weeks, and the latter also treated Bianchi for nothing when she was ill . . . He spends practically nothing though he earns a lot. He lives with acquaintances and takes his meals with friends and is always bringing strangers along with him.

As to Paganini's occasional impoliteness, or even impertinence, on one occasion he turned up at a very posh *conversazione* – definitely a full evening dress occasion – at the house of one Count Perucchini, in an outlandish yellow nankeen coat over a black suit. Yet at the same time he was obsessed with his status to the point of ridicule. In 1832 he bought himself a title 'as empty as his violin' of Baron and Knight of the First Class of the Order of St Stanislas from an exiled and impoverished German princeling, Frederick IV of Salm-Kyrburg.

Love as the Food of Music

As a Romantic composer Paganini is unusual in that hardly any of his droves of women inspired him to compose. Unlike, say, Schumann, Brahms and Berlioz, whose works were endlessly inspired by romantic longings or attachments, Paganini's love life impinges hardly at all on his compositions. He regarded writing music as a commercial enterprise rather than as any kind of soul-baring or mission statement. But one rare exception is his *Duetto Amoroso* of 1807 for a high-born lover at the court of Princess Baciocchi, the genesis of which he himself succinctly described to his friend and reliable first biographer Professor Julius Schottky whom he first met in Prague in 1828:

> Princess Elise did not always attend or else did not remain all through the concert, because my music placed too great a strain on her nerves. However, another charming lady ['he mentioned her name' added Schottky in parenthesis] who was attracted to me – or at least so it seemed – never missed them, while I had admired her for a long time. Our interest in each other gradually increased, but had to be concealed, which only intensified it. One day I promised

her a surprise at the next concert – a little musical prank having reference to our relations. At the same time I announced to the court an amusing novelty entitled 'Scena Amorosa' [later known as *Duetto Amoroso*]. Everyone was very curious till I finally appeared with my violin, from which I had removed the two inner strings, leaving only the E and the G strings. The first string represented the girl, the second the man, and then I began a sort of dialogue depicting little quarrels and reconciliations between my two lovers. The strings first scolded, then sighed, lisped, moaned, joked, expressed delight, and finally ecstasy. It concluded with a reconciliation and the two lovers performed a *pas de deux*, closing with a brilliant coda. The musical Scèna received great applause. The lady for whom it was intended rewarded me with the most friendly glances; as for the Princess, she was extremely gracious, overwhelming me with compliments and at last saying: 'Since you have already performed something so beautiful on two strings, couldn't you let us hear something on one string?'

The movements of the *Duetto* were: Flirtation; Request; Consent; Timidity; Gratification; Quarrel; Reconciliation; Love Token; Notice of Departure; Leave Taking.

Princess Elise's suggestion was duly taken up and resulted in the famed *Napoleon Sonata for the G string* – and, of course, the above-mentioned present. This commission marked the beginning of the maestro's life-long predilection for the G string.

De Courcy suggests that the enamoured recipient of the *Duetto* was probably the princess's beautiful lady of honour, Mme Laplace, dutifully emulating her royal mistress in her cavalier disregard for monogamy!

Musical Gallantry

Paganini did, however, make many acts of gallantry in the form of inscriptions, in words or music, which may well have hastened his entrée to upmarket boudoirs and bedrooms. When he was in Birmingham, England, in 1833 the 21-year-old authoress Louisa Anne Twambley sent him, after hearing him play, a 'rapturous poem' entitled 'Extemporaneous Sonnetta, with variations, composed for, and dedicated to Baron Paganini' (published in a volume of her poems in 1835). This brought him 'immediately to her feet', the maestro responding by presenting her with a suitably inscribed picture of himself and by writing the first eight bars of his *Campanella Rondo* in her album.

He was even more effusive to a Mrs Benjamin Curtis, wife of a wealthy American silk merchant in Paris, writing in her autograph album: 'O Love – why ignite this sweet flame in my breast if you are then to rob me of this dear object?' And to a Mme d'Obrée he wrote rather clumsily: 'How happy the original of this second portrait would be if he could express orally what the pen can never utter.' There was also an unknown lady in London who received this 'inflammatory' dedication on 29 July 1832: 'If some day it will be granted me to know the adorable object who will preserve the present [portrait] I shall esteem myself happy.'

Paganini seems never to have been very at ease with the written word, though when it came to eye contact and body language there were obviously few to equal him.

Marriage-itis: Carolina Banchieri and Others

... a person given to promising credulous girls to marry them with the object of accomplishing his libidinous aims, though he never had the slightest intention of honouring his promises ...

Lawsuit, Civic Archives, Genoa

For a rake to bed an unmarried girl from a respectable family invariably meant having to dangle the promise of wedding bells, and it is amazing how often Paganini the nympholept voiced transient notions of blissful matrimony. His interest was often as short-lived as a male pigeon on heat. On spotting a hen, he would puff himself up and strut about her, only to see another, marginally more attractive, and flutter to her, the original one quite forgotten.

Thus he wrote to Germi on 10 October 1818, of a certain Marietta from Bologna whom he adored:

I told her ... that no other city means so much to me as Bologna ... a city that will be blessed for me if Heaven lets me unite my destiny forever with that of my darling Marietta ...

She is very soon displaced in his affections! On 4 November he has gone off the idea of marriage and is asking Germi's advice on how to break the news of his 'indifference' because another has stolen his heart. On 23 December he writes from Rome:

Yesterday evening I saw the most beautiful Englishwoman, to whom

I lost my heart on the spot, but when I learned that she was a Jewess, I sighed and could almost have wept, knowing that a union was virtually impossible ... the young lady in Bologna, who is sighing for me, sees from my last letter that I've cooled off a bit so she wants to know the reason. Tell me what to say to her. I don't want to tell her that she no longer occupies my thoughts, but I've got to tell her something.

Here is another passing fancy from Palermo in 1820:

[31 January] In Naples I made the acquaintance of a very charming girl of eighteen, beautiful as an angel, with the education of a princess and a heavenly voice and an interpretative gift that bewitches everyone. She sings divinely and her name is – guess! Catalani, daughter of one of the leading and most successful lawyers in Naples. The young lady would gladly marry me but I don't know if her parents would consent, because the Neapolitans don't like to see their daughters leave home. Well, we'll see. I too will think it over before tying myself up. *Liberty is the best of all things.* [Libertas optima rerum!]

In August 1820 he reports from a Naples sweltering in heat:

The other day I saw a nice young girl in a church and I fell a little in love with her. I followed her to see where she lived. She's the daughter of a notary. What do you advise? Shall I marry her or remain a bachelor?

Inevitably his repeated enthusiasms did not go unnoticed and were the stuff of wild misrepresentation: a notice in the Vienna *Allgemeine Musikalische Anziger* of 15 August 1829 announced that he had actually married a young lady of 21 with a dowry of 130,000 francs who 'had long been in love with him'.

There are more brief spasms of conjugal speculation in a letter of 30 August 1830 when another two women are considered:

As for myself I often think of marrying! In Frankfort, I asked the most charming girl to marry me. She's the daughter of a businessman, not rich, yet well off. However, upon reflecting that she is too young and beautiful, and doesn't love music – or rather, has no music in her soul – so that she wouldn't be able to dedicate herself to me except under false pretences, I'm beginning to abandon the idea.

It would be far more fitting if I should marry another ...

However, the most colourful of these fleeting episodes reveals him to be the real bounder he was in these matters. It concerned a young lady named Carolina Banchieri whom he seems actually to have promised to marry purely in order to have his wicked way. He wrote to Germi from Naples on 22 June 1821:

> I have finally decided to follow the dictates of my heart and also of my station and take a wife – a charming girl, the daughter of a most excellent family, who combines beauty with the most thorough education, has really touched my heart and, though she has no dowry, it has pleased me to choose her and be happy with her . . . If you could make an arrangement with the parish priest of S. Salvatore and it were possible to put me on the sunny side of forty, it would please me immensely . . . You know my nature and can well understand the physical orgasm that has taken possession of me, excited by the most hypersensitive nerves and an exalted imagination. Now, if you don't want me to be devoured by desire carry out my wishes with the utmost despatch, and crown the sweet destiny that is in store for me . . . I'm looking forward to presenting my Venus to you and making you confess that Paganini shuns mediocrity in everything . . .

And again on 10 July:

> I see indications everywhere that God wants to make me happy in this way . . . Heaven seconds my desires . . . You, my mother, and whoever sees the object of my affections cannot help but admire her and join in with me in praising heaven for having created a girl embodying all the physical and moral graces.

When he finally managed in early winter to persuade her to join him on a trip from Naples to Rome, after a formal betrothal, his lust was obviously sated for good within four days!

> For you alone I'll say that I found that object a real *sans-souci*, who disappointed me on every score; which is why I freed myself after four days which seemed like four years to me.

He was careful to cover his traces, though, by bribing an accomplice to lie through her teeth:

> She's now with a peasant who will swear to everyone that she's been with her from the very moment she left home, so maybe in this way they'll think that nothing has occurred.

It had all been 'an elaborate ruse to break down maidenly defences'. Formally engaged couples were often allowed to live together.

The Whore, The Harridan, and The Minx

The 'Wily and Tenacious' Whore: Angelina Cavanna

– a tale of pinkish white powder, Divine Providence, and a loaf of spiced bread –

Paganini certainly took on more than he bargained for when at the age of 32 he was hooked for a trick back home in Genoa, in 1814, by the prostitute Angelina Cavanna. He had returned home from Milan where he had enjoyed a triumphal debut – a 'furore' – in 1813 with his brilliant and sensationally popular *Le Streghe* variations, followed later by eleven more concerts. It was in Milan and other cities that Paganini sowed his wildest oats; in his own words enjoying life 'in rich, full draughts' with heavy gambling, 'little love affairs', and, we can be sure, heavy drinking. Altogether he was to roam around Italy on and off for some 27 years between first establishing himself in Lucca in 1801 and venturing north to Vienna and beyond in 1828.

The Angelina story, recorded in vivid detail in the city archives, upstages the creakiest and most far-fetched *opera buffa*. Accomplished amorist as he was, our hero met his first known come-uppance. The whore's father eventually had him arrested for rape and abduction and thrown into gaol. The ensuing shock-horror court cases, held in camera, were packed with suits and counter-suits as convoluted as a huge bowlful of well-tossed *spaghetti carbonara*.

Recognising that her famous punter had fallen for her charms, and was almost certainly good for a few grand, Angelina, aided and abetted by her tailor father, refused him any further 'business' until a promise of marriage was made. Thinking she was a push-over, Niccolò, according to Angelina's father, enticed her into the room of a convent school 'under the pretext of more readily reaching an agreement regarding the proposed marriage' and there enjoyed 'anything but platonic relations with her'. He then rushed her off to Parma in the diligence only to become alarmed after a few weeks by her bouts of morning sickness. Taking advantage of Angelina's ignorance – she thought she had worms – Paganini gave her some pinkish-white powder he had obtained, told her to swallow it mixed with sweetened barley water, then gallantly left her to it for the day. Alas, this supposed anthelmintic caused her to vomit repeatedly and she gave the maestro a very hard time indeed when he returned. More drastic measures were now called for, so he told her that the police had instructed him to send her home. Believing him, but preferring to go to her sister's wet nurse in the Polcevara valley, Angelina submissively consented to be bundled off there in great haste without even her belongings, which Niccolò promised 'to bring her in a few days'. De Courcy and the archives continue:

> 'He gave her a loaf of spiced bread for the journey' and this, according to her father, was 'all she had to live on for several months in Fumeri, where she almost died of hunger and cold in the hut of charitable but miserably poor people . . . a couch of straw here served as a bed and every day she had to dry her chemise and tattered clothing before the fire because the rain had dropped down on her all night through the leaky roof. Indeed, she would have perished had not Divine Providence revealed her whereabouts to her disconsolate father who hurried to her and found her in a half-dying condition.'

The following May, 1815, Signor Cavanna lodged rape, abduction and breach of promise charges at court and the real fun started. Paganini was arrested and clapped in the Tower. He immediately confessed to elopement but not abduction, asserting that Angelina had been a willing accomplice in his plans. His lawyer Figari proved that Angelina was twenty rather than eighteen and then delivered his glorious opening salvo, claiming that the girl's father

> had turned her out on the streets to earn her living; that she was free to go out alone both day and night; that profiting from such liberty, she had often been seen at advanced hours of the night in public dance halls with foreigners and soldiers, unaccompanied by any member of her family; that the neighbours had frequent cause to complain of her conduct and that she was the object of a great deal of gossip; further that while residing in her father's house she received callers clandestinely at suspicious hours; and on several occasions had passed the night away from home, in places of ill repute, even during her friendship with Paganini . . .
>
> *Testimoniale di Remissione*, 28 September 1815, and *Testimoniale di Presentazione di Comparsa*, 31 November 1815. Civic Archives, Genoa

Naturally, Cavanna's lawyer retaliated, claiming that Paganini

> was a person given to promising credulous girls to marry them with the object of accomplishing his libidinous aims, though he never had the slightest intention of honouring his promises . . . that her reputation was now ruined and she could no longer follow her profession or hope to find a husband, to say nothing of the heavy expense to which her father had been subjected during her pregnancy and her dangerous and difficult confinement.

The upshot of all this was that Paganini was released from his eight-day spell in prison on condition he paid out 1,200 lire in two stages. However, he in fact paid out nothing until the verdict on a counter-suit he had initiated was delivered. In the mean time, somewhat bafflingly, he resumed cordial relations with the Cavannas and promised to marry Angelina and provide for the child – which proved however to be stillborn. In yet another twist to the plot Paganini now tried to wriggle out of all his responsibilities, thus provoking Cavanna into initiating a new chain of writs which were, of course, followed by counter-writs. It was at this point that his Germi appeared on the scene as his adviser. Alas, Germi's legal skills didn't match his reported talents as a musical amateur and Paganini ended up the loser. After a protracted series of stalling devices were finally routed, the Court ordered him two years later to pay out 4,400 lire including costs.

Did this case of a breach of promise featuring an Angelina, wonders de Courcy, have anything to do with W.S. Gilbert's *Trial by Jury*, also featuring a jilted Angelina?

The Harridan: Antonia Bianchi, 'an iniquitous beast'
a 'sordid story'

Antonia Bianchi was a much bigger thorn in Paganini's flesh than Angelina. She bore his only child and he was saddled with her for some four years before she finally released him from her clutches after securing a satisfactory settlement.

He first probably met Bianchi in 1824 while convalescing in Como, where she lived. By then he had acquired his cadaverous look following his first serious illness in 1822, which came in the wake of a busy period on the road in Italy from 1816, one highlight being his expert conducting at short notice of the final rehearsal and first two performances of Rossini's *Matilde di Shabran* in 1821.

Vivacious, good-looking, and a very decent singer, Bianchi made an immediate impact on the ever impressionable Niccolò when they met. In 1824 she accompanied him as his pupil and supporting act or 'guest *virtuosa*' for concerts in Milan, Pavia and Genoa, where she would have met his family. She was also his mistress, of course, in the time-honoured manner of travelling artists. After Genoa they made an extended tour of Venetia and the towns on the Adriatic, then continued via Naples to Rome, arriving there in early 1825. Not surprisingly, she had by this point become pregnant and inevitably started to dig her claws into her 'terrible weird man'. They went back to Naples, returned again to Rome, then took a sea journey to Palermo where on 23 July Antonia bore, on the wrong side of the blanket, a son, Achilles Cyrus Alexander. Paganini was to lavish untold affection on Achilles for the rest of his life, particularly after nursing him through his recovery from a broken leg while he was still a toddler. (The choice of names may have been influenced by French revolutionary theories Paganini assimilated in his youth, when parents were urged to give the future heroes of the republic the names of the heroes of antiquity.)

To be fair to Bianchi, her position was far from envious and it is hardly surprising that she gave him a very hard time. At no stage did Paganini show any inclination to make an honest woman of her. At the first whiff of matrimony he 'shied away like the bronco that hears the swish of the lasso'. And his prolonged ill-health at this time (he had a fierce cough and suffered acute attacks of suffocation arising from influenza and catarrhal fever) can only have weakened or killed off her limited reserves of affection for him. A later remark Paganini made to Germi implies that the couple stopped having sexual relations in 1826. De Courcy sums up their situation:

> As sensual passion subsided, sharp differences in character manifested themselves. On her side, avarice, inordinate ambition, and overweening jealousy. On his, reckless self-indulgence, harshness, with probably a touch of cruelty, brusqueness, and tremendous pride.

The family threesome were together for less than three years, with Bianchi becoming ever more career-minded, fractious, and prone to violent tantrums. Paganini's letters to Germi provide endless vignettes of domestic havoc. 'His repeated scenes with Bianchi were alone sufficient to keep all his organs in a chronic state of spasm,' says de Courcy, and no wonder:

> [Paganini to Germi, 17 December 1825] . . . By the way, Bianchi, who's still with me, has one great fault. She flies into a rage over nothing. The other evening she took my violin case and banged it up and down on the floor four times till she smashed it to pieces, just because I didn't take her along with me to a merchant's where I only had to go for a quarter of an hour on business. Fortunately my manservant grabbed it, or rather tore the violin from her hands, and saved it; and by a miracle I found it safe and sound, though a little shattered.
>
> [Later, while out visiting friends]
>
> Bianchi interrupted us (I think from jealousy perhaps) and asked me to take her home. On my asking why, she gave me a violent slap, accompanying it by infernal shrieks that shocked all the company. She screamed till she nearly burst, and none of us thought she would come to her senses.

In early March 1828 they set off in a brand new travelling carriage to cross the Alps for Paganini's grand tour of Europe, arriving in Vienna for his first concert at the Redoutensaal on 29 March. The maestro's hopes that visiting new countries in a round of concertising might soften the lady's hard and brittle edges were dashed. She gave him no peace until she had secured a life annuity from him of 100 Milanese scudi. By mid-April 1828 they had parted on bitter terms, and by mid-August Paganini had renegotiated a one-off settlement on her of 3,531.02 florins (10,953 lire) and had obtained legal custody of Achilles. Bianchi returned to Italy where she married a Signor Brunati in 1830 and never saw Achilles or his father again.

Bianchi can in no wise be criticised for relentlessly pinning him down. He was, after all, a shyster in these matters and would have had no qualms in summarily dumping her if he could have got away with it. As well as being sexually frustrated, Bianchi would also have resented Paganini's hogging of the limelight at their concerts, and also her exclusion, being only his mistress, from the aristocratic circles into which he was frequently invited, especially in Vienna. (Marie d'Agoult felt similarly snubbed when she came to England with Liszt as his mistress in 1840 and was likewise excluded from royal circles.)

Paganini's memories of Bianchi remained bitter and painful. He wrote to Germi on 5 July 1828:

Bianchi has been separated from me for some time because she is an iniquitous beast and I never want to hear her name again. But I'll tell you the rest when things are more tranquil.

And later, from Berlin in 1829, to the Milanese banker Carlo Carli who helped bring Bianchi and Brunati together:

My friend, it's just when I'm ill that I realise what an advantage it is to me not to have her about! Whether through lack of heart or intelligence, at such times she never did anything she should have done. I don't wish to reopen at this time the many painful wounds. The wretched creature never wanted to practice or do anything at all. When she had to undertake even the slightest task, she complained that I treated her like a slave. She told God and all creation of her ignominy. I tried in vain to restrain her; but again and again everything she did provoked me. This sad story would be too long and painful to relate here. When I met her she was an insignificant little singer and I taught her so that she could appear in concert. She had scarcely a rag to her back. Now she has a magnificent wardrobe, jewels, and money in the bank! She embittered my life as long as she was with me and now that I'm rid of her she has, as I know, only one aim in life – to blacken my character. Honourable men will judge between us. To a friend like yourself I wanted to explain my position once for all – not to justify myself, but to relieve my feelings.

Deep down it is just possible that he actually loved her, and may have been bruised by the rupture. Certainly, nine years after their parting he left her an annuity in his will of 1,200 lire.

Interestingly, living openly over the brush with Bianchi didn't prevent Paganini from receiving, from Pope Leo XII, the Order of the Golden Spur on 3 April 1827. He was thus following in the footsteps of Gluck, Mozart, Morlacchi and Liszt.

The Minx: Charlotte Watson

This 'thoroughly frigid, calculating little minx', with 'a beautiful, laughing, Hebe-like face, [Hebe was the goddess of youth and spring] irradiated by a bewitching pair of eloquent blue eyes', had the distinction of being the woman to monopolise Paganini's attention exclusively for longer than any other woman – a total of seven years. Theatre gossip soon had our hero, pushing 50, losing his marbles to yet another singing pupil and assisting soloist – whose singing was described by French critic Fétis as 'not entirely bad'. She was just sixteen when they met, and the story of their notorious and botched elopement is another penny dreadful, here stripped to the bare bones.

It is clear that Charlotte used the great man to further her own career and showed no signs of falling for him. They had first met in 1831 when her father John Watson, a palpable rake, had become Paganini's rather wayward and incompetent manager for his first English tour. Very possibly illegitimate, Charlotte was chaperoned, somewhat incongruously, by her father's mistress and singing pupil, Miss Wells, and was the recipient of the expensive jewels mentioned earlier. Paganini's name first seems to appear with the two singing ladies at a concert at the Lion Hotel in Shrewsbury in August 1833.

In 1834, the year of the decline and end of Paganini's inter-national career, Charlotte, still chaperoned, accompanied him first to Paris, and then, as his assisting soloist, on a tour of the Low Countries, which included a disappointing reception in Brussels but some enthusiastic receptions elsewhere. As well as being out of practice, having injured the third finger of his left hand while cutting some cheese, Paganini was also, according to Fétis, in need of 'that repose [which] is sometimes necessary to the greatest of artists'. His touring days were over anyway. Few would want to be slogging it on the road at the age of 52, no matter what the rewards.

He returned to England to give some poorly attended London concerts, which included a début on his viola, and followed these with a brief provincial tour which proved to be a wash-out, due partly to Watson's penny-pinching promotion. Watson actually ended up in the debtors' prison and Paganini, no doubt after pleadings from Charlotte, bailed him out.

Before leaving London again for the Continent, the rascal set up an elaborate elopement plan with Charlotte, arranging a rendezvous in Boulogne. It seems that Paganini set out on 21 June 1834, and that Charlotte left her home the following morning, pursued, unsuccessfully, by Watson *père* 'in his slippers'. Watson then made haste to Boulogne and arrived there on the packet before his daughter, much to the consternation of the waiting maestro 'and his followers', who beat a hasty retreat. Watson immediately sought out the co-operation of the French police and the British Consul. When Charlotte arrived at the port the next day, according to Watson's version of events to the press,

> a dramatic scene took place in the custom house. Paganini's valet rushed forward and attempted to seize Miss Watson, whereupon the police and gens d'armes beat the fellow out with their staves and muskets. Miss Watson was then conveyed to the Royal Hotel, and in the morning the consul escorted father and daughter to the packet, and saw them depart. On her return to London, Charlotte saw her error and repented her indiscretion – for, happily, it was no more, of which she has been guilty.

A long report of the scandal which appeared in Boulogne's *L'Annotateur* on 26 June sparked off a sequence of shock-horror stories on both sides of the English Channel. Once again in desperate straits as a result of his insatiable libido, our agitated hero summoned the assistance of an Irish friend, one Cornelius Marcus Sempronius O'Donaghue (*sic*), 'Ensign of the late 18th Royal Irish', to play spin-doctor and help him clear his name. With O'Donaghue's eloquent literary assistance, Paganini issued the following hilarious apologia, casting aspersions on Watson's probity and trying to disguise his own tacky designs as honourable intentions:

> Mr Watson and a Miss Wells (who is not his wife), along with Miss Watson (his daughter), entered into an agreement with me to give some concerts together. This contract (which in no way ruined M. Watson, since he had been in this condition for some time) I not only fulfilled to the letter but contrary to my own best interests. On my last journey to London, I was obliged to pay the hotel bill, which ought to have been met jointly. In settling our accounts I reduced my share 50 pounds, which sum Watson still owes me. When he was imprisoned by his creditors for the fourth time in five years, I paid 45 pounds out of my own pocket to secure his release. By the terms of my contract I was entitled to a farewell 'benefit' concert, but at his request . . . I waived my right and gave one on his daughter's behalf so that his creditors could not seize the receipts, reserving for myself only 50 pounds. His daughter turned over to him 120 pounds as the net takings of this concert.
> This, Sir, was the way I treated Mr Watson, whose antecedents, as I learned only too late, are so indicative of his character. In fact, he is a man who for fifteen years has allowed his lawful wife to suffer

abject misery in Bath, a man who drove from home a son whose mother would have looked on the latter's death as a blessing in concealing from him the infamy of his father – a man who treated his daughter in the most inhuman way and in whose presence he lived a life of disgraceful licentiousness, this man – of whom I am now only presenting a faint sketch – does he merit the slightest consideration and the credit you accord to his slanderous tales, which you call *official information?*

I now come to the charge of abduction, through which he wishes to give the impression that an *amourette* was what impelled Miss Watson to join me at Boulogne. On seeing that this young woman had decided musical talent, which her father could not afford to cultivate, I suggested taking her as a pupil, assuring her after three years' study she would be in a position, with her gifts, to make herself independent and be able to help her family, particularly her unhappy mother. My offers, turned down one moment and accepted the next with lively expressions of gratitude, finally came to nothing. I left England, renewing to Watson my offers of assistance to his daughter.

After pointing out that Charlotte was treated as a base menial with 'the heaviest housework' to perform, he emphasised that

to get away from it all she came to me *of her own accord* to ask protection from one whose counsels and benevolence had encouraged her to hope for a brighter future. Thus I did not abduct Miss Watson, as her father has dared maliciously to accuse me; for if I had had that criminal intention, nothing would have been simpler since while Watson was in prison his daughter was free and alone because Miss Wells went out every night to join the prisoner . . . Now after this did you conscientiously think that a young woman, maltreated by her father and an outsider who has no claim on her, need continue to bear the burden of such a humiliating existence? Is Miss Watson not justified in leaving such a disorderly and depraved household? And do you not see that in shamelessly coming here with his confederate, Miss Wells, to take back his daughter, Watson again cynically insulted public morals under the guise of asserting his parental rights?

The letter was published, but its effect enfeebled by the editor questioning the truth of Paganini's allegations and pointing out that his scandalous track record gave him little right to impeach the morality of others. Paganini had the last word, correcting the editor on the point that Miss Wells most certainly *did* accompany

Watson to Boulogne, disembarking the boat wearing 'a yellow straw hat and a green coat with which I am perfectly familiar', and that Charlotte 'joined me because I intended to marry her and give her jewels and a handsome dowry'.

Yet suddenly, as in the Angelina case, within a matter of a week or two Paganini was able to make his peace with Watson 'as if nothing had occurred'. Was the whole furore, indeed, a manufactured publicity stunt? In the middle of July Watson whisked Charlotte off to New York, whither Paganini sent his friend Urbani on the steam packet *North America* in December to negotiate a marriage proposal! This having failed, Germi was entrusted with the negotiations, emphasising that the maestro would like Charlotte to become a Roman Catholic! Alas, matters dragged on too long for Charlotte, who married a Mr Bailey in 1837, causing Paganini to abandon his own projected trip across the Atlantic.

Charlotte became a star turn in New York, appearing at Niblo's Garden where her 'fair face and lovely voice' had 'susceptible New York of all ages and sexes at her feet' during the summer (according to Paganini) and where the following winter she did a season at the Park Theatre. In following seasons, she and 'her bulky stepmother' Miss Wells (who presumably had become Mrs Watson) were 'immensely popular drawing cards' until the end of 1839.

Paganini's troubles were still far from over. When he arrived in Paris from Boulogne he had to face a barrage of criticism in the French press, led by the young critic Jules Janin in the *Journal des débats*, over his alleged refusal to give a charity concert for the flood victims of St-Etienne. And later, in 1837, he became embroiled in a disastrous Casino Paganini venture. Betrayed by his friends and advisers, he sustained considerable losses in a prolonged lawsuit which pursued him almost to his deathbed.

True Love, If Only Fleetingly

La Ragazza Eleanora

Undoubtedly Paganini's most serious and never forgotten love was his very first one. She was *la ragazza* Eleanora, a dressmaker considerably younger than himself, whom he first met while lodging with her sister and brother-in-law in Lucca after his arrival there at the age of eighteen in 1801.

Eleanora Quilici was clearly one of the most tender and loving memories of his life, the undoubted proof being that he later gave her money: 300 lire, certainly, in 1838 and very possibly on several other occasions as well, since she never married. He also remembered her in his will with an annual pension of 600 new lire. Whilst they were lovers Eleanora became the dedicatee of his Op. 3 compositions, comprising six of the twelve sonatas for violin and guitar he composed between 1802 and 1809: light-weight, certainly, but beautifully melodious and easy on the ear – real serenading music, although of course needing an exceptionally dab-handed performer.

> She was evidently [writes de Courcy] his first love (perhaps the magnet that drew him to Lucca!) – an experience that left him with tender memories that he always cherished; her girlish laughter, zest for fun, and some sweet, lovely quality in her devotion and surrender that was ever present with him and that from thenceforth drew him so strongly to young girls barely on the threshold of womanhood – a mixture of gratitude and penitence, perhaps.

The Broken-hearted Baroness: Helene Dobeneck

If his affair with Eleanora was a rare case of reciprocal feeling, we know for certain that the dusky, languid-eyed Baroness Helene Dobeneck broke her heart over him after he said a final goodbye to her when he departed for Paris from Baden-Baden in 1831, during his European tour.

A daughter of the famous criminal law theorist Paul Johann Anselm von Feuerbach, who seems to have spawned a family with more than its fair share of depressives and melancholiacs, Helene was a talented painter, portraitist, singer and composer and was locked in a loveless marriage of convenience to Baron von Dobeneck. After hearing and seeing the maestro in action in Nuremberg in October 1829, Helene was instantly felled and simply threw herself at him. Here is the 48-year-old Casanova recounting the adventure himself in some detail to Germi:

> [Baden-Baden, 30 August 1830] It would be far more fitting if I should marry another. This is the daughter of a famous (or rather *the* most famous) writer on jurisprudence in Germany (M de Feuerbach), a knight of many orders, the intimate counsellor of the

King of Bavaria, and president of the city of Ansbach. His daughter, whose name is Helene, is a baroness, having married a baron three years ago – but not for love. She is passionately fond of music and sings extremely well. She came to Nuremberg to hear me and begged her husband to bring her again to my second concert. After having heard, seen, and spoken to me, she fell so much in love with me that she no longer knows any peace of mind and will die if she doesn't eventually get me. I've had the pleasure of knowing her nine months now. She has a nice appearance and a most excellent education. Her letters, of which I have more than twenty-four, are worthy of being printed and are inspired by a sentiment far surpassing that of Heloise and Abelard. I have them all in Frankfort and if you'd like to see them I'll send you copies. In this young woman I should have a fine wife, Achilles an excellent mother. Meanwhile, read the enclosed letter.

Upon its receipt I went to Ansbach, where in order not to be recognised, I arrived at midnight and didn't go to the posting station but got out in the middle of the road, and under the assumed name of an architect of His Majesty, the King of Prussia, stayed three days at an inn without anyone remarking me, strange to say. The Baroness visited me there and I left again at night to return to Baden. I am so impressed by the sentiments of this lady that I must respect and love her. She has persuaded her father to get her a divorce in the hope of becoming my wife, and declares that she is ready to renounce all my wealth and wants only my hand! What do you say to that! It's very hard to find a woman capable – like Helene – of such love! True, when they hear the language of my music, the lilting cadence of my notes makes them weep. But I'm no longer young, no longer handsome. In fact, I've grown very ugly. Think it over and tell me what you think. She reasons like she writes. Her speech, her voice, are insinuating. She knows geography like I know the violin.

Alas, the maestro would not commit himself, either because he was insufficiently attracted to her or, 'ready as he was to "mesh his soul within a woman's hair", he had now at forty-eight', suggests de Courcy, 'laid aside his youthful fervour so that there was no longer the old tendency, as in his younger days, to be swept off his feet by some sudden attachment.' In addition Paganini, being very much a working musician with no intellectual or even creative aspirations, may have felt uncomfortable at marrying into a family so culturally and socially élite. Furthermore, although he was no model Catholic he may have been deterred by the Feuerbachs' rabid antipapism.

Poor Baroness Helene, having obtained her divorce, seems to

have pursued Paganini to no avail in Paris, and then continued to write to him for a further ten years. His death in 1840 triggered off a nervous breakdown, followed later by a conversion to Roman Catholicism and entry into a nunnery, where she failed to find peace of mind and aborted her noviciate. After years of aimless roaming, this sad, lost soul ended her life as a recluse in Treviso, dying at the age of 81.

The One Who Said 'No!' – Signora Lauretta
– 'a most unusual episode in his amorous career' –

One woman gets into the frame (we cannot possibly include them all by the way!) as being the only one to bug Paganini for a long time by actually refusing him or jilting him. To the maestro's pique, the singer Signora Lauretta turned out to be more interested in clandestine meetings with a painter named Carloni. She first turned him down in 1816 in Venice, where he had eyes for no-one else. In 1818 he told Germi that '[S]he's given up her music. She says she doesn't love me, that my friendship means nothing to her.' And here he is nursing his wounds to his friend Antonio de Pagliari in February 1819, and for once being out-manoeuvred:

> I agree with the last paragraph of your letter in which you say that women are too cunning, so that it is almost impossible to know what exactly is going on in their hearts. It often happens that a woman refuses the honours of a king to amuse herself with a mule driver, and whoever is ignorant of the latter considers her as a heroine. I don't want to put Lauretta in that class but very often refusals are publicised so as to enjoy more tranquilly secret love affairs . . . I'm breaking with Lauretta completely, owing to her proud and far from good character. But I intend to go on helping her . . .

He really must have been smitten, to be rejected by her and yet continue to pay out and support her career, however modestly. He was even enquiring after her 20 years later, in another letter to Pagliari.

The Real Love of His Life

Amidst all the enigmas of this secretive man and his necromantic performing powers, there is only one certainty: the core love of his life was his fiddle, in particular his favourite Guarneri del Gesù. This is crystal clear from an incident in 1834 London when it was damaged by two 'damned women' we have already met – Charlotte Watson and her chaperone Miss Wells!

[Paganini to Germi, 17 February 1834] . . . I don't know if I told you that while on tour in England my English singers – two damned women – on getting into the carriage to go to the concert in the theatre gave my violin to the coachman instead of holding it between their knees. The case fell down and damaged the violin, which I've now given to a famous man to repair. I hope for the best. Excuse this chatter . . .

He took it to Vuillaume who decided an operation was necessary. Paganini insisted on watching the work carried out, so the repairer took his tools to Paganini's hotel, the Neothermes. In the words of Louis Vidal:

The luthier consequently came to the Neothermes with his tools. Paganini sat at the end of the room . . . watching the operation with deep anxiety. The chisel was introduced between the table and the rib; a slight cracking noise – Paganini bounded from his chair. Every movement of the tool brought fresh beads of perspiration to the brow of the tortured man who loved this fiddle more than he cared for any other inanimate thing in the world. He said 'it was as if the chisel were entering his own flesh.'

In gratitude Paganini gave Vuillaume a gold snuffbox.

I've had two boxes like this made, one for the physician of my body, the other for the surgeon of my violin. My gratitude is equal in both instances and the souvenir should be the same.'

Have Coffin, Will Travel

Paganini died companionless on 27 May at about 5.00 p.m. after spending a lonely winter in Nice in rented rooms on the third storey of a house 'in the very worst part of the town', the apartment consisting of 'a salon and a bedroom with an alcove, a few chairs, no carpet'. Despite the efforts of various specialists he had been in a state of near total decrepitude, with trembling hands, unable to hold a pen or knife, plagued by a constant cough and insomnia, unable to speak and barely able to swallow. Yet even in this state he had not given up, planning to become a dealer in stringed instruments and also to write a violin method 'that would shorten the period of study'.

The story of his remains, rather like those of Donizetti, is really a separate chapter and speaks volumes for the hypocrisy within the Catholic Church whose Pope had, after all, made him a Knight of the Golden Spur in 1827. Suffice it to say that because he had steadfastly refused to see a priest before his death, the Bishop of Nice denied permission for burial and his embalmed body was shunted around endlessly: first to the cellar of the house in which he died; then to the leper hospital at Villefranche where there were soon mutterings of strange happenings; then to a temporary resting place near an olive oil factory, where leakages soon seeped into his grave; and then to another cellar where it remained for several years. In 1845 the Grand Duchess of Parma authorised his interment at his splendid Villa Gaione (which he had acquired in 1834). Finally, in 1876, 36 years after his death, his remains were buried in a cemetery in Parma. Even after that, his body was moved on several occasions for one reason or another.

Let de Courcy have the last elegant and poetic words on this unfathomable man:

> he never opened his heart fully and familiarly to anyone, presumably not even to his son . . .
>
> His nature was curiously uncommunicative, so we find [in his 500-odd letters] no confessional outpourings, no inclination to put 'on the cloak of penitence' to disclose his faults or reveal the root causes of his suffering. As far as the world could see, he was never disquieted, like ordinary mortals, by conflicts of sense and soul. No spiritual, philosophical, abstract problems of life are solved in these laconic epistles; they manifest no fury of conviction, tell us nothing of the subterranean movements of his soul. Even in his lonely moments, and they must have been veritably legion, he never dropped the bucket into the deeper water of the well to expose his religious convictions or his attitude toward life, to communicate in Goethe's phrase, *das Unmittelbare des Daseins, den schönsten unmittelbaren Lebenshauch* [the immediacy of being, the most beautiful, most direct breath of life] . . .
>
> He had achieved so many of the glories of this world and still, like Donne, had never known the 'Centrique Happiness' that para-

doxically comes to quite ordinary mortals: the companionship of a sympathetic heart with whom in times of acute despondency he could throw off all disguise.

CHOPIN

'The Ariel of the Piano'

Born: Zelazowa Wola, nr Warsaw, 22 February 1810
Died: Paris, 17 October 1849

*Of all the artists of our day, it is Chopin who most took possession of
the soul and spirit of women.*
Jules Janin: *Journal des débats* (obituary), 22 October 1849

*Women buzz round me like flies round a honey pot, you know I'm not
exaggerating . . . I am subjected to the most cruel temptations.*
Chopin to his friend Tytus Woyciechowski, 1833

*What an unpleasant woman that Sand is! . . . Is she really a woman?
I am ready to doubt it.*
Chopin to his friend Ferdinand Hiller, autumn 1836, after first meeting
Sand

inconstant sylph
Marquis de Custine to Chopin, New Year, 1840

*As he grew older, he revealed the intimacies of the solitary heart with
an ever-increasing precision.*
Alec Harman and Wilfred Mellers: *Man and His Music*

He was dying all his life.
Berlioz

It is surely no coincidence that the three women, outside of his family, to whom Chopin was closest were older than he: Countess Delfina Potocka by three years, George Sand and Jane Sterling each by six. As a young man he was as nervous of women as he was of appearing on the concert platform. When once suspected of seduction at the age of 21, he expressed his astonishment, in a letter to his close friend Tytus Woyciechowski, 'that anyone could imagine me *capable* of such a thing'. And as to public performance, he once told Liszt that 'the crowd intimidates me and I feel asphyxiated by its eager breath, paralysed by its inquisitive stare, silenced by its alien faces'. The scourge of pre-concert nerves led him to abandon the concert platform altogether, when he was only 28, for ten years. Shortage of cash forced him to brave the seas of faces again in the penultimate year of his life when he went to England. It is indeed astonishing that he built his legendary reputation on the strength of barely 30 concert-hall performances throughout his lifetime; a far cry indeed from pianistic giants like Thalberg or, especially, Liszt, with his 1,000 or so shows in the space of eight years in cities as far apart as Cork and Kiev.

If they were going to get anywhere with him, women had to be as upfront, determined and skilled in their tactics as the very loveable firecracker George Sand, furious feminist, utopian socialist, prolific novelist and notorious devourer of nearly a dozen men before she took a shine to Chopin in 1836. Although she was no sex symbol of her generation, in many other ways Sand was a forbear of the notorious Hollywood screen goddess Tallulah Bankhead (anyone seen *Lifeboat*, 1943?), also a tireless social campaigner, feminist icon and sexual omnivore who worked her way through Montgomery Clift, James Dean, Gary Cooper, 'half the British aristocracy and a good slice of Hollywood womanhood'.

However, it took even Sand nearly two years of plotting to entice Chopin between her sheets before she took him under her wing for nine years.

Although he was certainly not conventionally handsome as a young man, Chopin was nevertheless drop-dead gorgeous to his scores of female fans, with his frail, small-boned frame (he never topped the scales much beyond seven stone), graceful bearing, very small feet, long, tapering fingers, beaky nose, gaunt face, bright, although increasingly sunken eyes whose colour is still in doubt – blue? bluish grey? brown? – fair-to-auburn hair which he grew long, and sideburns. One contemporary cameo of the composer in his late twenties, taken here from André Maurois' richly documented biography of George Sand, *Lélia*, also reveals that Chopin had

> a very sweet smile, a rather husky voice, and something about his general air so noble, so indescribably aristocratic that those who did not know him took him to be some great Lord in exile.
> Wladimir Karénine: *George Sand, her Life and Works*

Chopin's prominent nose, by the way, once won him, hands down, a contest in which the object for each contestant was to use his nose to lift a ring placed on top of a pyramid of flour.

The crucial aphrodisiac in the alchemy of his appeal was, of course, his infinitely delicate, spell-binding playing – in Liszt's words, that of 'a poet, elegiac, profound, chaste and dreaming'. The popular, old-school virtuoso pianist Moscheles, Chopin's senior by fifteen years, had always been baffled by the young Pole's music, but nevertheless put his finger on why his playing had the ladies swooning:

> [October 1839] Now, for the first time, I understood his music and why women go into raptures over it. Those harsh inartistic modulations which I have never been able to master, no longer shock me, for he glides over them imperceptibly with his elf-like fingers. His touch is as soft as a breath. His *piano* is so ethereal that no *forte* is needed to create the necessary contrast . . . Listening to him, one yields with one's whole soul, as to a singer who, oblivious of accompaniment, lets himself be carried away by his emotion . . . In short, he is unique among pianists.

And here, by way of comparison, is the response to Chopin's playing in the last years of his life, of a Scottish lady, Fanny Erskine. She was a distant relative of 'Chopin's widow', Jane Stirling, of whom more anon:

> and how can I describe his playing – Anything so pure and *heavenly* & delicate I never heard – & so mournful; his music is so like

himself – & so original in its sadness . . . His preludes & his nocturnes composed at the moment were so delicious I could have
jumped up with joy! & he played us a Mazurka after. He is a Pole &
seems very fond of his country. I was quite sorry to come away but
had his exquisite harmonies in my heart for long.

One might well believe one is hearing small fairy voices sighing
under silver bells, or a rain of pearls falling on crystal tables.
    Léon Escudier, reviewing a Chopin recital in February 1842

Chopin's style of playing was certainly by no means to everyone's taste, because of its alleged lack of guts and sonority.
Essentially self-taught, he saw the piano primarily as a singing
rather than percussion instrument. He drew his inspiration particularly from Bellini, whose abundance of extended *bel canto*
melodies he adored, from popular forms like the waltz, and from
his intense national pride in the polonaises and mazurkas of his
homeland. ('You know how I have wanted to feel and in part
have approached the feeling of our national music,' he wrote in
a letter to a friend on Christmas Day 1831.) It was the rhythmic
flexibility in these dances which influenced his highly rubato
style of playing – a rubato stretched to the point where, on
different occasions, his friends Meyerbeer (whose operas he much
admired) and Charles Hallé were convinced he was playing his
mazurkas in (respectively) 2/2 or 4/4 time instead of 3/4 time!
Other formative influences included the music of Moscheles,
Hummel and Czerny.
    Chopin's music isn't all easy-listening salon music, with a for-
mulaic mix of languid dreamy tunes and bravura passage work.
He turned out scores of such 'social' pieces, of course – songs,
waltzes, polonaises, mazurkas, écossaises – but he himself was
clear about their status, describing such a piece as his Polonaise
in C major (Op. 3) for cello and piano as 'nothing but glitter,
for the drawing-room, for the ladies'. Conversely, no less a mod-
ernist than Mily Balakirev (leader of Russia's nationalist avant-
garde group, The Five) hailed Chopin as a radical and progressive
innovator, a view shared by Balakirev's circle and by leading
Slavonic nationalists in the later nineteenth century. Balakirev
even composed an orchestral suite based on melodies by Chopin.
    Particularly ear-bending and adventurous are some of Chopin's
overall key designs and chiaroscuro harmonic effects. Listen, for
example, to the Etude Op. 10 no. 3, where the harmonies modu-

late so rapidly that the tiller of the boat seems to be unmanned. In the last movement of the B flat minor Sonata tonality disappears altogether for a considerable proportion of its one and a half minutes' duration. And in the 'twilit and phantasmagoric private world' of the late mazurkas entire tonal structures seem to disintegrate.

No wonder Schumann referred to Chopin as 'a revolutionary cannon buried in flowers'! The toughness and power in the later compositions belie the frailty of their creator. The scherzos and ballades, the last polonaises, especially the one in F sharp minor, and the two piano sonatas all contain moments of true grandeur, while the stupendous Scherzo in B flat minor Op. 31, for instance, is 'an explosion of passion just waiting to be unleashed'. There is nothing wishy-washy in any of these later works, which are also feats of astonishing compression. Not a single note in the iridescent cascades of demi-semiquavers is redundant anywhere.

A breathtaking evocation of the enchanted and enchanting females who flocked to the Parisian salons and *soirées intimes* where Chopin played in his thirties appeared in February 1842 in *La Revue musicale*, a journal founded by the music critic Fétis:

> Chopin has given in Pleyel's rooms a charming soirée, a fête peopled with adorable smiles, delicate and rosy faces, small, shapely white hands; a splendid fête where simplicity was wedded to grace and elegance, and good taste served as a pedestal to wealth. Gilded ribbons, soft blue gauzes, strings of trembling pearls, the freshest roses and mignonettes, in a word, a thousand of the prettiest and gayest hues, mixed and crossed in endless ways on the perfumed heads and silver-white shoulders of the most charming women for whom the princely *salons* contend.

Even when he was on his deathbed, so Chopin's friend, the diva Pauline Viardot cynically remarked, 'all the grand Parisian ladies considered it *de rigueur* to faint in his room'.

As well as being bewitched by his playing, women were also enchanted by his supreme *bon ton* – call it snobbery in his case, if you like – his charm, ultra-refined sensibilities, his extraordinary gifts for caricature and mimicry, his exquisite taste in furnishings and interior decoration, and his immaculate grooming. His furnishings, Ruth Jordan tells us in her richly documented biography *Nocturne*, included a grand Pleyel piano, delicate chairs, a *canapé* (i.e. sofa) and side tables, heavy grey outer curtains and impeccably white muslin inner ones at the window, dove-grey wallpaper, a portrait of a pianist playing to an admiring listener, knick-knacks everywhere, low vases with violets, rugs, polished parquet floors, candles round the piano . . .

As to the immaculate grooming, Chopin was a true dandy, patronising only the finest tailors. He would spend hours discussing the finer details of dress with one of his especial friends and fellow dandies, Eugène Delacroix, then the foremost Romantic painter and colourist in France. On 3 October 1839, he wrote to his faithful and much put-upon friend, copyist and general factotum Julian Fontana to order a hat for him from the tailor Dupont – 'he knows how light I like them' – and from his own tailor, Dautremont, 'a pair of grey trousers . . . a dark shade of grey; winter trousers, good quality, without belt, smooth and stretchy . . . also a plain black velvet [or, failing that, black silk] waistcoat, but with a tiny inconspicuous pattern – something very quiet and elegant . . . not too open in the front of course'. Such sartorial fussiness approaches that of Wagner in its obsession with detail, though not in eccentricity. What a contrast with Brahms, whose attitude to clothes was ever more to persuade his housekeeper Frau Truxa to make do and mend!

Even when out in the sticks Chopin was dressed for the boulevards. Arriving, for instance, with George Sand and her children on the then remote island of Majorca, he sported tight trousers, silk cravat, white gloves and black top hat – singularly overdressed for the grotty accommodation they initially secured over a barrel maker's shop reeking with the stench of rancid oil.

Later, in June 1841, he sent from Sand's country manor house at Nohant more detailed orders (enclosing 100 francs) to the long-suffering Fontana. This time his factotum had to trudge round precisely specified shops and send him his favourite brand of soap, a bottle of patchouli, an ivory hand with a black handle for head-scratching (a favourite habit also of Tchaikovsky), suede gloves . . .

In the year before his death Chopin was still described as a 'young man of medium height, slim, haggard, worn with suffering and dressed in the most elegant Paris fashion'.

The Marquis de Custine (1790–1857)

As you might expect, it wasn't just the ladies who fell for him. Chopin was for many years pursued by a besotted and protectively minded admirer, the rich, middle-aged, fashionable travel writer the Marquis Astolphe de Custine, who lived in a villa at Saint Gratien, not far from Paris. When Chopin was coughing badly in the spring of 1837, the Marquis fussed over him with genuine concern, however queenly:

> You must allow yourself to be taken in hand like a child and an invalid. You must bring yourself to see that at the moment there is only one task for you: your health . . . Three months' rest and sensible treatment would be enough to arrest your illness; but you must do it.

Chopin, however, was not tempted by the prospect of a month at de Custine's villa, nor by a further two months with him at a watering place, and in July was well enough to make the first of his two trips to England. However, on his return he did then take up de Custine's suggestion to spend some time at the watering place of Ems.

Although de Custine felt somewhat spare when Chopin and George Sand had settled down to a routine of domesticity in their independent but interacting ménages after their return from Majorca, he was nothing if not kind and persistent in his Auntie-like attentions. He sent Chopin a note reminding him of his 'constance', and when Chopin failed to respond, the Marquis sent him an antique inkstand and pen with a second note in the plaintive vein of unrequited love:

> Goodbye, bad year 1839! And you, inconstant sylph, promise me a better one to come. That is all I wish for myself. As for what I might wish for you, it is not for me to give it to you. I am delighted from the bottom of my heart that you have found it, but I shall be less pained by it if, in spite of all your happiness, I could still mean something to you.

The poor Marquis had endured more than angst for his homosexuality. Chopin must have been familiar with the story that fifteen years earlier the Marquis had been 'whipped to within an inch of his life' by the comrades-at-arms of a handsome Guards officer with whom he had arranged an assignation in a secluded stable. No longer an acceptable bachelor in high society, de Custine was forced to search for his Ganymedes among the theatrical *demi-monde*, and doubtless also (like Tchaikovsky when he was in Paris), among the clubs, *cafés chantants*, and bordellos or *maisons des hussards* serving the needs of homosexuals.

Chopin was far too much of a gentleman to ditch de Custine altogether, however, and spent a week in the summer of 1840 with him at Saint Gratien, albeit chaperoned by friends including Delacroix and the Polish financier Count Grzymala. De Custine continued thereafter to hover solicitously but at a distance in the background of Chopin's life.

Apropos of matters of gender and sexuality, in his fascinating but at times overly obscure book *Chopin at the Boundaries*, the American academic Jeffrey Kallberg draws attention to the hermaphroditic and androgyne imagery in contemporary reports of Chopin and his playing. They are permeated with references to the otherworld and the afterworld – elves, fairies, sylphs and angels. Furthermore, suggests Kallberg, the 'metaphors of hermaphroditism' that gathered around Chopin could have, according to nineteenth-century treatises on pathology and juristic medicine, reinforced a 'sodomitical interpretation' of his sexuality.

> Chopin's weakness, pallor and slight build, explicable as resulting from pulmonary or cardiac diseases, could also [Kallberg continues] have been read as a sign of sodomitical inclinations. So, too, his smooth skin and slightly developed musculature, when understood as indications of 'effeminacy', were available as indices of sodomy. . . . Tuberculosis [Chopin's illness] was thought by many to be connected with the practise of masturbation, and . . . masturbation and sodomy had been understood as closely related practices.

Enough! All this seems to go no farther than saying that some of Chopin's contemporaries probably thought he was a homosexual, active, suppressed, or otherwise. This is no surprise to anybody. But although Chopin was obviously attractive to men like de Custine, there is no evidence that he had sex with them.

Virginal Love

As a child prodigy, Schoppin – as he was dubbed at the age of eight, in the Warsaw *Gazette* – took adulation in his stride after being introduced by his first important and beloved teacher Albert Zywyny (who fed him a diet of Bach and more Bach) into the aristocratic salons of Warsaw. He basked in the adoration of countless dazzling, bejewelled countesses and princesses bearing exotic-sounding Polish names: the Czartoryskis, Potockis, Sapiehas, Zamoyskas, Lubeckis, Radziwills. Other admirers included the legendary soprano Angelica Catalani who gave him an engraved watch that he treasured all his life. Coming himself from a solid bourgeois background, young Fryderyk was also in demand in the salons of the middle or minor landed gentry. (His father Mikolaj had risen to the rank of Lecturer in French Language and Literature at the Lyceum school which Chopin himself attended from the age of fourteen.)

As a young teenager, Chopin seems to have captivated the hearts of several pre-pubescent girls who belonged to the families who sent their sons to the Lyceum, where his father also boarded pupils. Chopin recalled that he was in love with a young girl from the convent school and used a Jewish lad, Leibush, who, in exchange for free piano lessons, used to act as 'a messenger of love' when arranging secret rendezvous. Another early romance was with Countess Alexandrine de Moriolles, a childhood playmate to whom, as an act of keyboard gallantry, he later dedicated his early *Rondo à la mazur* in 1828. To Emily Elsner, daughter of his second and most important teacher Joseph Elsner, he played many of his latest compositions and copied some of them into her album. Such innocent love!

One story goes that at the age of sixteen, young Fryderyk showed his chivalry by organising a charity concert for a pretty Czech waitress who had, with her brothers and sisters, been left destitute after her father was killed in a factory accident. Another version has as the object of young Fryderyk's chivalry a pretty nursemaid left with two young orphans on her hands after the death of their father.

When wrongly accused at the age of eighteen of seducing and impregnating a young resident governess at the house of his hostess Countess Priszak, Fryderyk's reaction was rather one of pride than resentment at wrongful accusation. 'Fool that I was, I had no appetite for her. Just as well as it turns out,' he wrote to his close friend Tytus.

In the summer of 1828, before he left for Berlin, his first-ever venture abroad, he refused a resident young governess 'with a free heart and a vacant bed' because he was not attracted to either. And when he arrived in Berlin shortly afterwards he displayed decided preferences in his tastes for females. He was very unimpressed by young German ladies, compared with their Polish counterparts with their 'peach complexions and lovely hair'.

> Tell Marylski [he wrote to his sisters] he does not know what he is talking about if he thinks Berlin women are beautiful. They have sagging cheeks and toothless mouths. They dress well enough, but what a waste of lovely muslins, they look like painted puppets.

However, while other young men were chasing petticoats, Chopin was composing, and by 1830 he had notched up some 50-odd piano pieces which sooner or later were published.

Tytus Woyciechowski

I am afraid of you as if you were some kind of tyrant. I don't know why I'm afraid of you, God knows you are the only one who has power over me, you and . . . well no one else.
Chopin to Tytus, autumn 1830

Chopin's classmate at the Lyceum, Tytus Woyciechowski, son of a squire in the Ukraine, seems to have been the composer's first real love. Certainly Chopin's attachment to his elder peer was very intense, even erotically charged, although there seems to have been no doffing of shirts nor downing of breeches in the darkest recesses of the school stables or the squire's rhododendron bushes. It was the type of deep homoerotic friendship that surely still goes on between adolescents today in boarding schools, before they feel confident enough or have the opportunity to relate to the opposite sex. Taller and a year or two older than Chopin, Tytus was a role-model for him. Temperamentally they were antipodal. The thin, nervy, indecisive younger man, in constant need of affection and reassurance, was powerfully drawn to his placid, virile and stable elder, also a pianist. All the emotional dependence that Chopin revealed some fifteen years later in his nine-year affair with George Sand was already evident in his reliance on Tytus.

After completing his university studies, Tytus lived the life of a country gentleman on the family estate at Poturzyn, near

Tomaszow, and received many letters from his admirer with all the latest social gossip, and news on his compositions and cultural activities. Chopin's letters during 1828 and 1829 sometimes seem to go a little beyond the characteristically *schwärmerisch* or gushing style of the period between two close friends – or what Ruth Jordan calls the 'Polish epistolary courtesy of the age' – into the language of romantic infatuation:

> [9 September 1828] Take pity on me and write sometimes. A word, half a word, a syllable, a single letter, it will mean such a lot to me . . . Give a kiss to your faithful friend.
> [4 January 1829] You do not like to be kissed. Allow me to do so today.
> [12 September 1829, from Vienna] I kiss you heartily, right on the lips if I may.
> [1829] Don't kiss me for now, for I haven't washed yet. How silly of me. You wouldn't kiss me even if I were to bathe in all the perfumes of Byzantium, unless I forced you to by some supernatural power. I believe in such powers. Tonight you shall dream you are kissing me.
> I kiss you lovingly. This is how people usually sign themselves off, but they don't really understand what they are writing. I for one mean what I write, for I love you dearly.

Tytus was the dedicatee of the Variations on *Là ci darem la mano* (the ones so handsomely praised by Schumann in his famous remark 'Hats off, gentlemen! A genius!'). 'I have put your name on three Variations,' he wrote to Tytus on 9 September 1829. 'Perhaps it was presumptuous of me to do so, but my heart dictated it, our friendship seemed to allow it, please do not take it amiss.' Fryderyk need have had no misgivings because Tytus accepted the compliment with pleasure.

However, when Tytus didn't show up at Chopin's important début at the Warsaw Theatre in 1830, Chopin was downcast:

> My own sweet heart,
> Never have I missed you so badly as I do now [a few days after Chopin's second Warsaw concert]. You are not here and I have no-one to talk to. One look from you after either of my concerts would have meant more to me than all the praises of the press, the Elsners, the Kurspinkis and the Solivas put together.

Chopin's letters were brimful of his vividly etched day-to-day experiences and intimate thoughts. A new dimension emerged in

1829 when Chopin confessed the heartache of his unexpressed love for the singer Konstancja Gladkowska. 'It is dreadful when something weighs on your mind, not to have a soul to unburden to. You know what I mean. I tell my piano the things I used to tell you.' As a solace for his unfulfilled longings for Konstancja, Chopin tied a ribbon round his latest letter from Tytus and carried it with him everywhere.

The last period of time they spent together, following a blissful summer holiday on the Woyciechowski farm in 1830, when they played the piano and practised the crossbow together, was during Chopin's tour to Germany, Bohemia and Vienna later that year. (This was Chopin's second visit to Vienna, but he failed markedly to capitalise on the success of his début there in August 1829.)

During their tour Tytus, who had never previously witnessed any of his protégé's early triumphs, planted himself in the audience in order to provide Chopin with feedback. One discovery in Breslau was that whilst the Germans admired his light touch on the piano, they didn't go a bundle on his compositions. In Dresden and Prague the two men packed in hectic rounds of courtesy calls and soirées, particularly amongst the Polish communities. Indeed, it was in Dresden that Chopin first set eyes on the ravishing but unhappily married Countess Potocka who was soon to play, perhaps, an important although hotly disputed role in his love life. In Vienna, the two men soon parted company when Tytus returned to Poland to join up in the insurrection against Grand Duke Constantin, then Commander-in-Chief of Warsaw, which was still under Russian tutelage. Tytus survived the fighting with only superficial wounds although he was never again to meet his life-long admirer. Chopin originally intended to dedicate to Tytus the most popular of his polonaises, the one in A major (Op. 40 no. 1) of 1838, but this plan never materialised.

'I still love him as much as when we were at school,' wrote Chopin of Tytus to Fontana, in 1839. 'He has a second son. He is calling him after me. Poor baby.' Not long before Chopin's death Tytus attempted to visit his acolyte in Paris after a break of some eighteen years. Alas, Tytus had to write and say he was unable to obtain a French visa and had been forced to abort his journey at Ostend. Chopin replied, apologising for being too ill to make the journey to Belgium.

To some extent, the pianist-composer Ferdinand Hiller took over Tytus's role as main confidant to Chopin after his arrival in

Paris. Hiller was also a close confidant of Berlioz and seems to have known everybody who was anybody in musical circles.

Konstancja Gladkowska (1810–89)

I have my own ideal which I have been faithfully serving for half a year now without talking of it; I dream of it, the adagio of my concerto [Op. 21] was a souvenir of it, and this morning it inspired the little waltz [Op. 70 no. 3].
Letter to Tytus, 3 October 1929

After returning to Warsaw from the heady triumphs of his Viennese début in 1829, Chopin felt hemmed in by its lack of opportunities and cultural provincialism. It was a far cry from the magic of Vienna, with its palatial apartments and exotic blend of German, Slav, Latin and Magyar cultures.

Although seemingly eager to venture forth from Warsaw again, Chopin was racked by indecision, repeatedly announcing his day of departure and then not going through with it. It was a time of acute emotional stress for him. Political troubles were part of the problem, as also was his anxiety about his capacity to cope with the strains of public performance. However, the major cause of his dithering was his unfulfilled longing for the first woman to touch his heart in any really serious way, the fair-haired, blue-eyed mezzo-soprano Konstancja Gladkowska, a student at the Conservatoire. The same age as himself (nineteen), Konstancja first excited Fryderyk by her singing, and even while a student was appearing as a soloist at the National Opera. Confiding to Tytus that she was his 'ideal', the pining, shy and dumb-struck swain never once during a whole year, from the spring of 1829, got around even to fixing himself an introduction to her. He mooned miserably while more macho Russian officers presented their compliments at the stage door.

In spite of lover's heartache, Chopin gave what was effectively his début as a public pianist in Warsaw on 17 March 1830, at the National Theatre, the programme including his F minor Piano Concerto, performed piecemeal during the concert, and his ecstatically received *Fantasia on Polish Airs*, Op. 13. He was now acquiring, although not by specific design, a new status as Poland's premier national composer, a symbol of hope for frustrated nationalist aspirations. Yet still he languished as a lover.

Even after an introduction to Konstancja was finally fixed in the spring of 1830 at one of the Conservatoire concerts, Chopin was quite unable to make any headway. He composed songs for her, practised them with her, all to no avail. What's more, she seemed to be inseparable from her companion Panna Wolkowa, also a soprano. Even if Konstancja recognised and reciprocated Fryderyk's feelings, she was either unable or unwilling to encourage him. She was certainly no Countess Potocka or George Sand.

Chopin sent Tytus an enthusiastic report of the operatic double-début of Konstancja and Panna, preferring Konstancja's delivery and purity of tone to her friend's markedly off-pitch efforts. That Panna enjoyed the more enthusiastic reception, the loyal Chopin put down to her all-conquering curves! But still the romance hadn't progressed beyond Konstancja's gift of a ribbon which Chopin wore next to his heart. No wonder he eventually began to doubt even his own feelings. 'Even if I were in love,' he wrote to Tytus, 'I would probably conceal my ineffectual and incommunicable fervour for several years more.'

Dressed in white with roses in her hair, Konstancja appeared with her friend in Chopin's last concert in Warsaw on 11 October 1830, when he premièred his E minor Piano Concerto (Op. 11) with resounding success, but little press response. In spite of his four curtain calls and his first successful partnership with an orchestra, Chopin's most vivid memory of the occasion was Konstancja's heavenly beauty and her performance of excerpts from Rossini's *The Lady of the Lake*. Soon afterwards, he was rash enough to invite her for a walk in the Saxon Gardens and offer her a thin wire ring with a shiny stone. But even though the lady reciprocated with a ring, they remained tongue-tied! Shortly before his departure she wrote some valedictory verses into his album which may have obliquely reflected her feelings for him, particularly in the last line: 'None could love you better than those here.' Some years later, Chopin added wryly: 'You could.' Despite her later disclaimers, Konstancja can hardly have been unaware of his feelings for her.

Chopin left Warsaw on 2 November for his second visit to Vienna, Tytus having arranged to meet him *en route* on the Austrian–Polish border at Kalisz. The tongue-tied lovers never met again and within fifteen months Konstancja married a resolute suitor 'for the sake of a palace' – at least, according to one of Chopin's younger sisters Izabella. Like many women even today, Konstancja gave up her singing career and settled down to a comfortable life in the sticks, bearing her husband five children. Although she lost her eyesight at the age of 35, she lived on to the age of 79, outliving her ineffectual suitor by 40 years.

Chopin readily admitted to Tytus that his feelings for Konstancja were poured into the slow nocturne-like movement of his F minor Piano Concerto, with its delicately ornamented, Mozartian melody, and also in his slender D flat Waltz Op. 70 no. 3. Many later works were also, according to *Grove's Dictionary of Music and Musicians*, inspired by this same passion. He was certainly missing her intensely in Vienna in December 1830 when he wrote to his friend from Lyceum days, Jan Matuszynski, 'I cannot even write her name, my hand is not worthy.' And in Stuttgart the following September when he heard that the Russians had crushed the Polish insurrection he wrote in his album 'What has become of her, where is she now, poor girl? . . . Perhaps she is already in Russian hands? The Russians may be touching her, stifling her, murdering her!'

However, during these Konstancja years Chopin was not so lovesick as to be impervious to the charms of others, including the daughters of his patron Prince Radziwill, and, in particular, to the beautiful appearance as well as singing voice of Henrietta Sontag.

By the time Chopin left Warsaw his tally of some 59 compositions included all his six works for piano and orchestra, several Studies from Op. 10 and several Nocturnes from Op. 9 and 15 (derived from the compositions of the gifted English eccentric, John Field).

In July 1831 Chopin left Vienna for Paris after a stay of eight months, having composed his *Grand Polonaise* in A flat, his popular mazurkas of Op. 6 and Op. 7, some songs, and several waltzes including the famous Op. 18 in E flat. While in Vienna, or on his journey thence, he seems to have had an enigmatic encounter with a certain Teresa, possibly a Tyrolese singer, about whom nothing is known except that, according to a letter Chopin sent to his friend Norbert Kumelski, her 'legacy' made it impossible for him to taste the 'forbidden fruit' so readily to hand in Paris. It would seem that either a whore or a tart had beckoned him for a trick which gave him a mild dose of the pox.

He arrived in Paris, which was to be his home for the rest of his life, in mid-September 1831, by way of Munich and Stuttgart. It was in Stuttgart that he was pitched into acute despair when he learnt of the re-capture of Warsaw by the Russians, although there is no evidence for the popular myth that this news sparked off the 'Revolutionary' Study Op. 10 no. 2. It is no wonder that Chopin later turned down a lucrative offer to become Court Pianist in St Petersburg, even though his financial needs would have been met for life. The struggles and sufferings of his fellow Poles had become a focus for the melancholic side of his nature. He lamented keenly that his friends such as Tytus and Jan Matuszynski were risking their lives in the fighting, and that his sisters were nursing the wounded while he could not 'even beat a drum'.

> Oh God! [he wrote in his album] You are there and yet you do not take vengeance! Have you not witnessed enough crimes from Russia? Oh father, so this is how you are rewarded in old age! Mother, sweet suffering mother, you saw your daughter die, and now you watch the Russians marching in over her grave to oppress you! ... I am helpless, sitting here powerless, suffering through the piano, in despair ...'

One effect of his suffering was that composition became ever more important to him as an outlet for his very deepest feelings. The results speak for themselves.

Paris

You find here the greatest splendour, the greatest filthiness, the greatest virtue and the greatest vice.
Chopin

In spite of a successful though poorly attended début concert in February 1832, when he played his E minor Concerto and his *Là ci darem* Variations, Chopin took a while to establish himself. His first digs were in the boulevard Poissonière on the Right Bank, and altogether he was to live in nine different apartments during his eighteen years in the capital.

However, with help from many quarters including several aristocratic Polish émigrés (Prince Walenty Radziwill among them), Dr Malfatti (one-time doctor to Beethoven), the composer Paër, the critic Fétis, and the Rothschilds, Chopin established himself as the supreme darling of the Parisian salons. Certainly by the end of 1834 he had a successful career, a close circle of friends, and an unassailable reputation as a composer. 'I sit with ambassadors, princes and ministers; and I don't even know by what miracle this is, for I have never crowed about myself,' he wrote to Dominik Dziewanowski, another friend from his school-days. He commanded the highest private tuition fees in the capital, with Mme de Rothschild having headed the queue for lessons: 20 to 30 francs a session, placed discreetly on the mantel-piece by his adoring pupils while he, even more discreetly, looked out of the window during such sordid transactions. This was more money than Liszt, Thalberg ('he plays famously but he is not my man') or even the doyen he most admired and briefly studied with, the 'conceited popinjay' Friedrich Kalkbrenner could make. But coining it though he was, Chopin, like Mozart, seems to have spent up to his income. 'I have five lessons to give today,' he wrote to a friend. 'You will imagine I am making a fortune – but my cabriolet and kid gloves cost more than that, and without them I should not have *bon ton* . . .'

He befriended many musicians including Liszt, who actually wrote a glowing biography of him in 1852, Berlioz (a vivid chronicler of the times), Ferdinand Hiller, the short-lived Bellini, whose music he adored, and Meyerbeer. Liszt's admiration of Chopin was by no means fully reciprocated, however, for while the Pole had a high regard for the Hungarian's playing, he found his compositions vulgar, and the man himself increasingly unlikeable.

Chopin also enjoyed the company of the Romantic poet Alfred de Musset, the master novelist Balzac, the German-born Romantic poet Heinrich Heine, the 'messianic' Polish nationalist poet Adam Mickiewicz who was Professor of Literature at the Collège de France, and, especially, Delacroix. When all or most of these talents were crammed into the same room in the capital city for salons and soirées, what mind-blowing parties they must have been! Paris in the 1830s was experiencing a renaissance not unlike the ferment of artistic activity in London towards the end of the reign of Elizabeth I.

However, it is noteworthy that Chopin's interests were not cross-cultural in the manner of so many other nineteenth-century composers – Berlioz, Mendelssohn, Schumann and Wagner, to name but four who were avid readers and inspired to compose by what they read. He was 'just' a musician, with little real interest in literature or, despite his friendship with Delacroix, in painting. He was never really happier than when in the company of fellow-players, making music and talking about it. Even his route to composition was firmly through and from his fingers. He could not compose save at the piano. Fétis summed it up well when he wrote that whereas Beethoven composed pianoforte music, Chopin wrote 'pianists' music'.

All in all, Chopin's prestige as a musician in Paris was unique and unrivalled by the 1840s. Liszt's keenly observant review, for *La Gazette musicale*, of a semi-private concert given by Chopin at the salon of the piano maker Camille Pleyel in April 1841 is an evocative picture not only of Chopin's status in Paris but of concert life there in general:

> Last Monday evening at eight o'clock the salons of M. Pleyel were brilliantly lighted; a ceaseless stream of carriages deposited at the foot of the steps, carpeted and decked with fragrant flowers, the most elegant ladies, the most fashionable young men, the most famous artists, the richest financiers, the most illustrious lords, the élite of society – a complete aristocracy of birth, wealth, talent and beauty.
>
> An open grand piano was on the platform; crowding around, people vied for the closest seats; composing themselves in antici-pation, they would not miss a chord, a note, an intention, a thought of him who was about to sit there . . . the one they wanted to see, hear, admire and applaud was not only a skilled virtuoso, a pianist expert in the playing of notes – he was not only an artist of great renown – he was all this and much more, he was Chopin.

1833 Countess Delfina Potocka – Yes or No?

'the greatest sinner of them all'
the Polish poet, Mickiewicz

I wish I could die listening to your singing.
Chopin to Delfina, 1833

Amongst the society women he befriended after his arrival in Paris were the highly exotic Princess Belgiojoso – briefly lover of Liszt and organiser of the legendary contest between him and Thalberg – and the cultivated and very seductive beauty Countess Delfina Potocka, one of the most sophisticated women in Paris. Born in 1807 in the district of Podole in Poland, Delfina made an unfortunate marriage at the age of eighteen to Count Mieczyslas Potocki, an out-and-out rake seven years her senior, and bore him five children. Duty performed, she walked out and went back to mother's where, in Dresden, she first met Chopin and Tytus in 1830. A year later she set herself up in Paris with a negotiated allowance of 100,000 francs a year to keep the wolf from the door. She was soon a pupil of Chopin. But did they, in time-honoured fashion, put the piano stool through its paces by the end of 1832?

Her tally of conquests reportedly included the middle-aged Count Flahaut, the Dauphin himself (Duke of Orleans, brother to the king), the Duke of Montfort, Viscount This, Prince That . . . There were dozens of them, but as a full-time player in the Theatre of Love, Delfina, 'the greatest sinner of them all', lost count. And no wonder! – with her 'dazzling white shoulders and generous breasts, dark blue eyes and golden hair worn in ringlets or piled into a bun'. To Krasinski she was a 'Don Juan in petticoats' frequently given to capricious behaviour because frustrated in her restless search 'for a higher condition in the world, a nobler sphere for the mind'. To the enchanted Delacroix she was 'a woman in the prime of her years, stately as a Greek statue', with a delicately contoured nose, eyes sweet and gentle, and lips on which there was 'a passionate desire for kisses that promise a heaven of delight . . .'

What's more, Delfina was not just a very pretty face, being well read, a pianist, composer and beautiful singer. Inevitably, behind the brazen mask was a much more vulnerable woman underneath, otherwise she would hardly have maintained a tender life-long friendship with Chopin.

But now to the vexed questions. Did Delfina have an affair with Chopin? Did she, in the words of the Romantic biographer G.F. Pourtalès, '[offer] him what he wanted long before he thought of asking for it'? And did Chopin write her those much disputed pornographic letters, some of which are quoted in Ruth Jordan's *Nocturne*? Was there, as I have so far fondly imagined after reading Jordan, a scenario of tantrums and reconciliations, flying vases (well, at least, the violets in the vases), ripped-up manuscripts and frenzied abuse? Were these followed by ecstatic clinches, gasps, gyrations, rucked-up dresses, split breeches, fallen and rumpled stockings, and, finally, frantic ruttings on the *chaise-longue*, the four poster, the legendary piano stool, or even against the Graf grand itself? All this, of course, witnessed by the servants with their eyes at the keyholes and ears pressed to the door?

Suffice it to say that according to *Grove's Dictionary of Music and Musicians* (1980) 'evidence from friends and acquaintances seems to leave little doubt that they were lovers.' One lady in particular, the widow of Dr Alexander Hoffman, an old Silesian acquaintance of Chopin, reported 50 years later that composer and countess *did* have an affair. At that time Dr Hoffmann lived with Chopin for a while in his apartment. Even one of the most sceptical of all commentators on this matter, Jim Samson, in his very recent, highly enjoyable study of the composer in the Master Musicians series (1996), doesn't rule out the possibility of an affair.

> That he admired Delfina and was close to her is beyond question. That he was infatuated with her is likely. Nor can we rule out absolutely the possibility of a liaison during this period. But it is hard to understand how biographers have found it possible to weave the story of Delfina into their narrative without a shred of reliable evidence to support it.

But what about those pornographic letters? Well, to cut a long story short, no-one has seen the originals. The correspondence had been mentioned by two early Chopin scholars but it was not until 1940 that a certain Paulina Czernicka announced her 'discovery' of them. She claimed to have received them from a descendant of Delfina whose family had withheld them from publication. The trouble was that as more and more letters emerged – over 100 of them in photocopies only – the sceptics became deriders. However, experts were still hotly disagreeing with each other in the *Chopin Studies* published by the Warsaw-based Frederick Chopin Society in 1985. One expert, a Dr Zbigniew Czeczot, 'Head of Department of Criminalistics' was prepared to assert that 'the writing in the disputed manuscripts is that of the person who wrote the comparative materials, i.e. Frederick Chopin.' (Nobody disputes that some of the letters are in the hands of a copier, by the way.)

After a detailed study of the handwriting of the disputed photocopied letters, Ms Jordan is (or was in 1978) also convinced that they are authentic. She points out in addition that they are written very much like Chopin's other missives in his native tongue in their chatty, open, spontaneous style and disregard for the niceties of grammar. Indeed, it was only in his letters to his fellow Poles that Chopin fully revealed himself.

All this is surely at least more than a 'shred' of evidence, however circumstantial. The stand of Grove on the matter is that 'it is generally accepted that there is an authentic nucleus to the correspondence but that Mme Czernicka forged *some* [my italics] of the erotic passages and the amateurish musical comments . . .'

So, with renewed acknowledgements to Ruth Jordan and her publishers Constable, let's publish once again and be damned! If Delfina had initiated Chopin in the School of Love, regular, rampant sex with her was, if you accept the authenticity of this letter addressed to her and attributed to him, disastrous for his creative urges:

[c. 1833] I have been thinking a great deal about inspiration and creativity and I have very slowly made an important discovery. Inspiration and ideas only come to me when I have not had a woman for a long time . . . A creative person must keep women out of his life, the energy collecting in his system will not go from his cock and balls into the woman's womb but into his brain in the form of inspiration and will perhaps give birth to a great work of art. Think of it, the temptation which drives us men into a woman's arms can be transformed into inspiration! But this only holds for those who have talent, for if a mere nobody decides to do without women he will only go mad with frustration and still won't be able to produce a work of art before God or man . . .

Longing for a woman, desiring her passionately, there's a way towards creativity. When I long for you, musical ideas come rushing into my head. Love and unrequited passion excite us men when we see the object of our dreams, they burn us alive, they can also give us inspiration . . .

Think of it, my sweetest Phindela [anagram of Delfina], how much of that precious fluid and energy I have wasted on you, ramming you to no purpose . . . Ballads, polonaises, even a whole concerto may have been lost forever up your *des durka*, I can't tell how many. I have been so deeply engulfed in my love for you I have hardly created anything, everything creative went straight from my cock into your *des durka*, you are now carrying my music in your womb . . . The saints are right when they say that woman is the gate of hell. No, no, I take back this last sentence . . . You are for me the gate of heaven, for you I will give up fame, work, everything.

> Loving you is my favourite occupation
> Bed is better than inspiration
> I long for your lovely tits
> So says your faithful Fritz.

... I know you like my cock and balls and after this dissertation you ought to respect them all the more because they are not only a source of pleasure but the source of my artistic achievement ...

... Oh Phindela, my own little Phindela, how I long to be with you. I am still trembling and shivering, it's as if ants are crawling all over me from my brain down to my cock. When the *diligence* [public stage coach] will at long last bring you back I'll cling so hard that for a whole week you won't be able to get me out of you. Bother all inspiration, ideas and works of art ...

... I kiss you all over your dear little body and inside.

Your faithful Frycek, your most talented pupil
who has mastered the art of love.

P.S. ... I have just finished a new prelude in which I have immortalised our eleventh frolic. There are eleven notes to indicate our favourite game ... I am sure the music will become our favourite, as the game has.

P.S. Yesterday I was made very angry on your account. Can you imagine it, evil tongues say you cannot have a baby because you have had too many lovers, grass won't grow on a well-trodden path and more such nonsense ... My own beloved ... let me give you a baby and silence those liars ... Answer quickly, your letters are my only joy and pleasure.

F.F.C.

What that 'eleventh frolic' was, can only be guessed!

The controversy will probably never be settled conclusively, rather like that over the cause of Tchaikovsky's death! But at the end of the day nobody disputes that Delfina's affairs were notorious nor that Chopin 'worshipped the ground she walked on'. It is surely not unreasonable to suppose that if Chopin and Delfina spent time together she would have wanted to enslave him, just as she did all the others. Nor is it far-fetched to suppose that Delfina was a supreme one-off in his otherwise quiet sex life, apart from the first blaze of passion with George Sand. That he had known no similar experiences with other women and that he wrote no similar letters to other women does not mean that with this one truly exceptional woman he did not enjoy passionate sexual ecstasy.

The *des durka* reference would take time to explain fully, but its meaning is clear enough. Although in Polish it means 'E flat' it was linked by Chopin with the Polish word *dziurka*, or 'little hole', and became a piece of love-speak between the two paramours for her 'notoriously hospitable vulva'. The complete story is told in Ruth Jordan's biography.

Chopin also had this to say to Delfina on the process of composition:

> Creating a work of art is like giving birth to a child. Some of you women die in childbirth, others spit a baby out like a pip. As for me, I have labour pains. I feel I have in my head a beautiful idea all ready to come out, but when I write it down I realise I have left gaps and it is not what I had in mind. On paper everything looks different and it drives me to despair.

Chopin continued to be jealous of Delfina's liaisons, especially one with a young male 'pupil' to whom she gave music lessons. 'Don't take me for a fool,' he wrote to her, 'I can see only too clearly what's going on, I am certain these lessons are only an excuse for an amorous adventure. If you want to break up with me, say so openly, and don't talk to me about so-called music lessons.'

Soon afterwards, in the summer of 1836, they did break up, but not because of Delfina's other affairs. Having reached the ripe old age of 30 and gained no lasting satisfaction from her string of men, she responded positively to a bid from her supposedly reformed husband to give their marriage another go. The break with Chopin was friendly, not least because his own parents' happy relationship had left him with a belief in marriage as an institution. To show there was no ill will, he dedicated to Delfina his F minor Piano Concerto. They spent their last few weeks together at her villa in Enghien, before Chopin bade her farewell in July and Delfina returned to her husband in August.

That was by no means The End, however. The Potockis' attempt to save their marriage failed, and a year after their reunion in 1836 Delfina again packed her bags and divorce proceedings were begun. In no time, of course, she plunged into another affair, this time with the young aristocratic Polish playwright and poet Sigismund Krasinski, one of whose poems Chopin later set to music. This was the Big One for both of them, with Krasinski sending Delfina enough letters to fill a mega-sized warehouse – well, more than 5,000 altogether. However, Krasinski's father would have none of it and after four years the poet married a very attractive Countess Eliza Branicka. This marriage, as you might have guessed, did not put an end to the affair, and Delfina and Krasinski remained a discreet item for years to come.

When Delfina returned to Paris in 1842, Chopin and Sand, who had first met in 1836, were no longer making love. Chopin *may* have made a passionate and successful bid to rekindle his flame with Delfina in another letter, also disputed and alas too long to reproduce here, which he may have written in response to her demands for an 'explanation or an apology'. They continued to correspond and retained a tender and intense friendship to the very end of Chopin's life. In 1848 he dedicated to her his Minute Waltz from Op. 64. In her only extant letter to him, dated the following year, she confided that 'I too have not been altogether happy in this world.'

Two days before his death Delfina arrived hot-foot from Nice at his apartment in the place Vendôme, reportedly to the greeting 'God has spared me so that I might see you again'. Let Ruth Jordan take up the poignant story, based on an account by Solange which inspired a somewhat romanticised oil painting of the scene by F.-J. Barrias:

> He then asked her to sing for him. The drawing-room piano was rolled into the bedroom and the Countess, fighting back her tears, began to sing. In the middle of the second song he had a violent fit of coughing. The singing was discontinued, Gutmann lifted the frail body of the patient in order to prop him into a less agonising position, the other people in the room knelt down in prayer.

1835 Maria Wodzinska

'Oh, we know Maria has won his heart.'
a family friend to Chopin's sister Louisa

Partly owing to Delfina's urgings that he should settle down with a wife, Chopin made the only marriage proposal of his life, to Maria Wodzinska, a girl from a Polish family which, with 50,000 acres of land around their home near Torun (to the north-west of Warsaw), was certainly wealthy if not truly blue-blooded. By the time Maria's family finally turned him down Chopin seems to have suffered considerable anguish, quite possibly a good deal more than his rather passive 'secret' fiancée. However, the lack of intimate letters between the couple makes it difficult to gauge

the feelings of either of them. Chopin sent Maria only one personal letter throughout the courtship, observing all the
proprieties by sending her 'stiff expressions of respect' through
her mother. In turn, Maria confined her written messages to brief
formal postscripts to her mother's letters to Chopin, whom Mrs
Wodzinska came to regard more as a 'fourth son' than as a
potential son-in-law.

After spending the summer of 1835 with his parents in
Karlsbad, Chopin had made his way to Dresden where by chance
he renewed his acquaintance with the Wodzinski family, whose
three sons had boarded with the Chopins while attending the
Lyceum in Warsaw. Chopin, then 25, immediately fell in love
with the family's pretty, dark-haired, olive-skinned daughter
Maria, then only sixteen. She was not only an accomplished
pianist and singer, but also, on the evidence of her watercolours
of Chopin, a talented painter as well.

Shortly before leaving Dresden on 28 September, he left with
her as love tokens the opening fragment of his Nocturne in E
flat, conceived some years earlier, and the tender, yearning and
dreamy Waltz in A flat, 'L'Adieu', Op. 69 no. 1 ('For Mlle Marie').
Interestingly, he was later to dedicate this same waltz to other
ladies after his pursuit of Maria came to nothing! During that
autumn his preoccupation with Maria drew from him the second
of his twelve Studies of Op. 25. In the key of F minor, it is
reportedly a musical portrait of her. (The first study was written
the following summer.)

Even if Maria's parents were initially well disposed towards the
match, they must have been alarmed to read in the Warsaw press
that December of Chopin's death, whither the news had finally
spread from Heidelberg where he had suffered a major bronchial
attack in October during his return trip to Paris. Throughout
that winter Chopin was frequently laid up as consumption tight-
ened its grip on him for the third year in succession.

In the following summer of 1836 Chopin, again in a fragile
state of health, spent the whole of August with the Wodzinskis
in Marienbad, where the sweethearts made music and went for
long country walks. He then followed Mrs Wodzinska and her
two daughters to Dresden, where it was probably love that
inspired him to write his beautiful Study in A flat, actually the
first of the twelve in Op. 25 and known as the 'Aeolian harp'
because of its gentle arpeggios. He also set another, rather
mournful, song to words, by the Polish poet Stefan Witwicki,

entitled 'The Ring'. The poem seems perhaps an odd choice for a musician to set to music on the eve of proposing to his sweetheart. While accepting that all attempts to link life with creativity are danger-fraught, perhaps nevertheless we might infer that Chopin intuitively, and maybe unconsciously, divined the slenderness of his chances of ever marrying Maria. The loss of Konstancja may also have been on his mind.

> And I already loved you,
> And for your left little finger
> A silver ring I gave you.
>
> Others have married girls
> I faithfully loved;
> There came a young lad, a stranger,
> Though I gave a ring.
>
> Musicians were invited
> At the wedding I sang!
> To another you became a wife,
> I still loved.
>
> Today the girls jeered at me,
> Bitterly I wept:
> In vain have I been faithful and constant,
> In vain did I give a ring.

Nevertheless, Chopin formally proposed to Maria at twilight on 9 September, the day after writing this song! Maria apparently accepted him, but Mrs Wodzinska, while winking at a secret engagement, made it clear that he was being put on probation pending a period of good behaviour in Paris and the future state of his health. 'You must go to bed by eleven,' she warned him after his return, 'and drink only *eau de gomme* [an aromatic syrup]. Do keep well, dear Fryderyk. I give you my solemn blessing like a loving m[other].' The sad fact is that for most of his adult life he suffered acute physical discomfort, especially during the Parisian winters.

Alas, the letters from the Wodzinski home became less frequent and less encouraging. Maria's parents can hardly really be blamed for not wanting their daughter to be tied up with a man who, however talented, was unlikely to reach the age of 50. True, his tastes and inclinations were indeed aristocratic, but his living was hand to mouth, and he was only, in his own self-deprecating words, 'a street musician'.

In the following summer of 1837, having refused George Sand's invitation to go to her country house at Nohant, Chopin went to London for two weeks in late July. Still anxiously awaiting news from the Wodzinskis, he was, according to a friend, 'in a dreadful state of mind' and went around largely incognito. While there he received a letter forwarded to him from Mrs Wodzinska which seems to have ended his hopes both of seeing Maria that summer, and of any prospect of marrying her.

Some time later he tied up all Mrs Wodzinska's letters, with Maria's occasional postscripts, into a bundle and labelled it, tellingly, 'My Sorrows'. Maria, of course, simply had no say in the matter – just like Liszt's early sweetheart of about the same age, Caroline de Saint Cricq, whose father, apoplectic at the thought of her marrying a piano player, dumped her on to some near-geriatric fogey with the requisite thousands of acres and a coach and six in which to drive round them.

Surely it was no accident that Chopin composed the Funeral March, later to be incorporated into the B flat minor Sonata, around this time. In the same vein, Jeremy Siepmann suggests that the concurrently composed B major Nocturne, Op. 32 no. 1, is a 'musical parable of love and loss whose surprise tragic ending is as powerful, in its way, as anything he ever wrote.'

Inexperienced with women as he undoubtedly was, Chopin had probably been more in love with love – or with the idea of getting married and becoming a family man – than with a real woman. Maria was, after all, only sixteen when he met her, and the couple had spent no more than a fortnight together in 1835 and just over a month in 1836. Nevertheless, in Jim Samson's words, 'the shattering of a dream is painful in itself.'

In 1841 Maria married Count Joseph Skarbeck, the son of Chopin's godfather – but not for long. The unhappy marriage was annulled after eight years, and Maria was married again to a man with a tubercular condition. She died in 1896 at the age of 77.

George Sand (1804–76)

She lived her truths one at a time, each cancelling the last.
Gastone Belotti

From the start it seemed an unlikely pairing.
Jim Samson: *Chopin*

Chopin is her evil genius, her moral vampire, her cross.
the Polish poet Mickiewicz

They are as far apart as the Antipodes are from France.
Countess Marie d'Agoult

a walking graveyard
Jules Sandeau

It's not difficult to see why Chopin was at first repelled by Sand, nor is it hard to see why he eventually succumbed and then became enslaved. After first meeting her at a salon given by Liszt and his mistress Countess Marie d'Agoult at their apartment in the Hôtel de France in the autumn of 1836 (Sand was living on the floor below), Chopin observed to his friend Ferdinand Hiller: 'What an unpleasant woman that Sand is! . . . Is she really a woman? I am ready to doubt it.' And to his parents he wrote: 'I did not like her face, there is something disagreeable about it. There is something about her which puts me off.' She was altogether unladylike; smoking, wearing trousers and taking liberties by addressing everyone informally as *tu*.

Their second meeting was on 5 November when Liszt arrived with Marie on one arm and George on the other at Chopin's apartment on the rue Chaussée d'Antin. Sand was particularly impressed by the fastidious elegance of Chopin's taste in furniture and fittings.

She was still searching for the Perfect Love to which she believed all women had a right and about which she so often wrote in her taboo-breaking novels – a relationship which would be completely satisfying in body and soul. Her first novel *Indiana* of 1832, the first to be written under her pen name of George Sand, pleaded for women's rights in extra-marital affairs; while her next one *Lélia* (1833) portrayed marriage as an unnatural state, an anathema, no less, to passion and, ultimately, love. 'The very thought of coupling without love is loathsome,' she later wrote in her *Histoire de ma vie*. 'A wife who turns to her husband with the thought of dominating his will is no better than a prostitute who plies her trade in order to live, or than a courtesan who sells herself in return for luxury.'

On that occasion in November, Chopin again was uninterested in her, leaving her to be entertained by the writer Ferdinand Denis. Nevertheless, persuaded by Marie d'Agoult, who seemed anxious to pair them off, possibly to deflect attention away from her own liaison with Liszt, Chopin invited Sand to a big soirée he held in his rooms on 13 December where the guests included the huge-nosed German pianist-composer Pixis, the top-ranking tenor Adolphe Nourrit, the aforementioned Custine, Heine, and Delacroix. Various Polish exiles were also there including the poet Grzymala – 'a gigantic Pole, of extremely smart appearance, frock-coated in the latest fashion in a monstrous, a pyramidal garment, all braid and trimmings' – who became a kind of father-figure to Chopin. Another fellow-Pole was the composer Josef Brzowski who has left a description of Sand in half-male, half-female attire:

> Madame G. Sand, dark, dignified and cold ... Her dress fantastic (obviously proclaiming her desire to be noticed), composed of a white frock with a crimson sash and a kind of white shepherdess's corsage with crimson buttons. Her dark hair parted in the middle, falling in curls on both sides of her face and secured with a ribbon around her brow. Nonchalantly she took her place on the sofa near the fireplace, and, lightly blowing out clouds of smoke from her cigar, answered briefly but seriously the questions of the men sitting beside her ... After Liszt and she had played a sonata, Chopin offered his guests ices. George Sand, glued to her sofa, never quitted her cigar for a moment.

Only Ferdinand Denis realised that she was actually wearing a Turkish peasant costume: a slit caftan over a tight bodice and baggy trousers.

The one certainty is that at this point there was no prospect of a future relationship between Sand and Chopin! Besides his immediate physical antipathy, they were poles apart in many respects. While Sand was consumed with a passion for various forms of utopian socialism, embracing illuminism, republicanism and many other 'isms', Chopin was, in his own words, 'no revolutionary' and refused ever to devote his talents to political causes – other than Polish nationalism, of course. With his conservative views, devoutly Catholic roots and fastidious respect for social proprieties the couple were indeed, as Marie d'Agoult said, 'as far apart as the Antipodes are from France'.

Chopin and Sand didn't meet again for almost sixteen months. We have seen that because he was preoccupied with Maria in the summer of 1837, he turned down the chance of a potentially recuperative holiday at Sand's spacious Louis XVI-style country mansion at Nohant (near Châteauroux in the Berry countryside, some 180 miles south of Paris). He elected instead to go to London.

It was at Nohant that Sand, the illegitimate daughter of Marshal de Saxe, had lived with her dull, unimaginative and long-nosed husband Baron Casimir Dudevant, a huntin', shootin' and fishin' type whom she had married at the age of eighteen. After sticking it out for nine years in what soon became a marriage of convenience, during which she bore a son Maurice by her husband and a daughter Solange apparently by a lover Stéphane Ajasson, she had escaped to Paris where she could spread her feminist wings to the full.

She was undoubtedly a woman of phenomenal talent, energy, originality and independence. 'What I want,' she wrote to her mother, 'is not society, noise, theatres, clothes . . . it's liberty. Here I can go out when I like, at ten o'clock or midnight, that's my business.' Literary works flowed from her pen like grape juice in a bumper *vendange*, many of them through the night when she had fulfilled all her domestic obligations. She was to write 104 published works altogether – including some 60-odd novels and several plays, all of them distinguished by a romantic love of nature and an extravagant, outspoken moral idealism in a world which was then (and still is) far less advanced than the visions to which she aspired. Her genius flowered during a time when France was in a state of intellectual ferment. Romanticism was a live issue in which 'Passion was King, as reason once had been, and the Irrational was worshipped as God.'

In addition, she wrote numerous essays and almost 20,000 letters. Not surprisingly, in England she was generally regarded as a force for evil and a wrecker of family values, but she was avidly read by such literary giants as Dostoevsky, Thackeray, Henry James and Marcel Proust.

She was also something of a polymath, being a decent painter and competent pianist – much to the chagrin of her piano-phobic husband, whose taste in music obviously never stretched beyond bellowing hunting horns to cries of 'Yoicks' and 'Tally-ho' (or whatever they are in French). Her other interests included butterfly hunting, phrenology, astronomy, folk medicine, embroidery, gardening, jam making, collecting folk songs – and collecting men.

The poet Heine, who penned such vivid portraits of other artistic figures living in or passing through Paris, was certainly fascinated by Sand:

> Her forehead is not high, her delicious chestnut brown locks reach her shoulders. Her eyes are somewhat languid, at least they are not brilliant, and their fire may have been dimmed by many tears, or may have consumed itself in her works, which have lighted conflagrations in all the world . . . Only her somewhat protruding lower lip suggests sexuality. Her shoulders are beautiful, no, magnificent. Ditto arms and hands, small like her feet. Her breasts I leave to others to describe, as I confess incompetence. Her body is a bit thick and seems far too short. Only the head bears witness to her idealism and reminds me of the finest examples of Greek art . . . She is monosyllabic because of pride, not thinking it worthwhile to waste her intellect on you, or because of self-centredness, taking in the best of your thoughts to incorporate them later in one of her books [. . .] And she endowed our much beloved Frédéric Chopin with a good deal of worldly wisdom.

Sand's Lovers

By the time she first met Chopin, Sand had mown through a meadow of men like a combine harvester in her avid, not to say desperate search for the Perfect Relationship. Here is Sand's list of men (and one woman), with snippets from André Maurois' *Lélia*, The Life of George Sand, translated by Gerard Hopkins:

• The writer and young lawyer **Jules Sandeau** whom she met when she was 26 and who became a trigger for her divorce. His shyness, his 'extreme youth, his pink and white complexion, his golden hair, the cast of his mind, the aura of Paris which surrounded him, his weakness for romantic dreaming' – all these acted as a stimulant to her pursuit. He then became enslaved by her 'wild beauty, the Quixotic, assertive character, the black and gleaming eyes, the lithe figure, of the mistress of Nohant'. After their affair he referred to her as 'a walking graveyard'.

• The volatile and fiery actress **Marie Dorval** 'brought up in a world of sordid passions', and the mistress of Alfred de Vigny when Sand met her. Although this was almost certainly not a full-blown lesbian relationship, Sand was, in her own words, 'utterly in thrall to her'. She was certainly infatuated, to judge by this note of 1833:

> I can't see you today, darling – no such luck! But on Monday, either in the morning or in the evening, at the theatre or in your bedroom before you are up, I must come and give you a kiss. If I don't, I cannot guarantee that I may not do something mad! . . . Goodbye, you loveliest of women.'

- **Prosper Merimée**, whose short novel *Carmen* formed the basis of Bizet's opera. According to Maurois, after Sand agreed to submit to his insistent advances they went back to her apartment where they ate a light supper, after which, with the help of her maid, she assumed her *négligée*, a confection reminiscent partly of Turkey, partly of Spain. Mérimée later declared that during this part of the proceedings she had been guilty of lack of modesty which had had the effect of killing all desire in him . . . the evening ended in a wretched and ridiculous fiasco.
- The Romantic poet **Alfred de Musset** ('the most effeminate lyric poet known to history') with whom she had a stormy mother–son relationship. De Musset's winning move was to declare that he loved her 'like a child'. 'He loves me like a child!' wrote Sand in her novel *Elle et lui*. 'Oh, my God, what is he saying! – and does he know the pain he is causing me?' She saw him again. He wept. She yielded, declaring afterwards: 'But for your youth, but for your tears which have made me weak, we should still have been to one another as brother and sister.' De Musset wrote an account of their liaison, including their trip to Venice, in his *Confession of a Child of the Century* (1836).
- The Italian doctor **Pietro Pagello** who had treated de Musset for brain fever during their visit to Venice. This was a calmer affair in which Pagello was essentially out of his depth with such alarming post-coital questions as these:

> When your passion has been satisfied will you give me thanks? When I have made you happy, will you know how to tell me so? . . . Do the pleasures of love leave you panting and besotted, or do they plunge you into a state of divine ecstasy? Does the movement of your heart outlive the prickings of your flesh when you have parted from her you love?

Although sad to lose his mistress when she left Venice, Pagello was also relieved to be able to appease his family and free himself from 'the load of a great sin'.

• The leading militant republican lawyer **Michel de Bourges** – 'a man cut from a block of granite, all straight lines and sharp angles, like the statue of an ancient Gaul' – who helped arrange her separation from Dudevant. A passionate eccentric who sported a kind of turban consisting of three knotted handker-chiefs, de Bourges was a complete match for Sand intellectually, and she saw no reason to delay the consummation of their extraordinary friendship beyond two days from their first meeting in April 1835. She had, after all, loved him 'from the day of her birth'.

• The Swiss poet **Charles Didier**, whom she seems latterly to have given a very hard time. According to his diary, their fraught affair ended in tears after a planned night of passion at the Hôtel de France in the autumn of 1836:

> The night ended with a scene of horrible frankness and a series of appalling confessions. What she said, far from giving me new life, froze my blood, so that I was little better than a corpse in her presence . . . There are depths of ferocity in her. She loves to make others suffer, and takes pleasure in the pain she causes.

• The tutor of her son Maurice, playwright **Félicien Mallefille**, an excitable créole 'with a beard seven foot long' whose presence in her life inconveniently overlapped with her acquisition of Chopin. Although initially finding him 'outrageous, ugly, vain and stupid', Sand had a lightning conversion, for within a matter of weeks, her 'physical repulsion' had metamorphosed into love. He was now 'a sublime character' with whom she settled down for a quasi-honeymoon at the Hôtel Brittanique in Fontainebleau.

• The lady-killing actor **Pierre Bocage** – 'the perfect type of a romantic "star", tall, slim and endowed with Byronic good looks' – who was the monologuist in the première of Berlioz's *Lélio*, and later Director of the Odéon Theatre. He and Sand had a fleeting romance in 1837 and he continued to pay court to her.

Conquest

The delicious exhaustion of a fulfilled love
Sand

'Tell him I adore him', Sand wrote from Nohant to Marie d'Agoult on 17 February 1837. And again, on 3 April, 'Tell him I worship him', both declarations as yet to no avail. Sand returned to Paris in April 1838, by then having obtained a legal separation from her husband, possession of Nohant and also custody of the children. She continued her pursuit by making sure she was invited to soirées where Chopin was present, notably at the salon of her friend Countess Charlotte Marliani, wife of the Spanish consul in Paris. She also met Chopin at the homes of Grzymala and the ever-solicitous Marquis de Custine. Gradually, it became obvious to their intimate circle that Sand's determined pursuit was succeeding. It could hardly fail after she threw a Cupid's dart at him in the form of a note on which she had scribbled the words '*on vous adore*' and Marie Dorval had added, three times, underneath '*et moi aussi*'. Chopin stuck this letter in an album next to other precious souvenirs.

Chopin was certainly weakening but still drew back from her bedroom, quite possibly because of his innate shyness, or because of his residual feelings for Maria. Baffled, after returning to Nohant in May, Sand sent Grzymala a letter exceeding 5,000 words expressing her predicament. Part of it reads:

> The other day, as we were leaving your house, he said something about resisting temptation . . . I do not remember his exact words. I think he said something about certain acts spoiling beautiful memories. This surely is nonsense. He cannot believe what he said, can he? Who is that wretched woman who has given him such ideas about physical love? Has he had a mistress unworthy of him? Poor angel! Those women should be hanged who degrade in men's eyes the most respectable and holy thing in creation, the divine mystery, the most serious and most sublime act in the entire life of the universe.

Chopin could hold out no longer. On 6 June Sand returned to Paris determined to follow Rousseau's 'moral standards of the heart' and get her man. 'I will be in Paris on Thursday on business,' she wrote to Grzymala. 'Come and see me and do not tell the boy.' Perhaps even then her feelings for him were primarily maternal! Whether or not, within days Chopin and Sand were lovers, having surrendered to what Sand described to Delacroix as 'the delicious exhaustion of a fulfilled love'.

'You think this happiness cannot last,' Sand also wrote to

Delacroix in the autumn of that year. 'If I consult my memory and my reason, then it certainly cannot. But if I trust my heart and feelings, it seems to me it can last for ever.' During this year Delacroix painted a double portrait (now cut in two) of the lovers, with Chopin seated at the piano and Sand standing 'curiously attentive and subdued' behind him.

The chemistry of this unlikely pairing is surely best left to an intuitive and highly perceptive woman to explain. The most vivid and convincing I have read is by Charlotte Haldane in her novelised biography of Liszt's relationship with Marie d'Agoult, *The Galley Slaves of Love*:

> [Chopin] was repelled by her pseudo-masculinity, by her fondness for men's clothes, for cigars and brandy. Yet he was almost magnetically attracted by her mental and physical vigour, her virility, which was complementary to his own frailty and sickliness. He was already consumptive. George herself was never so irresistible as when she decided to make a difficult conquest. She then became all woman, in spite of her masculine mannerisms; tender, maternal, affectionate, going to every length to make herself indispensable until gratitude became transformed into passion and the intransigence of the desired one melted into helpless dependence on her. So it was now with Chopin.

Once he was well and truly hooked, Chopin's musical imagination would take flight. It would soar to a level of excitement that would rarely flag for the next nine years. But just then, in the summer of 1837, they felt a need to escape from Paris to a place where Chopin could work over the winter in a climate kinder to his tubercular condition, and where Sand's fifteen-year-old son Maurice might recover from his rheumatism. Moreover, Sand needed to escape from her tiresome lover Mallefille, of whom Chopin was becoming ever more resentful.

The hot-blooded Mallefille's exit from the triangle is a story that was ready-made for the melodramas at the Théâtre des Nouveautés, where poverty compelled Berlioz to work for a time. In August, Sand sent the still unsuspecting Mallefille off to Normandy for a fortnight with her son Maurice. Realising on his return that he had been two-timed, Mallefille, so the story goes, waited, pistol at the ready, opposite Sand's apartment to wreak his revenge on her. Sand was only saved at the crucial moment by the fortuitous arrival of a large wagon. Mallefille was dismissed, but the episode sharpened Sand's determination to leave Paris.

Winter in Majorca

Being sick to death at Majorca, he made music that fully smelled of paradise.
Sand

I care for him like my child. He is an angel of sweetness and kindness.
Sand to her friend Charlotte Marliani, 14 December 1838

a truly extraordinary episode in both their lives.
Samson

After various deliberations they chose Majorca, notwithstanding the solicitous misgivings of Custine and Grzymala. Having met up in Perpignan at the end of October, the party of four (Sand's nine-year-old daughter Solange was also included) arrived at Palma on the small steamer *El Mallorquin* on 8 November. For the next six days they had to endure impossibly noisy and cramped accommodation over a barrel-maker's workshop – trestle beds with slabs of slate in place of mattresses, and just one straw-covered chair – together with a diet of fish and garlic, a pervasive stench of rancid oil, and the buzzing and nasty bites of mosquitoes. Eventually they moved to a primitively furnished 'villa' just outside Palma – an aptly named 'So'n Vent' (house of the wind) with thin damp walls, no window panes, no chimney, and an asphyxiating brazier.

Nevertheless they were happy in the spring-like weather. 'I am in Palma among palms, cedars, aloes, oranges, lemons, fig-trees, olives and pomegranates, etc.' wrote Chopin to Fontana in a letter that took well over a month to reach him in Paris. 'A sky like turquoise, a sea like lapis lazuli, mountains like emerald, air like heaven. Sun all day, and hot; everyone in summer clothing . . . In short, a glorious life . . . I am near to what is most beautiful. I am better.'

At the end of the month, Chopin embarked upon the completion of his 24 Preludes Op. 28. Alas, conditions soon deteriorated, with 'So'n Vent' becoming damp, cold, and full of acrid smoke from the charcoal burner. To make matters worse,

Chopin started coughing blood after over-exerting himself struggling against a violent wind which caused permanent damage to
his lungs. (His youngest sister Emilia had died ominously of TB
at the age of only fourteen in 1827.)

Perhaps (only perhaps) his E minor Prelude, completed at this
very time, reflects his feelings of despair at his condition. It is
certainly one of his saddest pieces, and, in a transcription for
organ, was to be played at his funeral only eleven years later.

The primitively suspicious locals were none too pleased at this
outbreak and potential 'plague' of 'consumption' (such had been
the diagnosis of the local doctors), and when the family's panic-
stricken landlord demanded exorbitant compensation for his
'soiled' summer house, they were forced to retreat. They crossed
heaths and fields of asphodel to a three-room cell Sand had also
rented in an old monastery seven miles away up in the hills –
the Charterhouse of Valldemosa, adorned with Arabic mosaics
and overlooking the sea on two sides. They arrived there on 15
December to find that their sole fellow 'guests' were an apoth-
ecary, a sacristan and a woman called Maria-Antonina who offered
her services as maid 'for the love of God' – which extended to
helping herself to their clothes and their food.

In spite of all these travails their spirits remained buoyant for
a while. Chopin was now truly and madly in love with Sand,
who, while describing her feelings for him as 'maternal', wrote
that 'His goodness and patience are angelic. We are so different
from most of the people and things around us . . . our family ties
are strengthened by it and we cling to each other with more
affection and intimate happiness.' In spite of the ever-swindling
locals who charged them exorbitant prices for fish, eggs and
vegetables, and the spartan conditions, Chopin was also looking
mainly on the bright side. He wrote to Fontana that in spite of
the 'queer place' in which they were living, 'no-one has yet scared
away the eagles that soar every day above our heads.'

He completed his Preludes and began his C sharp minor
Scherzo No. 3 and C minor Polonaise within a week of the
arrival, in mid-January 1839, of his Pleyel piano – the despatch
of which from Paris via the local customs, who wanted to charge
an import tax not far short of the value of the instrument, is a
riveting saga in itself. While at Valldemosa he also completed the
so-called 'Palma Mazurka' Op. 41, and probably worked on
the Op. 37 Nocturnes and the B flat minor Sonata. Sand valiantly
did all the household chores in spite of the primitive conditions,

even buying a sheep and a goat for basic sustenance. She also taught her children for several hours a day, worked on her new novel *Spiridion* and also on changes to *Lélia*. Both writer and composer had publishers who were breathing down their necks for manuscripts against which advances or loans had been paid.

Throughout their time at Valldemosa they had virtually no contact with the distrustful local peasants, who understandably regarded the presence of such an ungodly ménage in the monastery as a profanity. (The curé spread it about that they were heathens, Mohammedans or Jews.) It does seem that Sand and Chopin betrayed some of the lack of imagination and empathy of the 'English abroad', making no serious effort to understand such a primitive culture. Chopin had probably half expected to find room service with coffee and croissants *à la parisienne*.

Alas, as the winter deepened, so did melancholy. Chopin, according to Sand – who was certainly sometimes inclined to romanticise or melodramatise, although not on this occasion – became increasingly morbid and depressed when left alone, believing the monastery to be haunted by terrifying phantoms. (A sudden vision of 'those cursed creatures' was, indeed, to cause him to walk off the concert platform some nine years later during the middle of his performance, in Manchester, of the Funeral March from his B flat minor Sonata.)

Most of Chopin's Majorcan compositions are, indeed, imbued with melancholy or torment. They seem to reflect his increasing obsessions with his health, their isolation and the inhospitality of the locals. According to Sand, when on one occasion she and her children returned from a walk they found Chopin playing 'a wonderful Prélude with the tears streaming down his cheeks', beside himself with anxiety and convinced that they were dead. During their absence he had imagined himself to be dead as well.

He had a vision of himself drowned in a lake. Heavy, icy drops of water, he said, were falling rhythmically upon his breast, and when I made him listen to the raindrops which were, in fact, dripping with measured regularity upon the roof, he denied that they were what he heard. He even grew angry when I used the phrase *imitative harmony*. He protested as strongly as he knew how – and he was right – against the childishness of such aural imitations. His genius was rich in the mysterious harmonies suggested by natural happenings, but they were always transposed into the sublime equivalents of his musical thought, and were never a mere slavish repetition of sounds that had struck upon his ear from the outside world. What he had composed that evening was full of the sound of raindrops on the monastery roof, but they had been transformed in his imagination and in his music into tears falling upon his heart.

Un Hiver au Midi de l'Europe; Majorque et les Majorcains

The debate about the 'Raindrops' Prelude (usually thought to be the one in D flat major) will rage for ever. What is certain is that although no link can be proven between actual experience and the finished work of art, many people will believe there is one.

'For Chopin,' Sand wrote in *Histoire de ma vie*, 'everything beneath the Spanish sun was, for him, repellent. He was dying with impatience to be gone.' And she, for her part, had good cause to fear for his life. Once the depressing heavy rains had ended, they decided to abort what had now become a 'complete fiasco' and made for Palma. During the rough journey there Chopin suffered another lung haemorrhage. They crossed to the mainland on 13 February, again on *El Mallorquin*, with Chopin spitting blood in the worst cabin on the boat, thick with the stench of a cargo of live, screaming pigs. Then after spending a week or so in Barcelona and nearby Arenys-de-Mar, they made their way on *Le Phénicien* to Marseilles where they were based for about three months before eventually reaching the rural tranquillity of Nohant in June. They remained there until October.

Life at Nohant

The Majorcan episode had caused a marked and permanent deterioration in Chopin's health, but Sand's affectionate mothering of her 'little Chop' (or *le petit*) now nurtured him towards the full flowering of his genius. During that summer of 1839 at Nohant he completed one of his finest and most substantial achievements, the dramatic, stormy and doom-laden B flat minor Sonata, as well as the soft and tender G major Nocturne Op. 37 no. 2, and the F sharp major Impromptu Op. 36. The despairing mood of the Sonata, in particular what Chopin called the 'gossiping of demons' in the 90 second Finale, is another example, says Jeremy Siepmann, of 'that strange lack of synchronicity that often separates a work of art from the external circumstances of its composition'. (An example in reverse is Mozart's joyous *Eine kleine Nachtmusik*, completed just over two months after the death of his father in what was a traumatic year of misfortunes for him, 1787.)

On 19 June 1839 Sand carved the date on the window of her room at Nohant. Was it to mark the anniversary of the consummation of their love – such a lengthy relationship in itself being an unusual event in her life – or was it to signify that their love-making was at an end? We shall never know, but it seems reasonable to suppose that by this time Sand's metamorphosis from lover-mother to mother-only was complete.

The rest of the Chopin–Sand story must be telescoped into a few paragraphs. The modern writer Eleanor Perényi has described in her biography of Liszt the rural enchantment of Nohant:

> It was a plain, handsome manor house without pretension: the main gates faced the village square and the garden, at that season scented with white lilac, was informal. Imperfectly standardised shrubs stood in tubs on the terrace; shaggy archways of vine bordered the lawn; an old tower housed the flock of noisy doves. A farm belonged also to the property, and woods abounding in wild strawberries; nearby flowed the Indre, one of those ravishing miniature rivers that bind the landscape of central France like so many ribbons.

Delacroix and Marie d'Agoult were also entranced. 'This is a delightful place,' wrote Delacroix in 1842, ' . . . every now and then there blows in through your window – opening on to the garden – a breath of the music of Chopin who is at work in his room, and it mingles with the song of the nightingales, and the scent of roses.' Marie d'Agoult, whose relations with Sand became increasingly strained, recalled in her *Mémoires* enjoying 'a prom-enade along the Indre, the length of the woody path, across the meadows covered with forget-me-knots, nettles and English daisies, climbing many rustic fences, meeting with families of geese and herds of cattle, majestically ruminating'.

Sand herself etched their life-style there, making clear enough her role as mother rather than mistress to the man she now sometimes called 'Chip', 'Chipette', 'Chopinsky', 'little Chip-Chop', 'little one' or 'the boy' and whom even Solange was soon referring to as 'sans-sex Chopin':

> We lead the same monotonous, quiet, gentle life. We dine in the open; friends come to see us, now one, now another; we smoke and chat, and in the evening when they have gone, Chopin plays to me

at twilight, after which he goes to bed like a child at the same time as Maurice and Solange.

Sand would then sit up all night writing and then at dawn walk down to the river, undress, and lie naked on the sand 'with the water up to my chin, smoking a cigar and looking at the reflection of the moon in the stream around my knees'. Then she went home to bed and slept till noon.

Apart from 1840, Chopin spent all his summers at Nohant until 1849, and did most of his composing there – altogether, more than half of his entire output. He had the occasional company of friends like Delacroix and the famed singer Pauline Viardot as welcome distractions from the plethora of rather tedious 'artisan poets' whom Sand gathered round her. In the summer of 1844 he completed his third Piano Sonata in B minor, more serene than the earlier one in B flat minor, and unforgettable for the triumphant grandeur of its closing bars.

As an out-and-out townie, Chopin didn't ever really enjoy the realities of life in the country. 'He was always yearning for Nohant,' Sand wrote, 'but actually could never endure Nohant. . . . He would go for occasional walks, settle down under a tree, or pick a few flowers. Then he would go back to the house and shut himself in his room.' What is certain, however, is that whatever his reservations, Chopin was extremely well looked after there. After getting up late in his south-facing first-floor room, he would spend most of the day composing, until the family and guests assembled at six o'clock for dinner. From time to time the prevailing tranquillity was disturbed when he devised theatrical evenings and pantomimes in which he was able to display to the full his remarkable gifts of mimicry – gifts in which he had revelled ever since his schoolboy days.

Sand and Chopin in Paris

The winter seasons in Paris were generally too demanding for him to have much spare energy for composition. As the most pre-eminent pianist in Paris, he was all too often obliged to socialise with, and play for, grand families such as the Rothschilds and the Stockhausens. He also had to make time for all his pupils. Nevertheless his lifestyle in the capital, health permitting, was generally congenial and placid. Having settled in an apartment in the rue Tronchet from the autumn of 1839, in 1841–2 he occupied a luxurious summer-house adjacent to Sand's at 16 rue Pigalle. Balzac sent a graphic and vivid vignette of the Sand ménage to his mistress Eva Hanska, in March 1841.

> She is living at the bottom of a garden, at no. 16, rue Pigalle, over the coach-house and stables belonging to a mansion facing the street. She has a dining-room furnished in carved oak. Her boudoir is done in café-au-lait, and the drawing room, in which she receives, is filled with flowers in superb Chinese vases. There is a flower stand which is always kept full. The upholstery is green. There is a side-table covered with odds and ends of bric-à-brac, and there are pictures by Delacroix as well as a portrait of herself by Calamatta . . . The piano is a magnificent square upright in rosewood. Chopin is always there. She smoked only cigarettes – nothing else. She doesn't get up till four. At that hour Chopin is finished with his lessons . . . Her bedroom is brown. She sleeps on two mattresses laid on the floor, Turkish fashion. *Ecco, contessa!*

In 1842 they both moved to the square d'Orléans, where they also lived separately but in the same block of apartments. 'We have even arranged to do only one lot of cooking, and to have our meals in common, which is much cheaper and more amusing than each of us living separately,' wrote Sand. To seal their domesticity they had even acquired a stray puppy, Mops, who dirtied the salon and brought in fleas.

Some notable events in Paris during these years can be no more than mentioned. Chopin performed with Moscheles before the royal family in 1839. He gave lucrative private performances in 1841 and 1842. In the winter of 1843 he completed his valedictory works in three genres: the Ballade in F minor Op. 52, the Polonaise in A flat major Op. 53 and the Scherzo in E major Op. 54. The year 1844 saw the death of his ever-solicitous and dearly loved father, followed by a visit in the summer of that same year from his sister Ludwika, with whom his ties were as strong as ever. 'Often, when I come in,' he wrote to her on 18 September, after her departure, 'I look to see if there is nothing left of you, and I see only the place by the couch, where we drank chocolate . . . More of you has remained in my room: on the table lies your embroidery – that slipper – folded inside an English blotter, and on the piano a tiny pencil, which was in your pocketbook, and which I find most useful.'

The Bust-up

Although ultimately insufficient to withstand the eruption of a sordid volcanic squabble within Sand's extended family in 1847, the bonds between the couple remained strong and deep during their post-Majorca years. At the same time, however, tensions between them intensified, first and foremost because Sand had banished Chopin from her bed. Towards the end of their nine years together, in May 1847, she wrote about the matter to Grzymala:

> For the last seven years now I have lived the life of a virgin, both with him and with others. I have grown old before my time, and it has cost me neither effort nor sacrifice, so weary had I become of passions, so disillusioned and beyond all remedy. If any woman in the world could inspire him with absolute confidence it was I, and yet he has never understood . . . He complains that I have killed something in him by deprivation: but I know that I should have killed him altogether had I acted differently . . . in the midst of all my efforts and sacrifices this man whom I love with a chaste maternal love is dying of the insane love he has for me.

Her claim to have been celibate is not strictly true because she had a brief affair with a young social activist to whom she took a shine, Louis Blanc, in 1845. This revival of passion may even have weakened her feelings towards Chopin, who in spite of his increasing suspicion and jealousy never at any stage wished to split with her. He was too emotionally dependent, whereas within weeks of their final rift Sand was having an affair with the journalist Victor Borie.

Chopin's 'pin-pricks' of jealousy, as Sand called them, turned into huge blisters. 'At the age of forty,' she wrote to her friend Frédéric François, 'I make myself ridiculous by having a sort of jealous lover at my side.' Her brief former affair with Bocage became a serious bone of contention and she had to promise to restrict her contacts with him. 'Everything upsets him and gives him pain,' Sand wrote to the actor, 'and I will make unheard-of sacrifices for his peace.' Chopin became increasingly suspicious even of her friendships with like-minded thinkers whom he couldn't stomach.

Their widely differing political outlooks have already been mentioned. They tended increasingly to avoid each other's circles. Sand had an aversion to his élitist salon friends whilst Chopin, in some ways undoubtedly a snob, had little time for her socialist intellectuals and bohemian artists. If Elizabeth Barrett Browning's description of this arty-farty crowd in one of her letters is anything to go by, Chopin's revulsion is all too imaginable:

> Crowds of ill-bred men who adore her *à genoux bas* betwixt a puff of smoke and ejection of saliva . . . I did not mind much the Greek in Greek costume who tutoyéd her, and kissed her, I believe, so Robert said: or the other vulgar man of the theatre who went down on his knees and called her 'sublime'. '*Caprice d'amitié*,' said she, with her quiet, gentle scorn.

There were other sources of friction as well. In the summer of 1841 at Nohant, Chopin became paranoid about what Sand might be learning from her friend Marie de Rozières about his unhappy and aborted engagement with Maria Wodzinska. At that time de Rozières was in the throes of an affair with Maria's brother Antoni.

On the domestic front, Chopin's Polish valet Jan upset the household staff at Nohant and eventually had to be sacked. More seriously, Maurice became ever more jealous of Chopin's role in his mother's life, while Solange, whose wilfulness and lack of self-control turned her into a 'screaming hellcat' when thwarted, used her wily charms to secure Chopin's support in battles with her mother and brother.

Lucrezia Floriani

All these mounting tensions provoked Chopin into bouts of cantankerous behaviour which Sand recalled in what was demonstrably a *roman à clef* describing their relationship, her novel *Lucrezia Floriani*. Published in instalments in 1846, it prophetically mirrored the breakup of their liaison, with herself as Lucrezia and Chopin as 'Prince Karol'. The correspondences between truth and fiction are unmistakable. Prince Karol is an artist, delicate and refined, who is driven to kill his mistress Lucrezia, six years older than himself and no longer young and beautiful, because of intensifying jealousies and differences in outlook. The parallels don't stop there: Prince Karol has Majorcan-style hallucinations; Lucrezia has a past history of lovers; Lucrezia's son is a spitting image of Maurice, and so on. Even more tellingly, Sand's later autobiography contains retreads of chunks of *Lucrezia*, especially of the descriptions of Prince Karol. Liszt also quoted from *Lucrezia* in his own biography of Chopin.

Of *Lucrezia*, Jim Samson believes that in spite of the licence of fiction and the bias of current events 'some of it has the ring of truth' supported by other descriptions of Chopin. He quotes one particular extract on Prince Karol's (i.e. Chopin's) petulant and difficult behaviour:

> As he was predominantly polite and reserved, no one could really know what he felt. The more infuriated he was, the colder he would become, and the extent of his anger could be measured only by his ice-cold politeness. On such occasions he could be truly unbearable, as he would spoil for an argument and would subject real life, which he did not understand, to so-called principles, which he could not define. He would then use his wit, his false and ironic wit, to torture those he loved. He would be supercilious, haughty, precious and distant. He would seem to nibble lightly enough, but would wound deeply, penetrating right to the soul. Or, if he lacked the courage to argue and mock, he would withdraw in lofty silence, sulking in a pathetic manner.

It seems that in the summer of 1845 the friction between them had been enough to prevent Chopin composing a note of music, and it wasn't until that autumn that he felt able to get to work on the Cello Sonata Op. 65, the *Barcarolle* Op. 60 and the *Polonaise-Fantaisie* Op. 61. It was around this time that his thoughts turned increasingly to his family and homeland, as if to re-establish a source of emotional support.

And yet! In spite of all this, there were still times when the ties between them seemed to be unbreakable before they snapped so suddenly in 1847. Sand acknowledged Chopin's incalculable moral support at times such as at the opening of her play *Cosima* in 1840. 'Without his perfect friendship,' she wrote to her half-brother, 'I would often have lost heart.' In November 1843 she wrote to Maurice, 'I cannot live without you and my weakling. Tell me truthfully how is he?' Only two years before the bust-up she was writing to her eldest 'chick' from Nohant, 'I am desolate to think that you are in the coach facing a difficult night ... Love me dear angel, my dear happiness, as I love you.' She even included a lock of hair with this letter. Wladimir Karénine wrote, fancifully but attractively, in his biography of Sand of her continuing inspiration and their mutual love of beauty:

> One evening, at Nohant, she talked to him as only she knew how to talk, of the peace of the countryside and the wonders of nature. 'What you have been saying,' he told her, 'is beautiful.' 'Do you really think so?' she replied: 'then put it into music.' Immediately, Chopin sat down and improvised a genuine pastoral symphony. George Sand, standing beside him, with her hand laid lightly on his shoulder, murmured: 'Pluck up courage, velvet fingers!'
>
> Who can say whether, without that hand upon his shoulder, without the magic influences of Nohant, Chopin, in the course of his short life, would have composed so many masterpieces? Who can even say whether he would have gone on living?

On more mundane but no less important levels, Sand made sure hot water was ready for Chopin whenever he returned to Paris on his own, served him a bowl of soup between his lessons, wrote out prescriptions for his medicines . . . Chopin, in his turn, paid Sand all manner of reciprocal kindnesses: he had a black *lévantine* dress made for her to his specifications, he nursed her in sickness, supported her proposal to start a newspaper in Berry, supervised her renovations, even down to the cleaning of mirrors and chimneys.

The *casus belli* of the final breakup was Chopin's response to sordid feuding within the family, too tortuous to describe in any detail here. (Both Ates Orga's and Jim Samson's books contain riveting accounts.) According to *Grove*, Chopin was unscrupulously used as a pawn by Solange in the quarrels between herself and her recently acquired, gold-digging sculptor husband Auguste Clésinger, and between Sand and Maurice, who had already unsuccessfully tried to break up his mother's liaison. The dénouement as described by Jim Samson is yet another melodrama bordering on farce:

> In the end they all came to blows. Clésinger threatened Maurice with a hammer, Sand interposed herself and was hit in the chest by her son-in-law. Maurice then fetched a gun. This was high drama, and Sand, not unreasonably, resolved it by expelling the couple and forbidding them to return.

Chopin sided with Solange, whom he seems always to have

been only too ready to believe – perhaps because he had fallen for her – and refused to accept Sand's conditions for a restoration of their friendship. Finding him stubborn, and feeling herself victimised, Sand refused to attempt any reconciliation, as is clear from her final letter to him of 28 July 1847 which ends:

> I will not engage in a battle of this kind; it appalls me. I would rather see you go to the enemy camp than defend myself against an enemy grown in my womb and nurtured on my milk . . .
>
> Do look after her since you feel you have an obligation towards her . . . I shall not grieve over that extraordinary *volte-face* of yours. Farewell, my friend. I hope you will recover from all your ailments. I have good cause to wish you better; and I shall thank God for this bizarre conclusion of nine years of undivided friendship. Let me hear from you from time to time.
>
> There is no point in going over the rest.

After that, their only meeting, described by Chopin in a letter to Solange, who remained close to him until his death, was for a very brief exchange of news seven months later when he was leaving a party as Sand was entering. Chopin told her she was a grandmother. On reaching the lobby he then sent his Abyssinian companion Combes back upstairs to tell Sand that Solange's health was good. Sand then came downstairs and asked after both Solange and himself. 'I said I was well, and then I called for the concierge to open the door. I raised my hat and walked to the square d'Orléans.'

Inevitably, Sand's account of those moments is more emotive and self-exonerating.

> I should have liked to talk with him, but he took to his heels. It was my turn to say that he no longer loved me, but I spared him that pain. and left everything in the lap of the Gods and the future. I never saw him again. There were black-hearted people between him and me – and good-hearted, too, but they did not know how to help. There were also a number of trivial folk who preferred not to get mixed up in such delicate matters.

That [says André Maurois] is the way of the world . . . To the friend whom we once made the confidant of our every thought, we cannot bring ourselves to say a word. Silence covers all. The heart bleeds for Sand and Chopin meeting for a moment on the staircase of the house in rue de la Ville-l'Éveque, going their ways, and never, for a moment, looking back.

Although Sand neither forgot nor forgave, Chopin kept a lock of her hair at the back of his diary for the rest of his short life. Neither did he forget her when he was in Scotland in 1848, writing to his family with news of her troubles in Nohant where the peasants had turned against her, and of further domestic squabbles. 'Chopin,' says Jim Samson, 'was broken emotionally by the separation from Sand. He had nothing like her powers of recovery. Indeed he never recovered.'

Certainly, it seems, the profound and unresolved melancholy of his late mazurkas, particularly his very last one (Op. 68 no. 4) was due in part to their final rupture. Sand was the one human being who had been able to 'quell his tremulous nerves'.

On 1 September Sand wrote to Chopin's sister Ludwika, of whom she had grown very fond: 'Your memories of me must have been spoilt in your heart, but I do not think I have deserved all that I have suffered. Yours from the bottom of my heart, George.'

She was not invited to his funeral, although maybe she was consoled by the thought that the E minor Prelude he had composed in Majorca was performed at the service. She certainly left a resounding and perceptive if inevitably biased tribute to his music in her *Histoire de ma vie*:

Chopin's music is emotionally the richest and most profound that ever existed. He made one single instrument speak the language of the infinite. In ten simple lines which even a child could play he often created poems of immense sublimity, dramas of incomparable force. He never required large material means to give expression to his genius ... his genius ... has preserved an individuality more exquisite than Bach's, more powerful than Beethoven's, more dramatic than Weber's. He is all three put together, yet he is himself, more subtle in his taste, more austere in his grandeur, more heart-rending in his anguish.

The song 'Melodia' that he set in 1847 to words by Krasinski, with its melancholic outcry in the minor key after the opening in the major, was perhaps his last testament to a broken spirit. Chopin is said to have added after the music those famous lines from Canto V of Dante's *Inferno* which had so gripped Tchaikovsky:

There is no greater sorrow than to recall a time of happiness in misery.

Jane Wilhemina Sutherland: 'Chopin's Widow'

The critical point is that whereas Sand had facilitated his creative work, Stirling suffocated it.
Jim Samson: *Chopin*

They (Jane and her widowed sister Mrs Erskine) bore me so much they will be the death of me.
Chopin to Grzymala October 1848

Chopin's final emotional entanglement, if it can be called even that, was with his pupil Jane Stirling, a spinster six years older than he, attractive, wealthy, besotted and zealously solicitous. They had probably first met in the early 1840s when Jane made frequent visits to Paris with her widowed sister Katherine Erskine. The sisters had a house at Saint-Germaine-en-Laye. Certainly, in 1844, Chopin knew Jane well enough to dedicate his two Nocturnes Op. 55 to her. Having reportedly turned down as many as 33 proposals of marriage, Jane had undoubtedly at last found her Mr Right, the one she had been seeking for 20-odd years. If they were ever lovers, which seems most unlikely, it wasn't for very long, since Chopin made it very clear in his letters to friends that Jane, forever accompanied by her sister, induced boredom rather than thoughts of romance in him. Nevertheless, in his severely debilitated condition Jane undoubtedly had a strong hold over him and was a tower of strength to him in his last months, stumping up much-needed cash at a critical moment even when she had lost all hope of dragging him to the altar.

In 1848, glad of the chance to escape from the ravages of the February Revolution, he accepted her invitation to England and Scotland where he endured a punishing schedule which inevitably hastened his death. Arriving in London on 20 April he was at once in demand everywhere by fashionable society, of whose attitude to music he held a very low opinion. 'It is all the same to them,' he wrote to Grzymala on 21 October, 'whether the music they hear is good or bad, since they feel obliged to have it about them from morning till night. In this country they have flower shows with music, dinners with music, charity sales with music . . . Music is not an art and is not called art . . .' It is hardly surprising that he was exasperated by the banal comments and pianistic skills of his aristocratic hostesses. In the same letter he wrote: 'Every comment ends with the words "leik water", meaning that the music flows like water. I have never yet played to an Englishwoman without her saying: "Leik Water!!". They all look at their hands and play wrong notes most soulfully! What a queer lot! God have pity on them!'

He played at Lady Blessington's and in other blue-blooded households, most notably at Stafford House in front of Queen Victoria and Prince Albert at a soirée given by the Duchess of Sutherland. In June he gave a public performance at the house of the former soprano Adelaide Kemble (by then Mrs Sartoris, and a novelist). Then he played at Lord Falmouth's house in St James's Square, and so it went on. His playing, though still clear and elegant, had inevitably waned, as he himself undoubtedly realised when he refused, wisely, to perform one of his concertos with the London Philharmonic Society. He was impressed by neither the quality of the band nor their inadequate rehearsal time.

Although he was critically ill, Jane then proposed to drag him off to Scotland where he could supposedly rest. 'My Scottish ladies are kind,' he wrote to Grzymala on 17 July, 'but they bore me so that I don't know what to do. They want to insist that I go to their homes in Scotland. That's alright, but nowadays I have no heart for anything. Here, whatever is not boring is not English.'

Although Chopin undoubtedly enjoyed the hospitality of Jane's brother-in-law, Lord Torpichen, at Calder House, near Edinburgh ('it is quiet, peaceful and comfortable'), he was nevertheless compelled, by falling in with Jane's arrangements, to change hosts ten or eleven times in less than three months after arriving there in early August. 'My Scottish ladies give me no peace,' he wrote later to Grzymala on 1 October. 'Either they come to fetch me, or take me the round of their families (*nota bene* they make their fold invite them constantly). They are stifling me out of *courtesy*, and out of the same *courtesy* I don't refuse them.'

No wonder he was so exhausted that his loyal servant Daniel had to carry him upstairs to bed 'where I am free to gasp and dream until morning.' He was in a state of clinical depression. 'I am unwell and depressed,' he wrote to Grzymala on 9 September, 'and my hosts simply weary me with their excessive attentions. I can neither breathe nor work. Although I am surrounded by people, I feel alone, alone, alone. . . . All that remains to me is a long nose and a fourth finger out of practice.'

Shortage of cash obliged Chopin to do concerts over that summer and autumn in Manchester (on 28 August), Glasgow and Edinburgh. By this time his playing had died down to a whisper. Once back in London in November, he was not long free from his two ministering angels – some, indeed, have declared them to be vampires! – and he obviously felt it necessary to disabuse Jane of any thoughts she might be nursing of wedding bells:

They want me to stay and go on dragging me round the Scottish palaces [he wrote to Grzymala] . . . wherever I go, they come after me if they can. Perhaps that has given someone the notion that I am getting married; but there really has to be some kind of physical attraction, and the unmarried one Jane Stirling is too much like me. How could you kiss yourself – Friendship is all very well, but gives no rights to anything further. I have made that clear – Even if I could fall in love with someone, as I should be glad to do, still I would not marry, for we should have nothing to eat and nowhere to live. And a rich woman expects a rich man, or if a poor man, at least not a sickly one. It's bad enough to go to pieces alone, but two together, that is the greatest misfortune . . . I don't think of a wife at all, but of home, of my mother, my sisters. May God keep them in His good thoughts.

On 16 November he made his last public appearance at a concert and ball in aid of Polish refugees at the Guildhall. On returning to Paris, he was too ill to support himself, and was once again dependent on Jane. In March 1849 she sent him a staggering 25,000 francs (over £5,000, even then), but by one of those all too frequent and ridiculous quirks of fate that beset all human lives, he never saw the money for nearly five months because the concierge had hidden it in a room unopened. When the money finally came into his hands, he at first refused it, although Mrs Erskine eventually persuaded him to take 15,000 francs as a loan.

He spent his last summer (1849) at Chaillot where Jenny Lind sang for him, before dying in Paris in the presence of his sister

Ludwika and other mainly Polish friends, including Countess Delfina of course, at 2.00 a.m. on the morning of 17 October. Mozart's *Requiem* was performed at his funeral in the church of the Madelaine, along with two Prelude arrangements (one of them the E minor) for organ. Meyerbeer and Prince Adam Czartoryski led the cortège down the grand boulevards to the cemetery of Père Lachaise, the pallbearers being Prince Alexandre Czartoryski, Delacroix, Chopin's close cellist friend Franchomme, and his pupil Gutmann. A year after his burial alongside Cherubini and Bellini, a monument to him by Sand's son-in-law, Clésinger, was unveiled.

After his death, Jane, fanatical as ever, acquired the largest collection, outside Chopin's family, of mementoes and objects belonging to Chopin. She gave away some of these to his close friends, including the Pleyel piano he played on before his death.

$\mathcal{B}$RAHMS

'A Diamond washed out of a Sewer'

Born: Hamburg, 7 May 1833
Died: Vienna, 3 April 1897

One who had 'hummed along' to the chorus of love but always stood apart from it.
(Malcolm Macdonald: *Brahms*)

Music and love were, for Brahms, very closely allied – the women he loved were musicians; musical creation competed with his emotional life; his love was sometimes sublimated into composition. In this he was completely a Romantic . . .
Malcolm Macdonald

. . . by rights, I should have to inscribe all my best melodies, 'Really by Clara Schumann'. If I just think of myself, nothing clever or beautiful occurs to me. I have you to thank for more melodies than all the passages and such things you take from me.
Brahms to Clara Schumann, 1891

With this ring I pledge my love – all being well.
Brahms to Agathe von Siebold in David Pownall's play for radio: *Brahms on a Slow Train*

At the age of 20, he had the face of a child which any girl could kiss without a blush.
Hedwig von Holstein

Ladies never stayed long in his rooms, and the door always stood ajar so that I might have gone in at any moment.
Brahms's housekeeper Frau Truxa talking to Robert Schauffler

I never knew of his having an affair with a lady, but he often went with prostitutes.
Robert Kahn in Robert Schauffler's *The Unknown Brahms*

a shorter and seedier James Robertson Justice lookalike . . .
Peter Kingston, *Guardian*, 4 July 1997

The Singing Girls

'Only some unknown youthful trauma can explain Brahms's attitude to women,' writes Heinz Becker in the musicians' bible,
Grove's Dictionary of Music and Musicians. Like Beethoven, with
whom he had many traits and habits in common, Brahms seems
to have developed polarised fixations of women as Madonnas or
whores. But whereas Beethoven appears to have had no close and
continuing relationship with any woman throughout his life,
Brahms certainly had, of course, a long, although probably
unconsummated love affair (if that isn't a contradiction in terms)
with the composer and virtuoso pianist Clara Schumann, almost
fourteen years older than himself. She was, says Malcolm Macdonald, 'the supreme archetype of the talented, intelligent musical
women he was to love'. And whilst Beethoven pined repeatedly
in soulful fashion for such unattainable immortal beloveds as
Josephine Deym and Antonie Brentano, Brahms, although often
smitten and even once engaged, seems to have lost little sleep
over any women except Clara Schumann and his fleeting fiancée
Agathe von Siebold.

Yet, crucially, both men had a profound problem in integrating
love and sexuality. They only ever seem to have had sex with
whores. As a child, Brahms 'lived next door to prostitutes, rubbed
elbows with them at all hours on narrow tenement stairways and
in dark halls, and often until dawn made music for their orgies in
the lowest dives of the harbour', writes Robert Schauffler in his
highly readable if essentially anecdotal book *The Unknown
Brahms* (first published in 1933, and sadly out of print). These
dives were squalid, rat-infested 'stimulation saloons' (a literal
translation of *Animierkneipe*) which provided music, drink and
sex in the St Pauli dockside area of Hamburg. His father being
an impoverished, jobbing horn and bass player, Johannes had in
this way to help pay the rent for the family's cramped and dingy
two-room apartment (crammed with instruments as well as
humans) in the area of Hamburg known locally as 'Adulterers'
Walk'.

The 'unknown trauma' mentioned in *Grove* is surely not such
a complete mystery. Schauffler relates an account to him by

the distinguished baritone and teacher Max Friedländer of how Brahms endured child abuse by prostitutes which permanently damaged his attitude to women. Both men had attended a dinner party, given by a hapless Viennese hostess to celebrate Brahms's birthday, at which the composer had broken into a drunken and 'horrible, coarse tirade' about 'a beautiful and beloved woman' everyone present knew. Later, as the two men strolled together in the Prater, Brahms, having been implicitly admonished by Friedländer, asked his companion about his own upbringing. After Friedländer described his carefully nurtured childhood, Brahms's eyes 'grew bloodshot, the veins in his forehead stood out, and his hair and beard seemed to bristle' as he passionately defended his misogyny and foul language thus:

'And you,' [Brahms] cried menacingly, 'you who have been reared in cotton wool; you who have been protected from everything coarse – you tell me I should have the same respect, the same exalted homage for women that you have! . . . You expect that of a man cursed with a childhood like mine!'

Then, with bitter passion he recounted his poverty-stricken youth in the wretched slums of Hamburg; how as a shaver of nine, he was already a fairly competent pianist; and how his father would drag him from his bed to play for dancing and accompany obscene songs in the most depraved dives of the St. Pauli quarter.

'Do you know those places?' he asked. ' . . . They were filled with the lowest sort of public women – the so called "Singing Girls". When the sailing ships made port after months of continuous voyaging, the sailors would rush out of them like beasts of prey, looking for women. And these half-clad girls, to make the men still wilder, used to excite me on their laps between dances, kiss and caress and excite me. That was my first impression of the love of women. And you expect *me* to honour them as you do.'

'Small wonder, then,' comments Schauffler, 'that this species of premature introduction to the mysteries of sex helped to give little Johannes an infantile bias in favour of prostitutes from which he never recovered.' It appears that humble servant girls were to be the only other kind of women to arouse him sexually. One of these, a pretty woman who worked for the concert manager Kugel in Bad Ischl, went so far as to tell an informant of Schauffler that Brahms was 'a passionate but awkward' lover.

Small wonder, either, with such a punishing schedule of night work, in addition to his school work and demanding course of all-round musical instruction with his revered teacher Edward Marxsen, that Brahms developed migraines from which he suffered throughout his youth.

In his recent study of Brahms, Malcolm Macdonald relates another story originating from Friedländer that harks back to these early years. When Friedländer and Brahms were dining with friends in a shabby café, some whores came in with their clients. Recognising Brahms (whom they used to address as 'Herr Doktor'), one of the ladies asked him to play some dance music.

> Brahms went to the neglected upright piano and played while the couples danced; to their puzzlement it was dance music in an unfamiliar, quaintly old-fashioned style. Afterwards Brahms told Friedländer that it had been his nightly repertoire from the *Animierkneipe*; he had not played it for over 40 years and had wanted to see if he could still remember it.

In her reminiscences, *Impressions that Remained*, the British composer and suffragette Ethel Smyth, whose *March of the Women* (1911) was to serve as an anthem for the suffrage movement, also provides eyewitness evidence of Brahms's coarse chauvinism. She thoroughly disapproved of his 'detestable' reference to women as *Weibsbilder* (wenches? skirt?). Like many German men at that time, she wrote, Brahms regarded women as 'sweetmeats', and

> If they did not appeal to him he was incredibly awkward and ungracious; if they were pretty he had an unpleasant way of leaning back in his chair, pouting out his lips, stroking his moustache, and staring at them as a greedy boy stares at jam tartlets. People used to think this rather delightful, specially hailing it as a sign that the great man was in high good humour, but it angered me . . .

'The most beautiful thing in the world is to possess a mother,' Brahms once reportedly assured his friend Professor Robert Kahn. Inevitably, Brahms's relationship with his adored and adoring mother Christiane was another crucial ingredient in the enigma of his psycho-sexual personality and his relations with women. Partly because of Brahms's pyromaniac approach to his correspondence, information about Christiane is scanty. She was undersized, frail-looking, crippled in one foot, and limped badly. She was evidently a much stronger character than her easy-going, good-natured, stupid (some say), and rather passive husband

Jakob, younger than her by seventeen years. At least one psycho-analyst, a Dr Eduard Hitschmann, has even stated categorically, in his article 'Brahms and women' (*Psychoanalytische Bewung*, April 1933) that the affection Christiane lavished on her 'Hannes' induced in him a mother-complex. The evidence is inconclusive. Brahms was certainly also very devoted to his father, who took great pains to maximise his early musical development. However, if there is even some truth in the mother-complex theory, then it may partly explain Brahms's demonstrably polarised attitudes to women. Freud has suggested that such mother-fixations in a boy's childhood impede a later capacity in the same person to merge tenderness and passion in his adult relations with women. 'Where they love they feel no passion, and where they feel passion they cannot love.' This certainly seems to have been the case with Brahms, who, writes Schauffler, 'all through his life . . . often patronised houses of ill-fame', and was unable to integrate the 'stream of his sensuousness' with the 'stream of his tenderness' in the same woman.

Nobody has conclusively accounted for Brahms's arrested physical development. 'He was very short,' writes Schauffler.

> His beard was alarmingly late in growing. The worst handicap of all in impressing the other sex was vocal. When he was twenty, Hedwig Salomon confided in her diary: 'Brahms has a thin, boyish little voice that has not yet changed, and a child's countenance that any girl might kiss without blushing'. Up to the age of twenty-four [i.e. four years after he first met Robert and Clara Schumann] his voice remained pipish and girlish. These symptoms would indicate that in Brahms's case the normal changes of adolescence were deferred for something like a decade.

A physician named Dr Alfred Grüberger told Schauffler of his conviction that Brahms's 'exaggeratedly hirsute and virile appearance of his long-bearded middle age' was a 'psychic compensation' for the humiliation he had suffered on account of his smooth-cheeked twenties. (David Pownall includes a hint along similar lines in his powerfully evocative and carefully researched radio play *Brahms on a Slow Train*.) At the age of 24 Brahms had been so embarrassed by his girlish voice that he embarked on a course of vocal gymnastics which left it sounding rough for the rest of his life, as is evident in his brief squeaky greeting recorded on an Edison cylinder in 1889.

Schauffler attempts to sum up Brahms's psycho-sexual development thus:

> Brahms's early environment and life caused a psychopathic development which probably made him impotent to all but women of a low class. This probably defeated his projects for marriage with one respectable woman after another. He explained these defeats by rationalisation, salved his wounded pride with the healing balsam of wit, and grew expert in evading embarrassing advances of his lady admirers.

Whatever the implications of his retarded physical and emotional development, Brahms undoubtedly became very attractive to women, reportedly having to ward them off, for instance, when directing ladies' choirs in Hamburg and Vienna. Such was also the case in his summer resort of Pörtschach in Southern Austria, which he reportedly abandoned partly because of lady admirers after 1879 in favour of Bad Ischl, where he spent nine of his remaining summers from 1880.

'This is the usual order of events,' writes Schauffler, in illustrating the working-out of what has been termed Brahms's 'fate-neurosis' in his love-life.

> First Brahms's tenderness is aroused by some girl. But presently he begins to realise that something essential is lacking in the relationship. Finally he causes more or less wear and tear to the lady's heart, and his own, by brusquely drawing back.

It is certainly no accident, and comes as no surprise, to learn from Macdonald that Brahms's favourite tale in his adolescence was *The Wondrous Love Story of the Beautiful Magelone and Count Peter of Provence* – this title belonging to the version by the novelist and dramatist Ludwig Tieck (1773–1853) of a twelfth-century Provençal tale of Romantic chivalry. It centres on a young, idealistic, fair-haired knight, Peter, who leaves the parental home full of youthful ardour but inexperienced in love and the ways of the world. Having defeated all his rivals at the tournaments of the King of Naples, he wins the heart of Magelone, the king's beautiful, virtuous daughter. The lovers elope together, but become accidentally separated in the forest. While Magelone lies sleeping, Peter is cast adrift in the sea, only to be picked up by the Moors and sold into the service of the Sultan. Two years later

Sulima, the Sultan's sensual daughter, full of desire for Peter, enables him to escape with her by boat. Peter, however, manages to resist her seductive charms, leave her behind and set out alone, eventually returning to the forest and the shepherd's hut where the chaste Magelone has faithfully waited for him. They marry and live happily ever after.

As we shall see, the parallels between the fair-haired Peter and Brahms himself, who ventured forth from Hamburg and loved and parted from both Clara Schumann and Agathe von Siebold have, says Malcolm Macdonald, 'until their ends an over-obvious symmetry . . . We can hardly doubt that his own life-experience drew him consciously or unconsciously to this favourite tale of his adolescence.' Tieck interspersed seventeen poems between sections of his narrative, and it was fifteen of these that Brahms used for his large-scale song cycle, the *Romanzen aus L. Tiecks 'Magelone'* Op. 33, composed over the period 1861–9.

Psycho-sexual problems were not the only reason for Brahms's withdrawal from a full-on relationship with any woman. His need for creative freedom was absolutely paramount. 'I have always had plenty of time,' he reportedly used to say of his composing, 'because I have never frittered it away on cards and women.' On one occasion, in the summer of 1858, he deeply offended Clara Schumann when he actually told her he would prefer to remain at home in Hamburg and compose rather than join her on holiday in Göttingen. Twenty years later, she was even more put out when, deeply submerged in his Violin Concerto, he stayed away from the fiftieth anniversary bash celebrating her first appearance on the platform of the Leipzig Gewandhaus.

A further crucial clue to his bachelorhood emerges in this oft-quoted remark he made to his Swiss poet friend and frequent travelling companion Joseph Widmann:

> I missed my chance. When I still had the urge I was unable to offer a woman what would have been the right thing . . . at the time I was still willing to get married, my compositions were received with hisses or icy silence . . .
>
> Now I was perfectly able to put up with this because I knew exactly what they were worth and that the picture would eventually change. And when I returned to my lonely lodgings after such failures, I was by no means discouraged. On the contrary! But if at such moments I had had the chance to face a wife's anxiously

questioning eyes ... And if she had tried to console me – a wife's commiseration for her husband's failure – bah, I can't think what a hell on earth that would have been.

When once asked by Frau Simrock, the wife of his publisher, whether his sleeping alone in the double bed in her family's guest room had made him want to marry, Brahms 'cried in honest terror: "No, indeed! Why, I'd run away from her the third day!" '

Perhaps his friend and early torch-bearer, the virtuoso Hungarian violinist Josef Joachim who first made Brahms's cause his own in 1851, hit the nail on the head when he wrote some three years later that

> Brahms is the most intransigent egotist imaginable, although he himself does not realise it ... All he cares is to write music without interference; and his faith in a more sublime world of fantasy, and his manner of keeping all the unhealthy sensations and imaginary sufferings of others at arm's length borders on genius.

Brahms's English pupil Florence May left a vivid description of him in his late thirties, the most confident years of his life, after being introduced to him in the summer of 1871 by Clara Schumann, with whom she was already studying. In her two-volume biography of Brahms published in 1905 – the first to be written in English – Florence May observed that

> His most striking physical characteristic was the grand head with its magnificent intellectual forehead, but the blue eyes were also remarkable from their expression of intense mental concentration ... His nose was finely formed. Feet and hands were small, the fingers without 'cushions'.
>
> His dress, though plain, was always perfectly neat in those days. He usually wore a short, loose, black alpaca coat ... He was near-sighted, and made frequent use of a double eyeglass that he wore hanging on a thin, black cord round his neck. When walking out, it was his custom to go bare-headed and to carry his soft felt hat in his hand, swinging his arm energetically to and fro. The disengaged hand he often left behind him.
>
> In Brahms' demeanour, there was a mixture of sociability and reserve which gave me the impression of his being a kindly-hearted man, but one whom it would be difficult really to know ... His manner was absolutely simple and unaffected ... The intense pride which is equally inherent with intense modesty in the highest order

of genius had its share in causing Brahms's reticence about all things concerning himself.

Florence May might have added that there were sides to Brahms which would have made him very hard to live with. Although possessing great reserves of affection, loyalty and kindness, he didn't suffer those whom he considered to be fools gladly and could be difficult, moody, and tetchy even with his close friends. He was, indeed, a schizoid amalgam of opposites. 'If anyone,' wrote the Schumanns' daughter Eugenie, 'ever assumed that he held any particular opinion or judgement, he would always assert the contrary.' In Schauffler's words:

> The peasant in him fought the poet and the gentleman of culture. A fiery and aggressive temper and a malicious fondness for mischief offset a kindness tenderly thoughtful. His noble and delicate generosity was held within reasonable bounds by an imperious instinct for contradiction and an intolerance of every sort of constraint. His coarse brutal directness warred with a deep-seated instinct for secretiveness and a subtle obliqueness of tongue and pen.

He could be tactless in his rebuffs of aspiring composers, even to the extent of driving one poor unstable youth, Hans Rott, a friend of Mahler, to claim in a fit of insanity during a train journey that 'Brahms had filled the train with dynamite'. He could be blunt in both speech and writing to the point of withering offensiveness. His violent quarrel, for instance, in the middle 1870s with his erstwhile torch-bearer, Hermann Levi, the effervescent conductor of the Karlsruhe Court Theatre, for being 'too Wagnerian' lost him an invaluable supporter. He even fell foul for a time of such truly close and loyal friends as the surgeon and amateur pianist Theodor Billroth, the dedicatee of the Op. 51 String Quartets. Although motivated by a desire to see fair play, Brahms also infuriated Joachim for several years by thrusting a spanner in the wheels of the violinist's divorce suit in 1880. His wife, Amalie, produced a long letter from Brahms in court as a testimonial in her successful defence against her husband's charge of adultery. There was a gradual reconciliation of sorts between the two men, culminating with the composition of the Double Concerto for Violin and Cello in 1887.

It is doubtful whether any woman could have tamed Brahms's

bachelor eccentricities as he grew older, with, say (according to Schauffler), his country cousin's hat, cuffless, collarless and tie-less flannel shirts, sockless feet, curled-up, ankle-length black trousers with a brown patch on the seat and a black patch on the front, faded alpaca coat, large, old greyish-brown plaid shawl, untamed, chest-length beard, hands as 'rough as files', ungainly walk – and a cheroot clenched between his teeth. On one very public occasion, in Leipzig on New Year's Day 1879, he caused a stir when his trousers, tied up in haste with an old necktie, started to fall down while he was conducting the première of his Violin Concerto. Fortunately the piece ended before the worst could happen.

His table manners were sometimes those of a throwback peasant prototype, while his trencherman's palate was unashamedly plebeian in its preference for dishes such as white-bait, herring salad and beef pilaf. (Brahms's ancestry goes back to the tillers of the soil of the fens and moors of the Dithmarsh flatlands around the mouth of the Elbe on the Baltic.) At table he would drink the oil directly out of a can of sardines 'at a draught'. And although capable of extreme generosity to his family, friends, and children almost everywhere, he was predict-ably close-fisted in his domestic expenditure. His two-roomed permanent lodgings at Karlgasse 4 in Vienna (from 1864) were spartan in the extreme: there was no bathroom and the place was hard to heat. The study could be reached only through the bedroom which accommodated just a bed and wash-stand: it contained a bust of Beethoven, a laurel-wreathed photograph of Bismarck, a desk, a piano, and a rocking chair arranged to tip unwary visitors onto the floor. (Later, Brahms allowed himself the luxury of curtains in his study and rented an extra room to house his rare books and manuscripts.)

Frau Truxa, his second devoted housekeeper who replaced Fräulein Vogl in 1887, assured Schauffler that '[L]adies never stayed long in his rooms, and the door always stood ajar so that I might have gone in at any moment.'

For all his lack of husbandly qualities, Brahms would surely have made a good father. Anecdotes galore show how 'Uncle Bahms' (as Frau Truxa's brood called him) doted on children, with an ever-ready supply of candy and kreuzers (a small copper coin, 100 to the florin) in his pockets. He was in his element sharing their delight in snowballs, bonfires, bowls, gentle frog-baiting, hoaxes, practical jokes, whatever. And not surprisingly, his childhood passion for lead toy soldiers lasted all his life.

> You ought to see me here [he wrote to Clara Schumann from Ischl] in the role of children's friend. There are no more loveable and agreeable folks and little folks anywhere than in this neighbourhood. I cannot go for a walk without my heart laughing; and when I caress a couple of these adorable children, I feel as though I'd taken a cooling drink.

(In our own twisted times the poor man would probably have been run in as a suspected pervert.) On one occasion when Frau Truxa was obliged to leave her children in charge of the servant for some days, she was infinitely touched to hear that her master had checked every noon and night to ensure the children were properly fed and tucked up in bed.

'Behind the mask of his public and professional eminence,' concludes Macdonald, 'he clearly felt much unhappiness, frustration, shyness, loneliness, self-doubt and lack of emotional fulfilment.' Perhaps the sensual side of his nature could only merge with the spiritual in his rich, virile and powerfully Romantic, yet highly disciplined music – in such works as the 'sumptuously amorous' Double Concerto. Certainly the philosopher Nietzsche's jibe that his music was 'the melancholy of impotence' probably tells us more about Nietzsche than it does about Brahms.

There were (and are), nevertheless, others besides Nietzsche who disliked Brahms's music: Tchaikovsky found his symphonies 'colourless and boring', while the pro-Lisztian, Wagnerian, Brucknerian, Weimar-based faction known as the New German School, which Brahms, Joachim and others had publicly opposed in 1857 and 1860, could be positively scathing. One of the School's most vitriolic mouthpieces was Hugo Wolf, the last and perhaps the greatest of the 19th century *Lied* composers:

> Disgustingly stale and prosy. Fundamentally false and perverse. A single cymbal-stroke of a work by Liszt expresses more intellect and emotion than all three symphonies of Brahms and his serenades taken together.

The aversion was mutual. Brahms also didn't like Bruckner and his favourite modern work was *Carmen*.

It is interesting to note that the Brahms Centenary celebrations in the UK in 1997 in no way compared to those on offer for Schubert. In the words of *Guardian* journalist Peter Kingston, 'Compared with the grand whoopee around Schubert's 200th birthday, the Brahms anniversary bash has all the joy and pizzazz of a pub leaving-do for the office bore.'

Clara Schumann (1819–96)

'meine liebe Frau Mama' *(my dear Madam Mother)*
'I do love him like a son.'

One of musical history's longest and closest platonic friendships.
Malcolm Macdonald

Brahms's love for Clara Schumann was perhaps the central fact of his adult existence; in the nature of things hers for him, though very deep, could not be quite so central. Whether or not their early passions were ever consummated, whether either of them found it easy that their lives should essentially go separate ways, the tensions that clearly underlay their relationship were only an exacerbating factor for the more general unresolved tensions in Brahms's attitudes to women.
Macdonald

I think . . . I am in love with her. Often I have to hold myself back forcibly from just simply putting my arm round her: I don't know, it seems so natural to me, as though she wouldn't mind at all.
Brahms writing of Clara to Joachim in 1854

You have no idea how indispensable your presence is to me, you have not the remotest conception . . .
If things go on much longer as they are at present I shall have some time to put you under glass or have you set in gold.
Brahms to Clara, February 1855, May 1856

. . . every tone in your Serenade [Op. 11, 1860] has become part of me, just as everything you create is deeply and totally absorbed by me.
Clara to Brahms

To me he is as much a riddle – I might almost say as much a stranger – as he was 25 years ago.
Clara of Brahms to Max Kalbeck in 1880

The 20-year-old Brahms entered Clara Schumann's life in Düsseldorf when she was almost 34, on 1 October 1853. By then, due to her own talents and to the obsessively rigorous teaching of her domineering, hardboiled father Friedrich Wieck, she had become a pianistic phenomenon. She had received the kind of public adoration usually reserved for such virtuosos as Sigismund Thalberg and Paganini. Only Marie Pleyel (briefly the fiancée of Berlioz) among female pianists was in her league.

At one concert during her Viennese début at the age of eighteen, in 1837, she had been recalled to the stage thirteen times. Princes showered her with jewels and she was awarded the unprecedented honour, for her age, of 'Imperial Chamber Virtuoso'. Thereafter, after her prolonged and well-known legal tussle with her father, she married Robert Schumann in 1840 and, by the time she first met Brahms, had borne her husband seven children, one of them, Emil, dying at sixteen months. In spite of her family commitments and her husband's rather pathetic jealousy of her success, she managed to concertise occasionally in such places as Dresden, St Petersburg, Vienna, Prague and Berlin.

Armed with an introduction from his new-found patron and friend Josef Joachim, Brahms was visiting Schumann, whose music he admired to the point of idolatry, in the hope of getting encouragement and recommendations. A previous attempt, in Hamburg in 1850, to solicit his idol's opinions had come to nothing when Brahms had left Schumann a package of manuscripts at his hotel, only to have them returned unopened. This time Brahms had with him in his rucksack two completed piano sonatas Op. 1 and 2, and the beginnings of a third, Op. 5, as well as a scherzo, a violin sonata (now lost) and a miscellany of songs.

Although still composing frenetically, Schumann was mentally cracking up, having the previous year endured a paralytic attack, sleeplessness, depressions, an alarming new speech impediment, giddy attacks, 'remarkable aural symptoms', a slight stroke and goodness knows what else. He was also dabbling with table-rapping and other mysteries of the occult. Even the young Brahms was aware on this first visit of a 'slight nervous disorder'. Schumann's current job as Düsseldorf's municipal music director was, justifiably, on the line as there is abundant evidence that he was a hopeless case with a baton in his hand, indecisive and unclear.

Robert and Clara were enchanted both by Brahms the young man – still beardless, with his soft curly long blond hair, high forehead and voice not yet broken – and by his music. As Brahms began to play his C major Sonata (Op. 1), Schumann summoned his wife with some such call as: 'Clara, come quickly. We have a genius in the house. You will hear music unlike any you have heard before.' During the month Brahms stayed with them they even had the French painter Jean Bonaventure Laurens sketch a profile of their young acolyte, in which he looks quite girlish, with his long hair and soft, sensitive features.

Schumann successfully put in a good word for his new protégé with the publishers Breitkopf and Härtel, and with Senff. He even took up his professional pen again on the young man's behalf in the *New Music Journal* he had co-founded and edited, helping 'the young eagle in his first flight through the world'. As for Clara, a composer in her own right, Brahms was 'one of those who comes as if sent straight from God'. Not just because of his 'exuberant imagination, depth of feeling, and mastery of form' but also on account of his 'interesting young face' and 'beautiful hands, which overcame the greatest difficulties with perfect ease'.

In December of that year Brahms wrote to the Schumanns that his works had appeared in print: 'I am taking the liberty of sending you your first foster children, who owe to you their right to exist.'

By early February 1854 Schumann had 'gone', as is clear from this letter (among others) he sent to Joachim:

> It is a week since we sent you and your friends a sign, but I have often written to you spiritually, and will later reveal the invisible writing behind this letter. I will close now. It is growing darker.

The crunch came on the cold, very rainy day of 27 February in Düsseldorf after two weeks of psychotic hallucinations recorded by Clara or himself. On that day he wouldn't let Clara even touch him because he felt unworthy of her love. Then, while momentarily left under the surveillance of his twelve-year-old daughter Marie, the sobbing composer gave her the slip and left the house in a thin robe and slippers. A few minutes later he threw himself, reportedly squealing at the top of his voice, headlong into the freezing cold Rhine. Rescued by nearby fishermen, he tried to jump in again and had to be restrained and brought ashore by force.

Doctors decided to separate him completely from Clara, and on 4 March 1854 he made the eight-hour coach journey to the asylum at Endenich, a suburb of Bonn. Once institutionalised, Schumann gazed at the Laurens sketch daily and played and analysed many of Brahms's works, responding to them with unreserved delight.

The 'Werther Years'

'It was Johannes alone who supported me.'
Clara

Several members of Schumann's circle including Brahms, the young musician Julius Otto Grimm, the composer Albert Dietrich, and Joachim, helped to provide Clara with emotional and moral support at this time; but it was Brahms above all who was her anchor man and 'willing slave' for the next three years. As soon as he had heard of Schumann's tragedy, he had set out for Düsseldorf, arriving there on 3 March 1854 and taking lodgings nearby. Clara was expecting her eighth child (to be named Felix, after Mendelssohn) in a difficult pregnancy and money was tight. Nancy Reich and Joan Chissell have shown in their biographies of Clara how, free of any binding commitments of his own, the 'young eagle' took on a great deal of domestic nitty-gritty, supervising – as and when – the children's schooling and music lessons, and helping the housekeeper Bertha and servants with the care of the younger children. ('Ferdinand is too lazy, Ludwig is too self-willed, and Felix is even more so. Genchen [Eugenie] is for the moment just a little bit too passionate,' he wrote to Clara two years later.) He even kept the *Haushaltbuch* (household book), with its entries for stamps, servants' wages, school tuition, Schumann's income and investments, and so on. Except in the bedroom (it seems) Brahms played the role of husband. He also taught Clara's pupils when she was unwell, read E.T.A. Hoffmann to her and played both her own and her husband's compositions to her.

'Brahms does not say much,' Clara confided in her diary, 'but his expression shows how much he grieves with me for the loved one he regards so highly ... From such a young man, I am doubly aware of the sacrifice, for sacrifice it surely is for anyone to be with me at this time.' Johannes eked out a meagre income by teaching a few pupils and borrowing money from such friends as Joachim and Grimm. Not surprisingly, his mother became unhappy at such sacrifices, writing to him on different occasions: 'You're losing money and time ... Like it or not, only the man who has money will be respected ... When one has been so richly endowed by God with so many gifts, it's not right to remain sitting there so calmly.'

For her part, Clara showed towards the young man who had 'such a soothingly tender feeling for me' more love and understanding than anyone had done except his mother. Wanting 'the world to hear his voice', Clara was also soon making his musical cause her own (see below) by including his music in the programmes of her concert tours. These she resumed strenuously as soon as she had recovered from the birth of Felix in June 1854, having honoured and overwhelmed Brahms by making him a godfather. Throwing herself into her work was not only her main way of coping with her grief; it was meat and drink to a woman whose vocation as a pianist was probably always the single most important aspect of her life. And, of course, she needed the money.

It was while Clara was recuperating that Brahms completed his piano *Variations on a Theme of Schumann* (Op. 9) in which Clara was as much on Brahms's mind as her unfortunate husband. Clara had taken the same theme (from her husband's *Bunte Blätte* Op. 99) for a set of *Variations on a theme of Robert Schumann* of her own (her Op. 20), and this was Brahms's response to her set, written (she wrote in her diary) to 'comfort' her. The triangular dedications say it all. Clara's was *Variations on a Theme of Robert Schumann. Dedicated to Him*, whilst Brahms's rejoinder was *Little Variations on a Theme by Him. Dedicated to Her* (later retitled as the above-mentioned Op. 9). He also wove into one of these variations (the tenth) a 'Theme by Clara Wieck' from her *Romance variée* Op. 3. All a bit labyrinthine, but utterly fascinating in its revelation of the multi-layered relationship between a composer-genius in the madhouse, his grieving, very talented wife and her adoring 21-year-old acolyte whose voice had still not broken.

As a surprise birthday present for Clara that year, Brahms also arranged Schumann's Piano Quintet Op. 44 for piano duet.

'Why did you not allow me to learn the flute so that I could travel with you?'

While Clara was touring in the summer of that year (1854) Brahms set off on a walking tour of the Black Forest to try to sort out his feelings. But it was no good. Now deeply in love with his dark-blue-eyed, attractive, intelligent and supremely talented guardian angel, the young eagle very soon abandoned his holiday:

I cannot stand it any longer [he wrote from Ulm station]; I am coming back today . . . I should not have enjoyed a single moment of the trip. The names Tübingen, Lichtenstein, Schaffhausen which otherwise would have thrilled me with joy, leave me cold, so dull and colourless does everything seem to me.

Later, on 15 December, by which time they were addressing each other much more intimately as *du*, he finally came right out with it (albeit in the camouflage of a quotation from the *Arabian Nights*) in a letter from Hamburg:

Would to God that I were allowed this day, instead of writing this letter to you to repeat to you with my own lips that I am dying of love for you. Tears prevent me from saying more.

He continued in the same vein. On 25 January 1855, when he was back in Düsseldorf (having visited Schumann) and Clara was touring in Holland he wrote to her: 'I can do nothing but think of you . . . What have you done to me? Can't you remove the spell you have cast over me?'

'You have no idea,' he wrote in February, 'how indispensable your presence is to me, you have not the remotest conception.' On 25 June he was declaring that 'I can no longer exist without you . . . Please go on loving me as I shall go on loving you always and for ever.' Her shattering impact on him is all too understandable in the light of his inexperience with women and his deeply Romantic nature. He had already steeped himself in the ultra-Romantic works of writers such as E.T.A. Hoffmann, Jean Paul, and Joseph von Eichendorff, and it isn't surprising that he later referred to this time of his life as his 'Werther years', seeing many similarities between Goethe's susceptible young hero and himself. (In Goethe's epistolary novel *The Sorrows of Young Werther* (1774), based on his unrequited love for Charlotte

111

Buff, Werther shoots himself for love of the beautiful, motherly Lotte, whose husband he honours and admires.)

Clara was certainly not indifferent to Brahms's outbursts. 'There is the most complete accord between us,' she wrote in her diary. 'It is not his youth that attracts me: nor, perhaps, my own flattered vanity. No, it is the fresh mind, the gloriously gifted nature, the noble heart, that I love in him.' Her feelings were probably a confused and shifting blend of motherly gratitude, professional admiration and erotic attraction.

In August, Brahms moved into his own room in Clara's new apartment at 135 Poststrasse, where he could use the pianos for practising and composing, and satisfy his thirst for literature and music scores as he organised Schumann's huge library. On 4 December he wrote to her:

> I regret every word I write to you which does not speak of love. You have taught me and are every day teaching me ever more to recognise and to marvel at what love, attachment, and self-denial are . . . I wish I could always write to you from my heart, to tell you how deeply I love you, and can only beg you to believe it without further proof.

And again at the end of May 1856:

> I should like to spend the whole day calling you endearing names and paying you compliments without ever being satisfied. If things go on much longer as they are at present I shall have some time to put you under glass or to have you set in gold.

Joan Chissell believes that Brahms's First Piano Concerto (in D minor, Op. 15) written between 1856 and 1859, is 'unchallengeable proof' of the intensity of his inner conflicts over Clara at this time. Certainly Brahms himself made it very clear, as we shall later see, that what much later became his third Piano Quartet in C minor Op. 60 was entirely bound up with her.

'Well-tempered lust'
Brahms on a Slow Train

Did they or didn't they?

Did Brahms actually have an affair with Clara at some point after her husband had entered Endenich, as is so often mooted? The question is intriguing but unanswerable, although don't all the above declarations sound like those of a swain whose love for his 'angel' is still in his head and heart and hasn't raged uncontrollably in his groin? In June 1854 Brahms had written to Joachim (when he was 21 and Clara almost 35):

> I believe I do not respect her so much as I love her and am under her spell. Often I must forcibly restrain myself from just quietly putting my arms round her and even – I don't know, it seems to me so natural that she would not take it ill. I think I can no longer love a young girl. At least I have quite forgotten about them. They but promise heaven while Clara reveals it to us.

'If you had touched her in the right places, she would have been yours,' is how the mischievous railway conductor, in David Pownall's aforementioned radio play, sums up the situation to the composer during his fraught train journey to Clara's funeral 42 years later. And who can say the young wag is wrong, in spite of his many intriguing Freudian speculations in the play about this particular human triangle?

Back in real life, the gossip later actually went as far as suggesting that Brahms 'the young demon' had fathered Felix Schumann. One of Schumann's grandsons, Alfred, under the pseudonym Titus Frazeni, issued a booklet entitled *Johannes Brahms, The Father of Felix Schumann*, most copies of which were destroyed by the Nazis. They considered it to be 'sufficiently damaging to German honour to warrant being burned'. However, since Robert Schumann's household book shows that he and Clara had sexual intercourse seven times in the month before his committal, Alfred Schumann's accusation is unconvincing.

It seems on balance highly unlikely that a person so emotionally and sexually muddled up as Brahms would have been so positive as to lead, or attempt to lead Clara to the bedroom. 'For both of them,' writes Malcolm Macdonald, 'the situation was exquisitely complex.' Brahms had spoken characteristically, in December 1855, of the 'self-denial' that Clara had taught him to endure, while in May the following year he refrained from joining Clara in London for fear that 'it might be regarded as improper'. (What a far cry from Liszt and Marie d'Agoult or Chopin and George Sand!) If anything happened, it would surely have been Clara who would have taken the lead while they were living in the same house. David Pownall, in his play, has Clara enter Brahms's bedroom and offer herself to him as a one-off token of love and gratitude, rather than as a prelude to marriage. Brahms the idealist refuses her because he will accept nothing less than her total lifelong commitment. This she refuses for the sake of their art.

CLARA. What is here is mine. I give it to you.
BRAHMS. How long?
CLARA. Till the morning.
BRAHMS. It would have to be for ever. Go back to your room. I don't want the kind of morning you've got planned for me.

In such charged circumstances as theirs, a move by Clara along these lines is intriguingly plausible (just about), although on balance surely unlikely in such an honourable, practical, conscientious wife grieving for her revered husband. Perhaps one day the American scholar Maynard Solomon, who has revealed so much about the love lives of Schubert and Beethoven, will turn his attention to this teaser.

What is certain is that Brahms backed off when the chance to develop the relationship came. Clara didn't finally face her cadaverous husband until her second visit to the asylum with Brahms on 27 July 1856, having been cabled that her husband's death was imminent. Schumann died two days later, essentially from self-starvation. Then, in the late summer, Brahms and Clara went on a holiday down the Rhine and on to Lakes Constance and Lucerne, with two of her children (Ludwig and Ferdinand) and his sister Elise.

Nothing came of it. Perhaps the man steeped in medieval romances preferred to remain a knight yearning for an unattainable lady. Or perhaps the imminent prospect of marrying someone fourteen years older than himself with seven surviving children shed everything in a new light. Equally, perhaps Clara felt the obligation, at that stage, as the widow of the one and only man she had loved since she was twelve, to mourn him indefinitely. She did, however, later have a short discreet affair – 'one of the best-kept secrets in nineteenth-century music' – with one of Schumann's pupils nearer her own age, Theodor Kirchner.

The Schumanns' seventh-born child, Eugenie, states unequivocally in her *Memoirs* that it was Brahms rather than her mother who backed off:

That he broke away ruthlessly was perhaps also an inevitable consequence when one takes his inherent qualities and the nature of his situation into account . . . and he never got over the self-reproach of having wounded my mother's feelings at the time, and felt that this could never be undone.

This is also reinforced by Clara's remark in a letter to Joachim that her heart bled at the time of their crucial parting of the ways in the early autumn of 1857, when Clara sold her house in Düsseldorf and moved to Berlin shortly before Brahms began a piano teaching and choral conducting appointment at the court of Detmold.

In an extraordinary letter, Brahms adopted an almost fatherly role in trying to help Clara reconcile herself to all the traumatic changes in her life:

My dear Clara, you really must try hard to keep your melancholy within bounds and see that it does not last too long. Life is precious and such moods as the one you are in consume us body and soul. Do not imagine that life has little more in store for you . . . You must seriously try to alter, my dearest Clara . . . Passions are not natural to mankind, they are always exceptions or excrescences. The man in whom they overstep the limits should regard himself as an invalid and seek a medicine for his life and for his health. The ideal and the genuine man is calm both in his joy and in his sorrow.

Thus speaks the severe disciplinarian suppressing the ardent romantic; the man who wrote some of the most incandescent tunes ever written within rigorously confining frameworks. His instinct towards musical self-discipline became ever stronger, and accounts for his intensifying interest in all kinds of polyphony and counterpoint. Not surprisingly, his lifestyle in Vienna in his later years was to be the antithesis of that of the Romantic archetype. It was more like that of a retired banker: he rose early, worked in the morning, spent the afternoon strolling round the Prater or browsing in bookshops, and the evenings socialising: going to the theatre, eating and drinking at his favourite haunt, the Red Hedgehog – then perhaps rounding off the proceedings with a brief encounter in a brothel, as is and ever has been the wont of so many otherwise respectable and prominent men.

Despite ensuing jealousies, reproaches and frequent tiffs, Clara and Brahms both remained each other's closest friend, as the following overview, again heavily indebted in places to Nancy

Reich's detailed investigations, shows. Brahms's love for Clara was 'perhaps the central fact of his existence', suggests Macdonald, while 'in the nature of things hers for him, though very deep, could not be quite so central'.

Clara as Torch-bearer

Clara was a constant propagandist for the cause of Brahms's music, from his earliest to his last piano works. She premièred no less than ten of them, beginning with two movements of his Op. 1 Sonata in Leipzig in October 1854. In 1856 she was the first person to perform his music in England when she played a Sarabande and Gavotte 'in the style of Bach' in London. Nearly 40 years later, when she was no longer playing in public, she had her student Ilona Eibenschütz première his last works for piano, the *Klavierstücke* Op. 118 and 119, in that same city.

In 1855, when he was still in need of the support of an established virtuoso, she shared a concert with him and Joachim in Danzig. Six years later she did the same in Altona, near Hamburg. On another occasion she agreed to play in a charity concert (Vienna, 1860) only on the condition that his *Serenade* no. 1 would be included. Considering it her 'artistic duty', she canvassed the support of publishers and conductors on his behalf. She was also instrumental in securing the offer of the post he took for three seasons at the court of Detmold in 1857. In short, she did everything possible to promote his interests and to boost his morale when the going was tough, as was the case, for instance, when the première of his First Piano Concerto in D minor, in 1859, was almost hissed off stage. (Brahms spoke of its second movement as being a portrait of Clara.)

The professional support worked both ways. In the 1850s Brahms performed in several of Clara's works including her Piano Trio Op. 17, her unpublished *Volkslied* (folk-songs), and the first of her *Three Romances* Op. 21 which she dedicated to him.

'An exquisite harmony of soul'

Clara

> *'We were married in everything but the bed.'*
> Brahms in *Brahms on a Slow Train*

Each did for the other countless acts of loving kindness and generosity. Aware of his abiding interest in books of all kinds, her first gifts to him were literary works, including twelve volumes of Jean Paul, and editions of Ariosto, Dante, Schiller and Sophocles. (In his quest for self-education Brahms amassed during his life-time a huge library of some 850 titles of non-musical works, as well as over 2,000 volumes of music or studies of music. He also developed an intimate knowledge of the Lutheran Bible and the contemporary theatre, interests which tended to make Clara feel intellectually inferior to him.)

Coming herself from humble enough origins, although not as lowly as those of Brahms, Clara invited his unpretentious elder sister Elise to join them on their Rhine holiday in 1856 (after Schumann's death) and even advised her on such essentials as what kind of petticoats to pack! When Brahms's mother died in 1865 she reminded him to take warm slippers on his trip back to Hamburg. Having been inculcated by her tyrant of a father-teacher Wieck in the principles and practice of rigorously con-trolled domestic finances, Clara acted for some time as Brahms's financial consultant on such matters as fees, salaries and invest-ments. (He was one of the first composers to benefit from the introduction of royalties and gradually amassed a small fortune from the publication of his works.) She even instructed him in the complexities of coupon-clipping and the going rate for reasonably priced lodgings on his travels. Like Paganini, Brahms preferred humble accommodation to the grand hotels he could have afforded.

They unburdened to each other their personal, family and professional problems. In 1862 she was the first to know of his wounded pride when he was passed over, on the first of two occasions, for the directorship of the Hamburg Philharmonic Orchestra. After he was passed over again in 1867, she refused to accept a concert engagement to play there.

In 1863, he confided to her his acute distress after witnessing what had become open warfare between his father, then a youthful 57, and his much older mother, then 74, with whom his sister Elise had sided. Matters went from bad to worse when Jakob, obliged to practise his double-bass at home following his promotion to the ranks of the Hamburg Philharmonic Orchestra, was shoved up into the attic by a wife and daughter who couldn't tolerate the growlings of a none-too-talented rank-and-filer. 'That you,' wrote Clara to Brahms, 'who have been longing for a whole year to join your people should light upon just this unhappy juncture of affairs grieves me very much.' Soon afterwards Brahms helped his father move out, after 35 years of marriage, to a place of his own in the Grosse Bleiher.

When soon afterwards his dearly beloved mother died, Brahms inevitably unburdened himself to Clara, ever the repository for his deepest feelings:

> Time changes everything for better or worse. It does not so much change as it builds up and develops, and thus when once this sad year is over I shall begin to miss my dear good mother ever more and more ... the one comforting feature about our loss is that it ended a relationship which really could only have become sadder with the years.

He commemorated his mother's death in one of his most heartfelt slow movements: the deeply elegiac Adagio mesto, labelled 'sorrowful', of the Horn Trio Op. 40 (1865), incorporating a quotation from a German folk-song, 'Dort in der Weiden steht ein Haus' (There in the meadow stands a house). And, of course, his *Requiem* (Op. 45, premièred in Bremen Cathedral in 1868) was also very much a distilled reflection of his maternal bereavement.

Later that same year his father remarried a widow eighteen years younger than himself, Caroline Schnack, who had a sickly, crippled son of her own. After his father's death Brahms provided for both of them.

Meanwhile, soon after his mother's death Brahms was again fretting to Clara over Elise's plans to embark on what he thought was an unsuitable marriage.

Clara in turn also turned to her 'best friend' for personal advice and support – what books to read, where to find a good doctor for her son Ferdinand or what brand of Austrian cigars to buy him for a Christmas present ... She also reported to Brahms such brass-tack matters as her fees, the losses involved in concert cancellations and how she fared financially from season to season. He was generally her first resort when making crucial decisions on all sorts of professional matters: editions to be published of Schumann's music (apart from one very contentious exception, to be noted); how she should respond to letters from journalists and aspirant biographers; and deciding on moves to other cities and the offers of teaching posts. (In 1878 she became chief piano teacher at the Hoch Conservatoire in Frankfurt, setting up home in that city for the rest of her life at Myliusstrasse 32.)

Needless to say, Brahms's opinion of her playing meant more to her than anyone else's. She also confided to him her growing problems of stage-fright and fear of memory loss (aggravated by hearing troubles and rheumatism or neuralgia) during her performances – problems which eventually sometimes reduced her to tears in the Green Room. Her letter from London in 1871 is terrifyingly familiar to most musicians:

> God knows how I can begin to control the anxiety that is attacking me ... Though I am often so nervous from one piece to the next, I cannot make the decision to play without notes; it always seems to me that it is almost as though my wings were clipped.

Although Brahms was usually reluctant to get too involved as a surrogate father in the rearing and welfare of Clara's children, he was a constant moral support to her in her endless family troubles. In March 1874, for instance, after hearing of Felix's tubercular illness, Brahms assured Clara of his love in words he could have written to no-one else: 'Permit my fervent love for you to be of some comfort – I love you more than myself and more than anyone or anything in the world.' He also set one of Felix's poems to music (Op. 63 no. 5) and sent it as a surprise Christmas present to an overjoyed family. (Later he set two more of Felix's poems.) And when Felix finally died at the age of 25, Brahms consoled Clara as only he could:

> It is a good thing that Fate cannot assail me many more times. I very much fear that I should not bear it very well. But what I wish with all my heart is that everything that is given to mankind and which reaches them from outside, in order to comfort them, in their trouble and to help them to bear it, may be vouchsafed to you in abundance.

As to the rest of the Schumann family, Julie (with whom Brahms was to fall painfully in love) died after three years of marriage, during which she bore three children, in 1872; the 'gentle, eccentric, and erratic' Ludwig, a chip off the old block who suffered from a spinal disease which led to his insanity at the age of 22, was locked up in Colditz Castle and outlived both Clara and Brahms; whilst poor Ferdinand, Clara's only successful and healthy son, contracted a debilitating rheumatic disease while serving in the army and became a morphine addict for the rest of his life. Clara thus became responsible for his wife and three eldest (of six) children. Amidst all these agonies and misfortunes, there is no doubt that her work was her strongest lifeline to sanity.

Brahms's support was tangible as well as moral and emotional. In 1883, when Clara had almost ceased to perform in public because of her neuralgic arm, and was having to contemplate selling her Frankfurt home to pay for Ferdinand's medical costs, he pressed her to accept a gift of 10,000 marks as a 'belated contribution to the Schumann Fund . . . to disburden myself of some of my superfluous pelf.' Although she refused, Brahms sent the money anyway, stipulating that the gift should be kept secret. She used it, characteristically, to make investments for her grandchildren.

Above all, Brahms and Clara were soulmates, sharing in hundreds of letters their deepest and most crucial experiences in life and music – excluding their private sex lives, of course. Clara would surely never have divined Brahms's recurring clumsy 'quickies' in brothels and back alleys any more than he had any inkling of her fleeting, secret affair with Theodor Kirchner. Had he known of it, he would surely have regarded it as adultery, for, in David Pownall's words, 'we were married in everything but the bed'.

Whenever one of them was enjoying something, the need to share it with the other was imperative. Here he is writing to Clara from Pörtschach (in Southern Austria) in the summer of 1877, in expansive mood after the glorious success of the First Symphony in Karlsruhe the previous autumn:

> I have just been on a walking tour for two days in the Ampezzo valley . . . You would be enchanted . . . above all with the mountains (the Dolomites with all their strange shapes and shades which one never grows tired of looking at), the lakes, the flowers, the magnificent highways and everything.

And here he is writing to Clara from Siena and Rome in 1881 in the company of Bilroth:

> If only you stood for only one hour in front of the façade of the

cathedral . . .you would be beside yourself with joy and agree that this alone made the journey worthwhile.

On the following day in Orvieto you would be forced to acknowledge that the cathedral was even more beautiful and after all this, to plunge into Rome is an indescribable joy.

Altogether Brahms made nine trips to Italy, where he invariably exhausted his companions with his crippling itineraries. His fanatical attention to such details as the 3,000-odd statues on the roof of Milan cathedral was all of a piece with his perfectionist attention to the minutiae in his own scores.

Clara as Muse, Devotee, Critic

Brahms's need for Clara's continuous involvement in his work was a basic necessity of life. Likewise, his music was her lifeblood. Her supreme, though never idolatrous joy in it is to be found repeatedly in her letters to him and in her diaries. Altogether, Nancy Reich tells us, Brahms asked Clara for her comments and suggestions on at least 82 of his 122 works published with opus numbers. Unlike even Schumann, he kept her informed of what he was composing and planning to write, a confidence she may have valued more than any other. It is surely not excessive to suggest that without her presence in his life many of his glorious works would not have been written. Brahms himself said as much. On one occasion (in 1891) after she had belatedly and contritely asked his permission to acknowledge her use of his material in a book of cadenzas for Mozart's D minor Piano Concerto she was publishing, he wouldn't hear of it, replying:

> If you did that, by rights, I should have to inscribe all my best melodies, 'Really by Clara Schumann'. If I just think of myself, nothing clever or beautiful occurs to me. I have you to thank for more melodies than all the passages and such things you take from me.

Clara wrote repeatedly that his music 'filled' her (*erfüllt*, implying fulfilment). Nancy Reich has culled a string of Clara's phrases from her letters and diaries describing the effect of his music on her: 'the pleasures you create . . . the blissful hours . . . treasures I am gathering . . . my most beautiful hour . . . the sun-

shine you have bestowed on me . . . I understand and feel them
[his works] better than so many others do.' And of individual
works Clara wrote, for example:

Every tone in your Serenade [Op. 11] has become part of me, just
as everything you create is deeply and totally absorbed by me

[*Requiem* Op. 45] It was joy unlike anything I have felt for a long
time . . . [Afterwards] Reinthaler made a speech about Johannes that
moved me so much that (unfortunately!!!) I burst into tears.

[First Violin Sonata (*Reigenlied*) in G major Op. 78] After the first
delicate enchanting movement, and the second, you can imagine my
delight when, in the third movement, I found my beloved melody
again. . . . I say 'mine' because I don't believe there is another person
who can experience this melody as [both] blissful and melancholy
as I do . . . no-one could feel it more than I do – the deepest and
most tender strings of the soul vibrate to such music . . . This last
movement is what I would wish to accompany me on my journey
to another world

[Third Symphony Op. 90] What harmonious mood pervades the
whole! All the movements seem to be of one piece, one beat of
the heart, each one a jewel. From start to finish one is wrapped
about with the mysterious charm of the woods and forests . . . such
a wonderful creation . . .

[Violin Sonata No. 2 in A major Op. 100] It was a joy that removed
all my miseries for that evening.

[Piano Trio in C minor Op. 101] No other work of Johannes' has
transported me so completely . . . How happy I was tonight, how
long it has been!

[Third Violin Sonata in D minor Op. 108] Again I felt sheer rapture
[after performing it] and thought of you with a thankful heart. How
magnificent this sonata is and how my pulse still throbs for something truly beautiful . . . [Later, after playing it with Joachim] It was
a pure delight, something one is rarely given. In the surging of
harmonies in the first movement, I always have the feeling that I am
soaring in the clouds. I love this sonata indescribably – each movement of it!

[Clarinet Quintet Op. 115] What a magnificent thing it is and how it moves one! How the subtle fusion of the instruments with the soft and insistent wail of the clarinet above them lays hold on one . . . [Mühlfeld] might have been specially created for your works.

Brahms basked in such admiration with reciprocal telepathic warmth:

[1889, from Vienna] The thought of my D minor [Violin] Sonata proceeding gently and dreamily under your fingers is so beautiful, I actually put it on my desk and gently and deliberately accompanied you through the thickets of the organ point [i.e. the long held note in the bass part of the piano below the changing harmonies above it]. For me, there is no greater pleasure than to be always at your side, to sit or, as now, to promenade with you.

Clara's presence, indeed, permeated the very staves of scores of music other than his own that were most precious to him, such as Schumann's Second Symphony in C major (Op. 61):

[1854] I often visualise you as if you were here in person; for example, in the trills of the closing passages of the Andante of the C major Symphony, in the organ point of the Great Fugue, where you suddenly appear to me like the holy St. Cecilia.

And yet, even when indisputably established as a composer to the extent of elbowing out Beethoven in popular esteem, Brahms still had serious self-doubts when he had written a new piece, and dumped them on to Clara. The man who received many honours – including the Honorary Freedom of the City of Hamburg, the Order of Maximilian from Ludwig II of Bavaria, the Medal for Art and Science and the highly coveted Order of Leopold from the Emperor Franz Joseph, and an honorary doctorate from the University of Breslau – forever needed Clara's opinion and approval. As late as 1888, when he was awash with money earned from his music, he could write to her that 'I never have faith that a new piece could please anyone.' Earlier, he even lacked faith in his most famous-ever choral number 'How Lovely Are Thy Dwellings' from the *Requiem*, which he sent to Clara along with some songs and piano works:

Perhaps you will have a free hour to strum through these things and perhaps another to write me just a word as to whether there is any sense or purpose in my having two volumes of the Variations published. Please, just a word on that.

Sometimes his modesty hid behind insouciance, as when he asked her to mark out of ten some *Lieder* [Op. 69–72] he had sent her: 'You can just write the opus or number and mark it like this: op. X, 5, bad; 6, dreadful; 7, ridiculous, etc.'

Critic

Like all best and truest friends, if Clara thought he was capable of better work, she said so. The second subject of his Fourth Symphony in E minor was too 'wilful' and 'in no way adapted to what goes before'. Certain passages in the Double Concerto were 'disturbing'. Some works in part or whole – such as a motif from his First Piano Quartet Op. 25 – she criticised as being 'ordinary', while her response to his request for an opinion on the 23 songs in four sets comprising Op. 69–72 minced no words: 'Only about half should be published; the others are not worthy of your name etc.' On these occasions he disregarded her advice, but on others he accepted it, agreeing, for instance, not to publish his *Brautgesang* (Bridal Song) of 1858 for Agathe von Siebold. He also took her advice in making considerable revisions to the structure of the First Piano Concerto.

Ciphers and Codes of Love

'Brahms and His Clara Themes'
(Eric Sams, *Musical Times*, May 1971)

The ultimate and most enduring testimony to Clara's overwhelming presence in Brahms's life is the astonishing degree to which she infuses the very content – the actual notes – of his music. So much of it bears, in Eric Sams's words, 'the unmistakable undertone of autobiographical fantasy'. For instance, in the original Op. 8 version of his Piano Trio of 1854, it could well be, suggests Eric Sams, that the second theme of the first movement was one of many 'messages' to Clara because of its adoption of key phrases from Schumann's opera *Genoveva* (yet another grim tale of triangular love). We've already seen that in his Op. 9 *Variations on a Theme of Schumann* (originally the *Little Vari-*

ations on a theme by Him. Dedicated to Her mentioned above) Brahms wove a theme of Clara's into the tenth variation to symbolise, as Schumann himself had so often done, the fusion of their personal and musical lives.

Perhaps the piano quartets are the most passionate embodiments of Brahms's feelings for Clara. More specifically, Brahms made it very clear to his publisher Simrock that his third one, in C minor (Op. 60) – completed in 1875 but begun some 20 years earlier when his feelings for Clara were at their most intense – was conceived by a man sharing the plight of Goethe's Werther. ('On the cover you must have a picture, namely a head with a pistol to it.') In other words, the work expressed his unrequited grand passion for Clara. It was 'the rendering of his soul, the final act of homage'. Indeed, at one point in the first movement, Malcolm Macdonald tells us, 'one has the distinct impression that the violin's E♭–D semitone speaks the name "Clara" – an idea rendered less fanciful by the immediate unwinding of a transposed version of Schumann's "Clara-motif".' (Schumann's Clara-motif appears repeatedly in Brahms's works as the descending sequence C–B–A–G#–A or its transposed equivalents. One of its most recognisable shortened appearances in Schumann's own music is in the opening notes of the melody played by the oboe at the beginning of his A minor Piano Concerto, immediately after the bombardment of descending chords from the piano.)

There is also a version of the Clara-motif in the first movement of the First Symphony in C Minor (Op. 68), possibly the most painfully wrought of all Brahms's works, first conceived in 1855–6 and not completed until 1876. The motif first appears unobtrusively in an inner part but later assumes great importance at the most dramatic point in the movement – the climax of the development and the lead-back to the recapitulation. What a staggering feat of compression that movement is: such powerful feelings all the more intense for being reined in by the tight structural framework. And what marvellous melodies, built, as always, from the simplest and most familiar musical shapes.

As well as officially dedicating his Op. 2 and Op. 9 works to Clara (the Second Piano Sonata and the *Schumann Variations* respectively) Brahms presented the autograph of the Op. 24 *Handel Variations* to her as a birthday gift, 'For a beloved friend'. He also dedicated other works without opus number to her, including an arrangement of a Gluck Gavotte and two Preludes and Fugues. Countless other works, including the final piano pieces, were written for her as birthday or Christmas greetings, or, as we have seen, simply with her expressly in mind.

Rifts and Tensions

Brahms being Brahms, and Clara also being very proud and independent, it wasn't and could never have been all sweetness and light between them over a period of more than 40 years. There were even problems of 'the other woman'. The first of these erupted in 1858 in Göttingen. Although Clara had told Brahms she would like to see him happily settled with the right woman, she could not cope with the reality of seeing him with his arm round the waist of the lovely singer Agathe von Siebold, of whom more below. Clara was so upset she left the town the same day. 'My nerves were . . . in such a wretched condition that I could do nothing,' she wrote afterwards to a friend. She was also later miffed by his *amitié amoureuse* with Elisabet von Herzo-genberg (also profiled below).

There were prolonged difficulties between Brahms and Clara during and in the year before his serious but undeclared infatu-ation with Clara's daughter Julie. Through much of 1868 he generated an unprecedentedly bad atmosphere in the Schumann household – by his moodiness, inept teasing (which Clara could never let pass), uncouthness, curt manners, cutting repartees, and, most specifically, by tactlessly suggesting to Clara, yet again, that she should cut down on her 'strolling player' life. (Their first major quarrel had erupted seven years earlier over this same issue, the raising of which, for Clara, was a red rag to a bull.) Matters reached the point where Clara almost banned Brahms from her home. On 15 October she was provoked into writing one of her strongest-ever letters to him: he was (reports Nancy Reich) rude and boorish and inconsiderate of her feelings as well as of those of her children, who always hated to see their mother hurt. 'One cannot,' Clara wrote, 'have a friendly relationship with the mother which doesn't carry over to the children.' Moreover, she rammed home once more, 'the practice of my art is an important part of my ego; it is the very breath of my nostrils.'

Julie Schumann (1845–72)

In the following year, realising how beautiful she had become at the age of 24, Brahms fell speechlessly in love with Julie. (He had earlier dedicated his *Schumann Variations* for piano duet Op. 23 to her in 1863.) For her part, Julie regarded Brahms only as a loving uncle and in any case, in July, announced her engagement to a young Italian count, Victor Radicati di Marmorito whom she had met whilst visiting Italy to try to improve her health. Brahms was again generally rude and moody, merely adding to Clara's many other problems: Ludwig was then showing the first signs of his mental illness, Julie's health was still very precarious and there were already indications that Felix's tubercular illness might be fatal.

'Johannes is completely different,' Clara recorded in her diary after breaking the news of Julie's engagement to him. 'He rarely comes to the house and when he does he speaks in monosyllables. He also treats Julie this way, although he used to be especially kind to her. Did he really love her? . . . But he has never thought of marrying [her], and Julie has never had any inclination towards him.' Perhaps Brahms sublimated his dreams and fantasies about Julie into some of the lovely Viennese-style *Liebeslieder* Waltzes for vocal quartet and piano duet (Op. 52) he completed that summer. They were settings of love-songs by the poet Georg Daumer.

Brahms continued to be disruptive until September when Julie married. On her wedding day he turned up at Clara's house with what he called his 'bridal song' – in effect almost an exorcism of Julie's wraith in the form of one of his most frequently performed choral works, the richly melancholic and evocative *Alto Rhapsody* Op. 53, for contralto, male chorus and orchestra. The words of Goethe he chose to set (from the poet's 'Winter Journey in the Harz Mountains') reflect his bleak state of mind:

Who can comfort his pain if balsam be poison? if he drinks the hatred of men from the fullness of love? The scorned turns to a corner and devours all his worth alone in arid self-searching.

The mood, of course, was not lost on someone as close to his feelings as Clara, especially as Hermann Levi had told her that Brahms was 'devotedly attached' to Julie:

It is long since I remember being so moved by a depth of pain in words and music . . . This piece seems to me neither more nor less than the expression of his own heart's anguish. If only he would for once speak as tenderly!

Just how much Julie had affected Brahms is clear from the fact that he kept the score under his pillow and would not authorise a performance until the following year at Jena with Pauline Viardot as soloist.

In spite of Brahms's and Clara's recurring problems, Julie's death in 1872 at the age of 27, after a period of acute suffering, inevitably drew from Brahms some characteristic words of melancholy and love:

> It is obvious that we who go on living must see many things vanish with the years – things with which it is more difficult to part than with years of life . . . No one can be more attached or devoted to you than me

Another source of friction between Brahms and Clara erupted in 1873 when Brahms was unbusinesslike over the question of providing a piece for a Schumann festival concert in Bonn to help pay for his memorial statue. Brahms gave Clara no firm answer as to whether he would provide a new piece or prefer the *Requiem* to be used. In the event, no work of his was performed, although the rift was healed sufficiently, through the intervention of friends, for him to attend the festival.

In 1874, with the arrival of the 'childless, beautiful, wealthy, young, talented aristocrat' Elisabet von Herzogenberg into Brahms's personal orbit, the potential for friction between the two 'best friends' increased. When Brahms began sending manuscripts to Elisabet in 1877, Clara reminded him that *she* could not return manuscripts as promptly as he would like because 'I am not master of my time and energies so that I can burrow in a work for days, as Frau von H. does.' And in her diary she wrote that '[t]hey have all the time in the world while I have lessons to give in the morning, am entirely exhausted in the afternoon, and continually have a piano loaded with proofs for Härtel which also demands strength.' Brahms certainly fretted when Elisabet hung on longer than expected to the Third Violin Sonata he had sent her first, insisting it must be forwarded to Clara immediately. 'Frau Schumann must be jealous of our having had the pleasure first,' remarked Elisabet. 'You know Frau Schumann is very touchy,' he wrote to her on a different occasion, in the context of the D minor Violin Sonata.

After 1882 Brahms became less scrupulous in sending his manuscripts to Clara first, partly because, due to her arthritis and deafness (she was then 67), she was rather slow in returning them. Nevertheless she resented, sometimes bitterly, his consultation of others including, at varying times, Joachim, Grimm, Dietrich, Levi, Billroth, the critic Hanslick, the archivist Eusebius Mandyczewski, the baritones Julius Stockhausen and George Henschel (the latter also a conductor), the pianist Ignaz Brüll – as well as, of course, his adored Elisabet.

Perhaps the root cause of the tensions between Brahms and Clara was his recurring feelings of exclusion from the Schumann family circle, either as a surrogate husband or adopted son. His resentment surfaced most acutely in 1892. They had a bitter quarrel which was ostensibly about Brahms's publication of Schumann's original version of his D minor Symphony (side by side with the revised version), and Clara's omission of some unpublished pieces by Schumann, edited by Brahms, from the Collected Works. The real rub, however, is clear enough in his letter to her on her seventy-third birthday (1892), ending:

> to you more than to any other I am a pariah; this has, for a long time, been my painful conviction, but I never expected it to be so harshly expressed. You know very well that I cannot accept the ostensible cause, the printing of the symphony, as the real cause. Years ago I had a profound feeling that this was so, though I said nothing about it at the time when the Schumann piano pieces were not included in the Complete Edition. All I could think of on both occasions was that you did not like to see my name associated with them.
>
> In my dealings with my friends I am aware of only one fault – my lack of tact. For years now you have been kind enough to treat this leniently. If only you could have done so for a few years more!
>
> After forty years of faithful service (or whatever you care to call my relationship with you) it is very hard to be merely 'another unhappy experience'. But after all, this can be borne. I am accustomed to loneliness and will need to be with the prospect of this great blank before me. But let me repeat to you today that you and your husband constitute the most beautiful experience of my life, and represent all that is richest and most noble in it . . . Your devoted J.B.

Permanent Reconciliation, 1893

'Every day my most beautiful hour is the one I owe to you.'
Clara

Although Clara replied icily, she eventually saw she had gone too far, and thawed after he wrote to her that Christmas to say that he was going to start work (as Uncle Bahms) on the Christmas tree for Frau Truxa and her children, and to think of her as he did so. The reconciliation was permanent, with an increased tenderness on both sides. His visits to Frankfurt, resumed by the end of January 1893 (after a gap of two years), once again occasioned 'a quickening of pulse in the family as tastier dishes, choicer wines and prettier dresses were made ready in his honour'. During her last years Clara carefully reported to him all her hearing problems, rheumatism and stomach ailments and he responded with affection and solicitude, rushed published scores to her and arranged for her to hear his works, particularly the late Clarinet Trio and the Quintet (perhaps his most beautiful chamber work?) in comfortable surroundings. He sent her many piano pieces, some of which are lost or possibly in private hands, throughout 1892–4 and she delighted in playing them. Of these – which included his *Six Pieces* Op. 118, and his *Four Pieces* Op. 119 which he called 'your and my little pieces' – she wrote in her diary:

> In these pieces I at last feel musical life stir once more in my soul . . .
> How they make one forget much of the suffering he has caused
> one . . . It really is marvellous how things pour from him; it is
> wonderful how he combines passion and tenderness in the smallest
> of spaces . . .

In the Op. 119 Brahms had borne Clara's neuralgia especially in mind. 'I have,' he wrote to her, 'just finished a little piece that will at least suit your fingers.' She was thus able to play through these 'pearls' (as she called them) which are imbued with the gentle, mellow melancholy of so many of his late works. 'Every day,' Clara responded to her best friend, 'my most beautiful hour is the one I owe to you.' And she knew, of course, that the music's inner voice was for her alone.

Vier Ernste Gesänge (Four Serious Songs)

When Clara suffered a series of strokes in 1895 Brahms became all too conscious of her mortality. Their last meeting was a brief one in the autumn of that year. On the morning of his departure Clara played pieces he had written for her during the past few years, including the E flat minor Intermezzo from his Op. 118. 'When she had finished', writes Nancy Reich, 'Eugenie found them sitting together, obviously overcome by deep emotion. Brahms never saw Clara again.'

In late March 1896 Clara suffered another stroke. To Marie he wrote:

> When you believe that the worst may be expected, be so kind as to send me word so that I can come and still see those dear eyes – those eyes that, when they finally close, will close so much for me.

And to Joachim:

> The idea of losing her cannot frighten us any more, not even my lonely self, for whom there are far too few living in this world. And when she is gone from us, will our faces not light up with joy at the thought of this glorious woman whom it has been our privilege and delight to love and admire throughout her life?
>
> Only thus let us grieve her.

His final love token to Clara and to all his dear departed friends was his *Vier Ernste Gesänge* (Four Serious Songs) Op. 121. Actually dedicated to Max Klinger, and based on biblical texts from Ecclesiastes and Corinthians, they are his most profound meditations on death and 'last things'. In Brahms there is no spiritual transcendence of death – only an ever calmer acceptance of it, as in the *Requiem*. Love could not regenerate the world (as it could for Haydn and Beethoven) but was a dying man's solace for its inescapable follies.

Clara sent him a few confused words on his birthday from her deathbed, from which she was finally released on 20 May 1896 after suffering another stroke. Distressed and agitated, Brahms messed up his rail connections and never made it to her funeral in Frankfurt. After a 40-hour journey he arrived in Bonn only just in time to throw a handful of earth on to her coffin as it was lowered into her grave next to her husband. Utterly exhausted, he caught a severe chill, and after recovering he went to Ischl for the summer and wrote his very last pieces, the eleven Choral Preludes for organ.

After the *Four Serious Songs* were published in July, Brahms sent a copy to Marie Schumann with the words:

> I wrote them during the first week in May . . . Deep inside us all there is something that speaks to us or drives us, almost unconsciously, and that may emerge at times sounding as poetry or music. You will not be able to play through these songs just now because the words would be too affecting. But I beg you to regard them . . . as a true memorial to your beloved mother.

'Is life worth living when one is so alone?' Brahms asked afterwards. Her death may well have hastened his own. When Marie and Eugenie Schumann, to whom he had volunteered help, offered him a memento of their mother he replied: 'I must thank you . . . but I want nothing. The smallest trifle would suffice me, but I possess the most beautiful of all!'

He himself died, like his father, from cancer of the liver, eleven months after Clara – at 8.30 a.m. on 30 April 1897. He was buried in the presence of many mourners in the central cemetery of his beloved Vienna. Tributes poured in from all over Europe, especially Germany, and all the ships in Hamburg reportedly lowered their flags to half-mast.

The Others

Agathe von Siebold (1835–1909)

With this ring I pledge my love – all being well.
Brahms on a Slow Train

The summer of 1858 saw Brahms in Göttingen where he met Agathe von Siebold, the daughter of a professor at the University. Brahms was soon smitten by this blue-eyed, vivacious, intelligent young lady, the same age as himself, with long black hair and a voice which Joachim later compared to the tone of an Amati violin (praise indeed!). The couple seemed to be extraordinarily compatible in temperament and interests. They were both ecstatic lovers of nature and enjoyed long country walks. They were also well read and, of course, passionate about music.

We have already seen that when Clara discovered Brahms with his arm around Agathe's waist she left Göttingen in distress the same day. Although Clara had often encouraged 'her' Brahms to find 'a nice young wife', she couldn't cope with the reality of any move in that direction.

Returning in the autumn to his job at the court of Detmold, Brahms wrote many letters to Agathe via their mutual friends the Grimms, and sent her several intensely wrought new songs and duets in folk-song style, some of which became his opuses 14, 19 and 20. He was certainly on a creative and probably an amorous high when he wrote 'I was in ecstasies. I thought of music alone . . . If things go on this way, I will probably evaporate as a musical chord and float away into the atmosphere.' He also sent Agathe a setting of *Brautgesang* (Bridal Song) which he later destroyed. (His savagery towards compositions he was dissatisfied with never abated.)

In January 1859 he returned to Göttingen to try out his songs with his beloved, and the couple went so far as to exchange engagement rings in a secret ceremony. But being too preoccupied with the imminent première of his First Piano Concerto in Hanover, he left Göttingen without silencing the gossips by announcing an engagement. A timely letter from Grimm bidding him do just that elicited an insultingly evasive response to Agathe. Much later she recalled the gist of how he wanted to have his cake and eat it: 'I love you! I must see you again. But I cannot wear fetters. Write to me, whether I am to come back and take you in my arms.' Deeply wounded, Agathe released him from his promise but refused to see him ever again.

They were both traumatised for a long time, particularly Agathe, although ten years later she married someone else. Towards the end of her life she wrote an autobiographical novella in which it is very clear that her courtship with Brahms had been the crucial romantic event of her life. The novella was a kind of magnanimous exorcism in which she let Brahms off the hook by declaring that 'like every genius, [he] belonged to humanity . . . he was in the right to burst the bonds which bade fair to fetter him,' while 'she, with her great love, would never have been able completely to fill his life.' Agathe also probably knew that in so far as Brahms could ever belong to anyone, it was to Clara.

'Here is where I tore myself free of my last love,' Brahms said to his amateur cellist friend Josef Gänsbacher in 1865, referring to bars 162–8 of his Second String Sextet which contain Agathe's name in the coded sequence of notes A–G–A–D(=T)–H(=B)–E. Ironically, this is not the music of disappointment but rather of liberation! The same note pattern also occurs several times in the tenth of his *12 Lieder und Romanzen* for female voices (Op. 44), all of them about separation or the silence of lost love. Once again Brahms, influenced by Schumann, was using musical symbols to 'speak in his music'.

Agathe remained in Brahms's creative bloodstream, often, as Eric Sams has shown in great detail, 'seen but not heard' in the actual musical fabric of his works. (See *Musical Times*, 'Brahms and His Musical Love Letters', April 1971.) She was a kind of prototype for many of his songs and choral works featuring a girl abandoned by her lover. He also drew on his experience with her in his aforementioned *Magelone-Lieder*, which refer to the giving of rings and to a love triangle, and in his gorgeous choral work for tenor solo, male chorus and orchestra *Rinaldo*, with its enamoured knight freed from the manacles of love.

Brahms was never again to get himself into such a tight corner.

'My dear girls'

Bertha Porubsky, his first Viennese Sweetheart

Brahms was director of the Hamburg Ladies' Choir from 1859–62, and a favourite sweetheart among a variety of young women he met in the summer of 1859, while lodging in nearby Hamm, was the Viennese beauty Bertha Porubsky. Bertha nattered on delightfully about Vienna and sang folk-songs she had grown up with. 'Through her,' Brahms wrote to Joachim, 'Vienna, which is, after all, the musician's holy city, has taken on a double magic for me.' What happened between them is anyone's guess, although it probably wasn't much and is of no real importance, but she goes down in the history books as the dedicatee of the immortal *Wiegenlied* (Cradle Song or Lullaby, Op. 49 no. 4) that Brahms presented to her on the birth of her second son after her marriage to one Herr Faber. Is there any tune by Brahms more beautiful or better known? Surely none better known, although for me the most heartbreaking melody in Brahms, especially when the cellos get their crack at it, is the second theme of the slow movement of the Fourth Symphony. (It is almost unbearable!) The *Lullaby*, incidentally, is itself a freely invented variation on an old Austrian folk-song that Bertha sung to Brahms in those sweet Hamburg days. Brahms remained friendly with Bertha all his life.

Other young lady-choristers he cavorted innocently with that summer in Hamm included his former pupils and vocal quartet members the Völckers sisters (with whose aunt he was lodging), and Laura Garbe and Marie Reuter. Brahms even playfully told his sister that Laura might become her sister-in-law. All of them probably suffered soulfully from the all-too-common fixations of choir ladies on their choirmaster.

All in all, it seems to have been an idyllic summer. He wrote a lot of music for the choir, and Clara recorded that they went on a delightful excursion by steamer to the Blankensee where 'we found the loveliest trees in the garden and sang beneath them with Johannes conducting from a branch.'

A singer named Luise Dustmann also gets into the frame. Love between them flared up in 1863, but quickly went the way of all the others.

Happy days!

Elisabet von Herzogenberg (1847–92)
Amitié amoureuse

the woman of whom (after Clara) Brahms was undoubtedly fondest.

Macdonald

You must know and believe this, that you belong among the few people whom one loves so much that – as your husband is always there to read and hear – one can not tell you.

Brahms to Elisabet von Herzogenberg

His attitude was perfect . . . reverential, admiring and affectionate, without a tinge of amorousness. It especially melted him that she was such a splendid *Hausfrau*, and during his visits she was never happier than concocting some exquisite dish to set before the king; like a glorified Frau Röntgen [mother of the Leipzig-based composer Julius Röntgen] she would come in, flushed with stooping over the range, her golden hair wavier than ever from the heat, and cry 'Begin that movement again; that much you owe me!' and Brahms's worship would flame up in unison with the blaze in the kitchen. In short he was adorable with Lisl.

Ethel Smyth, *Impressions that Remained*, Vol. 1

We have no greater pleasure in the world than that we derive from your music.

Elisabet to Brahms, 1886

In the summer of 1864 Brahms lost his head to a 'very pretty' singer, Ottolie Hauer, who sang in one of his ladies' choirs and to whom he actually proposed in a giddy moment the following Christmas Day. Fortunately, she had already been 'snatched up' only hours earlier.

More importantly, later that summer he became briefly smitten with his very beautiful sixteen-year-old Bavarian-born pupil Elisabet von Stockhausen, soon to become Elisabet von Herzogenberg. Declaring it was impossible not to fall in love with Elisabet, Brahms soon made his excuses and abandoned the course of piano lessons he had been engaged by his Croatian friend Julius Epstein to give her, palming her off back on to him.

It was another ten years before Brahms could enjoy Elisabet's company and adore her from a safe distance. By then she was a young, childless *hausfrau* and fine amateur singer and pianist (having studied with Chopin), with an extraordinary rapport with Brahms's music. 'It was said' – a useful get-out phrase, this – that she could reproduce on the piano, from memory, a complete symphony after having heard it twice. Well, that's not as good as Mendelssohn who, 'it was said', could reproduce a symphony on the piano after hearing it just once.

In January 1874 Brahms visited Leipzig for a festival in his honour organised by Elisabet's husband, the Viennese-born composer and conductor Heinrich von Herzogenberg, who had settled there with his wife two years earlier. Herzogenberg was one of Brahms's most unswerving admirers, and shared his deep interest in early church music – affinities which Brahms reciprocated by readily helping Herzogenberg with his composing career. So it was that a deep and fulfilling – but totally above-board – friendship developed between Brahms and Elisabet, then in her late twenties. He basked continually in her admiration. Perhaps the lovely but essentially untranslatable French phrase *amitié amoureuse* best describes their relationship.

'This slender woman in blue velvet and golden hair,' as Brahms once described her, was another of those enchantresses we meet just occasionally in these pages – mercurial, witty, magnetic, sparkling, vivacious . . . but *not a femme fatale* bent on enslaving her admirers. (Puccini's Sybil Seligman was another such.) Nevertheless, Clara always remained remarkably cool to Elisabet. Described by Ethel Smyth as 'not really beautiful but better than beautiful, dazzling and bewitching', Elisabet may well have inspired or released in Brahms his great 'spring of song' of 1877, when he composed in a few weeks no less than eighteen songs of opuses 69–72. Certainly it seems that many *Lieder* of the 1870s and 1880s were associated with Elisabet. For instance, she may, suggests Macdonald, especially have been in his mind in his exquisite setting of Heine's *Sommerabend* (Op. 85 no. 1, 1879) in which a beautiful elf bathes in a brook, her arms and neck 'shimmering in lunar radiance'.

The correspondence between Brahms and Elisabet over nearly 20 years was voluminous, always benign, and wide-ranging. They delighted in sharing the kind of banter alien to Clara's temperament.

Here is Elisabet chatting to Brahms while he is on holiday on the Baltic island of Rügen in 1876:

> I remember hearing they give you nothing to eat but pale grey beef and indescribable wobbly puddings made of starch and vanilla . . . the person who told me her own bitter experiences was reduced to living on eggs which she boiled or fried in the privacy of her own room.

Reporting the before and after of the first performance of his First Symphony in Leipzig, 'that most fickle of musical centres', in January 1877, he fretted thus to her from Vienna:

> Three days before the concert I began to perspire and drink camomile tea; after the fiasco, attempts at suicide, and so on. You will see the lengths to which an exasperated composer will go!

She obviously enjoyed teasing him. After he had stayed with them for the successful première, she wrote:

> I was mad to ask you at all, you spoilt creature, with your mock turtles, your Prater manners and your constitution ruined by every conceivable refinement of luxury.

'Please have the symphony published soon,' she continued; 'for we are all symphony-sick, and weary of straining to grasp the beloved, elusive melodies.'

Here he is talking down his Second Symphony, knowing, of course, that she adored his music as much as he adored her:

I shall not need to play it to you beforehand. You have only to sit down at the piano, put your small feet on the two pedals in turn, and strike the chord of F minor several times in succession, first in the treble, then in the bass (*ff* and *pp*), and you will gradually gain a vivid impression of my 'latest'.

He continued in like fashion on the day before the Viennese première by the Philharmonic Society under Hans Richter, in a letter signed 'Ever your unwashed J.Br.':

The orchestra here play my new symphony with crêpe bands on their sleeves because of its dirge-like effect. It is to be printed with a black edge too!

Some of Brahms's banter trudges along in Teutonic boots. Here he is writing to Elisabet from Naples on his first Italian holiday with Billroth in 1878:

The undersigned begs to inform his esteemed patrons that letters addressed poste restante, Naples, will find him from 14th April to 20th. From 20th onwards – Rome. He travels with Bilroth, and requests orders for writing letters, amputating legs, or anything in the world.

Brahms bounced some of his ideas off Elisabet. Looking in July 1880 for a suitable text for a choral work, he remarked that 'they are not heathenish enough for me in the Bible. I have bought the Koran but can find nothing there either.' (The children's Bible he was given as a child was his book of books and his correspondence is 'remarkable for its grasp of scriptural problems'.) Elisabet suggested looking in Psalms but Brahms in the end settled on a 'pagan' text, Schiller's *Nänie*, for his work of the same name for chorus and orchestra. 'For sheer heart-breaking beauty of sound,' writes Macdonald, '*Nänie* is possibly the most radiant thing he ever wrote.'

Elisabet's response to her admirer's second set (Books 3 and 4) of *Hungarian Dances* for piano duet in 1880 shows clearly how completely she internalised his music. It was her lifeblood.

Delicious as the earlier ones were, I hardly think you hit off the indescribable and unique character of a Hungarian band so miraculously then as now. This medley of twirls and grace-notes, this jingling, whistling, gurgling clatter is all reproduced in such a way that the piano ceases to be a piano, and one is carried right into the midst of the fiddlers . . . you are able to raise it [the artistic whole] to the highest level without diminishing its primitive wildness and vigour.

(Dvořák, incidentally, was so impressed with the dances of Book 4 that he orchestrated them all, adding a Slavonic tinge to the gypsy elements.)

Admiring as she was, Elisabet was not afraid to voice her reservations about the obscurity of the austere and intensely compressed Fourth Symphony Op. 98, completed in 1885:

Your piece [she wrote after studying the score] affects me curiously, the more penetration I bring to bear on it, the more impenetrable it becomes . . . I have the feeling that this work of your brain is designed too much with a view to microscopic inspection . . . as if it were a tiny world for the wise and the initiated in which the common people 'that walk in darkness' could have but a slender portion.

In due course, she was won over and, writes Macdonald, 'the letters in which [Elisabet] came to terms with the symphony's greatness are among the treasures of the Brahms–Herzogenberg correspondence.' And when she received, in 1886, the Second Cello Sonata in F major Op. 99, the Second Violin Sonata in A major Op. 100 and the Third Piano Trio in C minor Op. 101, all in similarly austere vein, Elisabet and her husband assured Brahms that '[w]e have no greater pleasure in the world than that we derive from your music.' She believed that the mercurial Trio of the Cello Sonata was 'better than any photograph, for it shows your *real* self.'

Her influence even reached the point in the mid-80s where she was able to persuade him to suppress a setting of one of the Heine poems in his *Four Lieder* of Op. 96, in favour of a setting of Daumer's 'Wir wandelten', in which 'two lovers walk side by side, their inmost thoughts unspoken'. (Although Daumer wasn't a distinguished poet, Brahms often chose to use his work.)

Brahms celebrated his adoration of Elisabet by dedicating to her his *Four Quartets for SATB soli and Piano* Op. 92, all except the first written in 1884 and collectively his most ravishing settings of Daumer.

Elisabet did her best to console Brahms after Nietzsche's attack on him as 'the eunuch of music' enshrining 'the melancholy of impotence' in his book *The Case of Wagner* (1888). 'Really,' wrote Elisabet all too prophetically, 'this man's vanity will bring him to a lunatic asylum yet.' Melancholy in Brahms there certainly is a-plenty – it imbues, for instance, the Third (and largest) Violin Sonata in D minor (Op. 108) with its beguiling play of ever-shifting colours and moods, but where on earth is the impotence? Fortunately all his closest friends, whose opinions he canvassed anxiously about the work in the wake of Nietzsche's bilious outburst, assured him of its supreme quality.

One bright spot in Elisabet's final years of illness and depression was when she received the score of the String Quintet no. 2 in G (Op. 111). 'Reading it,' she wrote to her revered admirer, 'was like feeling spring breezes.'

She died at the age of only 44 in Italy on 7 January 1892. Brahms was devastated by the news. 'You know how unutterably I myself suffer by the loss of your beloved wife,' he wrote to the bereaved Heinrich. Although, as a measure of emotional self-protection, he had withdrawn somewhat from them during their illnesses, the fact that he kept a photograph of Elisabet on his desk for the rest of his life tells its own story.

That same year he also lost his sister Elise. With his brother Fritz having died in 1886, he must have sometimes been over-whelmed by feelings of isolation and loneliness.

Hermine Spies (1857–93)

Brahms was 50 when he first met Hermine Spies, an outstanding German-born contralto who specialised in *Lieder*. She had been engaged to sing in a performance of his new choral work *Gesang der Parzen* (Song of the Fates) in Krefeld. That summer, they enjoyed much time in each other's company in Wiesbaden, not least because Hermine, then a 'merry and invigorating' 26, had ready ripostes to Brahms's sallies and badinage. Brahms was undoubtedly enchanted with 'my songstress' whom he addressed by such pet names as 'the Rhinemaiden', 'Herma', 'Herminche', and 'Hermione without an o'. Hermine's letters show that, smitten as she was with a 'Johannes-passion', she longed for Brahms to declare himself. However, it now goes without saying that he stopped short of any such move and the relationship, writes Macdonald, 'never seems to have progressed beyond a particularly warm and mutually stimulating friendship'.

Nevertheless, Brahms's interest in Hermine both as a woman and as a singer bore rich fruit in the form of many of his late songs which were written with her especially in mind. Macdonald ascribes 'the greater contentment and sometimes youthful ardour' of such late *Lieder* as the Op. 106 set directly to his romantic friendship with Hermine. 'He can sing once again . . . of students serenading a fair lady, wittily rendering their affable music of "flute and fiddle and zither".'

Brahms actually had a friendly rival for Hermine's attentions in the 64-year-old poet Klaus Groth, many of whose texts he set to music. On Brahms's fifty-second birthday (1885) Hermine received in the same post a copy from Groth of his poem 'Komm Bald' (Come soon), and from Brahms his setting of it as part of his *Six Lieder* Op. 97!

Hermine died at the age of 36, having married only the previous year. The raft of composers and musicians dying under the age of 40 in the 18th and 19th centuries never fails to stun each time another instance crops up.

Alice Barbi (1862–1948)

Positively Brahms's last flirtation, begun in 1890, was with the 26-year-old Italian mezzo-soprano Alice Barbi. Naturally, like all the others, she was pretty, cheerful, intelligent . . . and one of his most favoured interpreters. 'It would be impossible to hear anything more lovely,' he wrote of Alice's singing to Clara, who by then must surely have indulgently taken his harmless infatuations in her stride. After hearing Alice perform some of his songs in April 1892, he declared: 'I had no notion of how beautiful my songs are. If I were young, I would now write love songs.'

Brahms often accompanied Alice in recitals, including her farewell concert of 1894 in Vienna, shortly before she married an Austrian nobleman. Rumour had it that Brahms himself had proposed, but that Alice had refused him because he was old and she wanted children.

In his 'retirement' after completing the Op. 118 and 119 piano pieces for Clara, Brahms was sufficiently inspired by Alice and her love of folk song to compare variants and annotate for publication folk songs he had collected throughout his life. And had he known it, he would have been gladdened that she was a mourner at his funeral alongside the twelve friends who bore torches round his coffin.

'If I don't catch it, straight away it goes.'
Brahms on a Slow Train

One final thought. Would we have had so much wonderful music if Brahms had actually been a partner in a settled long-term relationship? Very possibly not. Again and again, delving into composers' lives shows that so much great music has emerged from men unhappy in love. In these rather clumsily translated words of Max Kalbeck, who in later years became one of Brahms's most frequent companions and whose monumental standard biography of the composer was published between 1904 and 1911:

> Stilled yearning, satisfied desire, wish-fulfilment are seldom fortunate gifts for the artist, in whose works the eternally unattainable lives and resounds. And the fate which he so terribly denounces deals more kindly with him when it refuses that which, as a usual thing, it graciously accords to the least of mortals.

Kalbeck's magnificent description of Brahms 'in a veritable orgy of creative emotion', composing on the edge of the Ischl forest, perhaps reinforces the idea that it was in composition alone that he fulfilled himself; that he 'converted the greater part of his unutilized [sic] sexuality into lofty music ... through a sublimation as far reaching as any recorded in the history of the arts':

> Bare-headed and in shirt sleeves, without waistcoat or tie, he swung his hat with one hand, dragged his coat behind him in the grass with the other, and hurried as if to escape some invisible pursuer. Even at a distance I heard sounds of laboured breath and moaning. As I approached I saw his hair hanging down his face and the sweat running from it over his hot cheeks. His eyes stared straight forward into emptiness, and gleamed like those of a beast of prey. He seemed like one possessed. Before I had recovered from my fright he had shot by me, so close that we almost brushed elbows. I understood at once that it was a mistake to address him; for he glowed with the fires of creation. Never shall I forget that sight, and the terrifying impression it made upon me of elemental force.

TCHAIKOVSKY

Born: Votkinsk, 7 May 1840
Died: St Petersburg, 6 November 1893

You ask if I've ever been in love. Non-platonic love, I take you to mean.
The answer is yes and no ... If we rephrase the question slightly;
and ask whether I've ever known complete happiness in love, the answer
is no, no, and no again!!! *I think, in fact, that I answer that question*
in my music. But if you ask me whether I appreciate the full power,
the invincible force of this emotion, then I'll answer yes, yes and yes
again. And I would say that I have repeatedly tried to express in my
music the torments and bliss of love ...
Letter from Tchaikovsky to Madame Nadezhda Filaretovna von Meck, 21
February 1878[1]

... it is true that my damned pederasty does form an unbridgeable
abyss between me and most people ... I often dwell for hours now
on the thought of a monastery or the like.
To his brother Modest, 21 January 1875

This night [the third following his marriage] the first attack took place.
The attack proved weak; it is true it met with no resistance, but in
itself it was very weak. However, this first step accomplished a lot. It
brought me closer to my wife, since I resorted to various manipulations
which established intimacy between us. Today I feel in her regard
incomparably freer.
To his brother Anatoly, July 9 1877, describing the attempted
consummation of his marriage

As regards my source of delight, about whom I cannot even think
without being sexually aroused and whose boots I would feel happy
to clean all my life long, *whose chamber pots I would take out and*
[for whom] I am generally ready to lower myself anyhow, provided that
I could kiss, even if only rarely, his hands and feet ...
To Modest, of his sister's family's servant, Evstafy, 21 September 1877 –
two months after his marriage

1 All dates in this chapter are, I hope, according to the Western Gregorian calendar,
twelve days ahead of the Julian calendar which was in use in Russia until 1918.

The voyeur, in varying shades of blue, lurks inside many of us – well, surely, at least, in buyers and readers of this book, as well as in its writer! But even the most assiduous Peeping Tom might surfeit himself when prying into Tchaikovsky's gay love life. The man who still today packs in the punters and sends them wild at concerts across the globe with his *1812 Overture*, the *Capriccio Italien*, the *Marche Slave*, the First Piano Concerto, *Swan Lake* and *Nutcracker*, was what the tabloids nowadays do not hesitate to call a pervert. At the sharp end of his life-style, by today's shock-horror scale of moral values, there is sordid scandal a-plenty to come to terms with: brotherly incest, very possibly, or something close to it involving 'tangible sexual play'; hebephilia (attraction to adolescents), pederasty, paedophilia (to a lesser degree), 'abusive power relationships', and other practices now considered unsavoury.

At the other extreme there was his sublime and prolonged, purely epistolary, love affair with a very wealthy and beneficent widow, Mme Nadezhda Filaretovna von Meck, who, besotted by both the man and his music, was his distant muse and source of colossal funds. He was the 'artist-son of her neurotic imagination' whilst she was the 'lover-mother' he lost at the age of fourteen. Although they exchanged some 1,200 letters over nearly fourteen years, they never even met, except once by accident. Their relationship surely ranks as the most extraordinary known to the world of classical music. It must even be a front-running story in the entire History of Love as well.

Yet, in real life, in spite of his scores of sexual encounters, Tchaikovsky was unable to establish a stable and long-term equal relationship with any other human being. 'We shall,' he wrote at the age of 41 to his younger brother Modest, 'live out our whole lives without experiencing for a single second the full happiness of love'. In his later years his love life became a pattern of extremes: he either used and discarded rent boys and rough trade, or idolised bright and attractive young Ganymedes such as those in his circle who called themselves the Fourth Suite. With these men he enjoyed physically nothing more than a passing caress.

Recent investigations by such assiduous biographers as Alexander Poznansky and Anthony Holden – until very recently constrained by the inaccessibility of archives jealously guarded by loyalists at the Tchaikovsky Archive at Klin (north of Moscow) – fulfil the composer's own worst nightmares. 'The notion,' said Tchaikovsky in 1880, 'that one day people will try to probe into the private world of my thoughts and feelings, into everything that I have so carefully hidden throughout my life . . . is very sad and unpleasant.'

Yet many of us want to know, and indeed probably should know about every side of this deeply baffling but ultimately very loveable man if we are to get the utmost out of his music, which ranges from harrowing spiritual autobiography (by his own account), to escapist fairyland and rousing, sometimes hysterical public razzmatazz. Even the cause of his death matters. Controversy has raged on in recent years as to whether the man who became a world celebrity, and whose honours included the Order of St Vladimir, not to mention an honorary doctorate from Cambridge University and membership of the Académie française, was finally forced by a Court of Honour into taking his own life after allegedly having an affair with a young aristocrat. My own opinion on the matter appears at the end of this chapter.

Has there ever been a more neurotic composer in the pantheon? Certainly not, according to Edward Garden who writes of Tchaikovsky's 'propensity for nervous breakdowns unparalleled by any other great composer'. Has any of them encompassed such a bewildering mix of conflicting traits? Any summary attempt to present Tchaikovsky the man can only really be a distortion. For a truly exhaustive portrait, readers can do no better than to bury themselves in Alexander Poznansky's riveting psycho-sexual biography which runs to nearly 700 pages: *Tchaikovsky: The Quest for the Inner Man*. It exudes infinite love for its subject without ever sliding into idolatry. Poznansky's more recent *Tchaikovsky's Last Days* contains not only an 'inquest' into the composer's death, based on a cluster of contemporary documents, but also previously unpublished extracts from his correspondence. Anthony Holden's *Tchaikovsky* is certainly a compulsive read and concludes with an exhaustive justification of the case for Tchaikovsky's death by suicide so utterly rejected by Poznansky. David Brown's four-volume study of the composer concentrates more on the music than the man, while his *Tchaikovsky Remembered* is a collection of memoirs by the composer's contemporaries.

How prone to weepiness and gush Tchaikovsky was, often born of real heartache and despair but sometimes almost dismissable as fits of histrionic 'luvvies', living as he did in a culture then 'dominated by emotion and sensitivity' with a craving for sensationalism! How introverted he was, how morbid, habitually insecure, not to say frequently paranoiac. How painfully shy to the point of 'misanthropy' (his own word). How easily a prey to despair over his worth as a composer when slated by others. And how sadly susceptible to fits, probably mildly epileptic, when severely stressed.

Set against this the respectable bourgeois, the whimsical, versifying jester and heavily perfumed man-about-town flaunting, say, his grey overcoat, top hat, silk plastron with coral pin, and lilac gloves; the rigidly self-disciplined worker, the ultimate believer in his own greatness, the ardent lover of young men, the lecher, the dissolute hebephile, the heavy drinker, hypochondriac and compulsive gambler. Or take the caring and beneficent uncle, the kind, gentle and dependable friend with trusting eyes, the idealist, the Fatalist, the ever-departing, ever-more-homesick wanderer.

All this is no more than a smattering of the man. A sense of guilt on many counts also looms large, and showed its face at an early age. When only ten he was tormented by the death, for which he felt responsible, of his friend Kolyar, the eldest son of a family friend Modest Vakar. During an epidemic of scarlet fever at his preparatory school, Tchaikovsky blamed himself for infecting the Vakars' home while lodging there.

Many of these strands are reflected in his music. Contrast only the magic and intense innate charm of, say, the early opera *Vakula*, *Swan Lake*, the Violin Concerto, the *Serenade for Strings*, and *Capriccio Italien*, with the hysterical despair of the fate-obsessed Fourth, Fifth and Sixth Symphonies and the bleak frigid world of *The Voyevoda*. And surely his inspiration, for example, to compose a symphonic fantasia, in 1876, around Dante's story of Francesca da Rimini in the fifth canto of *Inferno* came from his immediate identification with Francesca's uncontrollable and fatal illicit lust for her brother-in-law Paolo Malatesta.

Any personal exposure of such a vulnerable human being cannot but be partly cruel, although nevertheless justified. The man himself, in his thirty-eighth year, told Nadezhda von Meck that his angst-ridden love life was the creative mainspring behind his music – was nothing less than the very content of it. He was then, of course, really referring to works as close to his heart as the Fourth Symphony which he dedicated to her, and which 'echoes' the anguish of his pre- and post-marital crises, rather than to the escapist world of *The Nutcracker* or the bespoke bombast of the *1812*. And his remark applies equally to such later works as the Sixth Symphony, the 'Pathétique', another sound-world of psycho-sexual confessions and reflections on mortality, dedicated to his young nephew Bob who had become the hapless object of his uncle's obsessive, unrequited passion.

No wonder Tchaikovsky himself declared he would have gone insane without the safety-valve of composition! If we love no more than some of his music – including altogether six symphonies, two piano concertos, a violin concerto, several tone poems and other orchestral works, a hundred or so songs, piano pieces, eleven operas, and the ballets – we must be thankful that such a frequently knotted-up melancholiac could release his maelstrom of frustrations and neurotic anxieties through his music.

A side-benefit of delving into Tchaikovsky's life might be to help eliminate the residual prejudices, of those who have them, against homosexuals. No-one can dig deep here and not believe that homosexuals' love lives are every bit as real and valid as those of heterosexuals. If only Tchaikovsky had been born into the culture of Ancient Greece in which male love affairs were an accepted and integral part of the social fabric! In Plato's *Symposium*, for example, a party of diners took it for granted that homosexual love between male soldiers was a virtue because their loyalty to one another and their mutual sense of honour would make them invincible.

Lilies of the Valley

Side by side with [his] adoration of Sergey Kiryev, Pyotr experienced many involvements of a different character, yielding to them unrestrainedly, and with the full fervour of his passionate and sensuous nature. Women were never the object of these infatuations; physically they evoked in him only detestation.... [On one occasion dinner guests at St Petersburg's restaurant Chautemps] were defamed throughout the whole city as buggers. Among them were Pyotr and Apukhtin, and they acquired forever the reputation of buggers ... It goes without saying that the Chautemps scandal did not change

Pyotr's inclinations . . . but he became more cautious in his amorous adventures . . . and to seek interests outside the beau monde.
    From Modest Tchaikovsky's unpublished autobiography

Throughout his adult life Tchaikovsky was forever searching for adolescents in their mid-teens. Returning, for instance, in 1886 to Paris from Batum (at the Caucasian end of the Black Sea) via Trebizond and Marseilles he wrote to his homosexual younger brother Modest that the people in Trebizond were 'very attractive . . . I do not know about the women, but the men and especially the boys are most beautiful.' Arriving later in Marseilles he 'wandered about the city . . . searching without success'.

Many of the adolescents and young men who crossed his path became, as we shall see, his protégé lovers, heart-throbs, passing flings, platonic friends, distant beloveds – or, let's face it, just paid one-night stands. Perhaps the most elegant revelation of the irresistible appeal of boys and young men for Tchaikovsky comes not in a letter or diary entry but in his 'deeply heartfelt' poem, 'Lilies of the Valley'. He wrote it in Florence in 1878 during the aftermath of his horrendous marital crisis. This poem is his only serious attempt at the medium and he was 'terribly proud' of it. Once confessing to Mme von Meck 'a sort of wild adoration' for lilies of the valley, Tchaikovsky seems in his poem to invest in them all his feelings about the transient beauty of young men, especially those in their mid-teens. (Significantly, lily of the valley in Russian, *landysh*, is masculine.)

Poznansky includes the poem translated in full for the first time in his wonderful book. He is surely right in feeling that 'Lilies of the Valley' is a 'depiction of the dynamics of erotic attraction from its beginning to its dying away, through languor, torment, hope, and expectation, and incorporating into this emotional spectrum sensations of the transience of youthful beauty'. Poznansky even feels that the poem echoes the cyclical patterns of the symphonies which express in their own language the composer's profoundest musings on love, life and death. (The Fifth Symphony, indeed, is surely one of the finest cyclic works of the 19th century.)

There is space here for just the climax of the poem, the all-too-brief florescence of the lily of the valley in all its heavenly beauty in spring – implicitly echoing, for Tchaikovsky, the fleeting allure of boys in mid-adolescence:

Where lies the secret of your charms? What do you prophesy
   to the soul?
With what do you attract me, with what gladden my heart?
Is it that you revive the ghost of former pleasures,
Or is it future bliss that you promise us?
I know not. But your balmy fragrance,
Like flowing wine, warms and intoxicates me,
Like music, it takes my breath away,
And, like a flame of love, it suffuses my burning cheeks.
And I am happy while you bloom, modest lily of the valley,
The tedium of winter has passed without a trace,
And oppressive thoughts are gone, and my heart in languid
   comfort
Welcomes, with you, forgetfulness of trouble and woe.
Yet now you fade . . .

The letters and diaries abound with references to young men
who might have inspired such a poem, from a beautiful boy
singer named Vittorio whom he met in Florence, to anonymous
youths such as this one mentioned in June 1884: 'Dreamed of
M. and consequently all day was a little, and even more than a
little, in love. [A cut follows.] Never mind, never mind – silence
– !!!' A more identifiable youth who provoked an erotic dream
recorded in September 1886 was Modest's servant Nazar Litrov:

> I slept fitfully, and had strange dreams (flying with Nazar in the
> nude, needing and at the same time being unable to do something
> with the help of Sasha, the deacon's son, etc).

'The Shadowy Underground Dimension'

Diary entries:

[16 June 1886] With Timosha [Timofey, a bathhouse attendant].
Somehow wasn't any fun. It's not the same any more.
[18 July 1886] Letters, about which Aloysha mustn't know (to
Tim[ofey] . . .).
[27 July 1886] Bruce [a Moscow restaurant and homosexual pickup
venue], even though it's Sunday. Pleasure and remorse.
[16 May 1887] Znamenskie [St Petersburg bathhouse]. Timofey.
[3 April 1889] In the café with [cut] and in [Café de la] Paix
[another cut]. Back home alone. A negro. They came to my place.

It might be as well to have done with it and dish the man's dirt first before scaling his loftier encounters – although, of course, there can be trace elements of the aesthetic or divine in the most casual flings, in one-night stands even. Conversely, long-term relationships can be sordidly exploitative. The frontier territories between lust, love and exploitation are very foggy and boggy. Part of Tchaikovsky's problem was that, because of his timidity and fear of embarrassing his family, he never followed the example of his more up-beat homosexual friends like Prince Golitsyn and the poet Aleksey Apukhtin in living openly with a male lover. His sexual needs therefore frequently propelled him towards the seedy flesh markets where sex was bought and sold.

His attitude to this underworld remained ambivalent. He needed it to satisfy his needs but also abhorred any public undermining of conventional standards of behaviour. He disapproved, but nevertheless joined in!

While visiting Paris, his favourite European city, in the winter of 1879 he sent Modest a graphic description of one of his encounters with a young rent boy:

[26 February] A bed, a pitiful little trunk, a dirty little table with a candle-end, a few shabby trousers and a jacket, a huge crystal glass, won in a lottery – those make the room's only decorations. Yet it did seem to me at that moment that this miserable cell is the centre of human happiness . . . There occurred all kinds of *calinerie* [tenderness] as he put it, and then I turned frantic because of amorous happiness and experienced incredible pleasure. And I can say in confidence, that not only for a long time, but almost never before have I felt so happy in this sense as today.

On the morning after came post-coital guilt and remorse and a desire to help the young man whose poverty he had exploited:

I woke with remorse and full understanding of the fraudulence and exaggerated quality of that happiness which I felt yesterday and which, in substance, is nothing but a strong sexual inclination based on the correspondence with the capricious demands of my taste and on the general charm of that youth. But, my God, how pitiable is he, how thoroughly debauched! And instead of helping to better himself, I only contributed to his further going down.

To salve his conscience, Tchaikovsky gave the young man 500 francs so that he could return to his family in Lyons.

Another stay in Paris early in 1883, when he was 42, drew from his pen some of his most indiscreet ever letters to Modest. He went on sexual binges that would have the eyes and ears of the grizzliest tabloid editor twitching. The letters contain enthusiastic although euphemistic descriptions (heavily censored) of how he spent his leisure time after working on the orchestration of one of his more nationalist operas *Mazeppa*: of his evening 'strolls' searching for boy pick-ups whom he enticed back to his rooms, and of his delight in finding 'a club, a real club' catering for the varied tastes of homosexuals. In Paris there were not only clubs and *cafés chantants* but also bordellos or *maisons des hussards* serving their needs. As early as 1876 Tchaikovsky had begun to contemplate casual pick-ups, writing to Modest that '[T]here is nothing more foolish than to travel avoiding any acquaintance with the locals, as I usually do.'

Poznansky quotes at some length from the research reports of a contemporary Russian physician, Ivan Merzheevsky, in his *Sudebnaia ginekologiia* (Court Gynaecological Reports) on male prostitution across Europe and the blackmail hazards involved for vulnerable clients like Tchaikovsky. They include a graphic portrayal taken from a French law journal of the kind of rough-trade Parisian rent boy whose come-on might have set Tchaikovsky's heart pounding:

> Is it a man? The hair is parted in the middle, falling in ringlets against the cheeks like that of a young coquette, a cravat is tied carelessly about the neck ... the collar of the shirt lies on the shoulders, the eyes are languid, the lips a little heart, he bends to the side like a Spanish dancer, and when he is arrested, he clasps his hands together and gets such an expression on his face that one might laugh if only this did not also arouse disgust and indignation.

Tchaikovsky did not, of course, confine his strolls to Paris. Back on his home territory in St Petersburg he and his ilk assiduously sniffed out similar meat in the Zoological Gardens, behind the Peter and Paul fortress, and in the gardens off the main thoroughfare, Nevsky Prospekt – 'this tasteless, libidinous and jubilant world ... a chaos of petty pimps and cheap courtesans'. In the early 1890s his nephew Bob was often with him, or other members of what became known as the Fourth Suite (Tchaikovsky only having written three orchestral suites known as such by then) including a special favourite, Count Alexandr

'Sanya' Litke, who acted as the composer's *général de suite* – translatable (says Holden) as 'procurer'.

Merzheevsky also includes in his reports a bluntly factual account of the goings-on in one favoured venue for male prostitution in St Petersburg, the bathhouses – which Tchaikovsky definitely frequented. (Certain restaurants in both St Petersburg and Moscow were also well-known pick-up places.) Having footed it to the capital from the sticks in search of their crocks of gold, some lads in their late teens ended up as bathhouse 'attendants'. One such peasant describes his supplementary services for punters such as Tchaikovsky:

> I began to engage in buggery (*muzhelozhstvo*) . . . with the visitors to the bathhouses from the day I started working at the baths. I was taught this by some former attendants at the baths, Aleksey and Ivan. . . . They themselves were also engaged in this . . . It happens this way: when someone comes who wants to do it, he asks for an attendant, me or anyone else, since everyone who works as an attendant in the bathhouses does this, and orders me to wash him, but meanwhile I already see that it is not washing he wants, and he starts embracing and kissing me, and will ask my name, and then will do with me either as with a woman, or, depending on what he wishes, will sit while I stand before him, or will lie with me as with a woman, or will order me to do with him as with a woman, only in the anus, or bending forward and lying on his stomach, with me over him, all of which I would do . . . I never allowed myself to be taken in the anus, because it is painful, that is to say, because I believe that it must be painful. I would receive payment for this from the people who came through, whatever they would give, a ruble or more, while those who gave less we would curse, because why sin for the sake of a trifle? All the money we got for this we would set aside together and then on Sundays would divide it.

The composer's preferred services are not recorded, though his inordinate passion for cross-dressing (especially as a female ballet dancer) and powerful perfumes perhaps suggest that he would have ordered the attendant 'to do with him as with a woman'. (In the wild period of his late twenties he attended a masked ball dressed in 'an exceptionally elegant domino of black lace set off by diamonds and an ostrich-feather fan'.)

Whatever, when the mood was on him his appetite was insatiable, as he himself made clear to Modest in October 1876, the year before his traumatic and disastrous marriage, when he admitted that he had already given way three times, in less than a month, to his 'natural compulsions'. It was 'impossible to fight one's weaknesses'.

It is possible, in the opinion of the cholera specialist Dr Valentin Pokrovsky, President of the Russian Academy of Medical Sciences, interviewed on film by Holden in July 1993, that Tchaikovsky may have contracted the cholera from which he almost certainly died in just such an encounter as the above. The homosexual practice of 'rimming', or tonguing, can lead to infection by the 'faecal-oral route'. A certain Dr Thomas Stuttaford made a similar suggestion in *The Times* on 4 November 1993.

It should not be forgotten either that one of the attractions for Tchaikovsky of his visits to Italy was that in the second half of the nineteenth century that country was, says Poznansky, 'widely considered an erotic paradise by European homosexuals'. (Interestingly, in Lully's seventeenth-century France the term 'Italian morals' was synonymous with sodomy. Likewise, the circles Handel moved in during his visit to Italy in the early 18th century were awash with homosexuals.) The Roman milieu Tchaikovsky moved amongst in January 1880, while he was working on the *Capriccio Italien*, centred round various locals including a singer Amici and a painter Giulio. These two were at the centre of a rampant, squabble-and-spat-ridden homosexual sub-culture of promiscuity and prostitution. Tchaikovsky had also previously made use, when in Florence, of the services of a pimp named Napoleone, 'in his eternally grey coat and a hat set back on his head'.

'Pederasty and pedagogy cannot live in harmony with one another'
Tchaikovsky to Modest, 31 August 1876

For the eager student of human waywardness there are reams of stuff to forage from Holden and Poznansky, but it nevertheless takes some fancy psychic footwork to remain non-judgemental about Tchaikovsky's abusive power relationships with some of his pupils while he held the post of Professor of Musical Theory at the Moscow Conservatoire from 1866 to 1878. Not only did his lectures become increasingly ineffective towards the end of his stint; he favoured those male students whose 'adolescent charms he valued so highly' over the females. Just as his skirt-chasing, heavy-drinking boss Nikolay Rubinstein took home female students for extra-curricular activities, so Tchaikovsky also began taking some young men home with him for extra tuition. Interestingly, a mischievous article in *Novoe Vremya* (New Times) of 26 August 1878 referred to numerous love affairs going on between professors and their female pupils. It also, alas, thrust the 'sword of Damocles' into Tchaikovsky's neck (as he put it to Modest) with what he took to be a concluding insinuation against himself:

> Love affairs of another kind also go on at the Conservatoire – but of these, for obvious reasons, I shall spare you the details.

Fearing public exposure of his 'secret vice' above all else, this made the composer 'sick at heart' and more than ever determined to quit the Conservatoire. His one overriding consolation for such an innuendo was the abiding love between Modest and himself. It is somewhat ironic that two years earlier, in August 1876, he had been warning Modest, who was by then a tutor to a young deaf mute, Nikolay Konradi, that 'pederasty and pedagogy cannot live in harmony with one another'!

Home for Tchaikovsky from the summer of 1871 was temporarily a modest Moscow apartment with two rooms and a kitchen vacated by his life-long supporter and close friend from Conservatoire days, the critic Herman Laroche. Tchaikovsky had at last freed himself from the constraints of lodging with Nikolay Rubinstein, whose more orthodox brother Anton ran the parent institution in the capital, St Petersburg. (Both institutions had emerged from the Russian Musical Society.) It was at St Petersburg that the composer had studied form, instrumentation, organ and flute while supporting himself with piano and theory pupils, graduating in 1866 with a Silver Medal. He had committed himself to a career in music in 1863 after quitting his cushy-sounding job at the Ministry of Justice – where he did, nevertheless, for a time strive diligently to improve his prospects – and enrolling full-time at the Conservatoire.

A Gallery of Lovers and Close Friends

His Servant Alexsey Sofronov

First and foremost among Tchaikovsky's lovers must come his servant Alexsey (Aloysha) Sofronov, who served his usually adoring master for over 22 years, excluding only a period of army service.

Alexsey joined Tchaikovsky from when he was a delectable twelve years old, initially alongside his elder brother Mikhail. Alexsey did a great deal more for his master than lackey for him and caress and scratch his head. 'There is no doubt that Alexsey performed sexual services for Tchaikovsky,' says Holden unequivocally, quoting a partly censored passage from a letter of 1877 from Tchaikovsky to Modest: 'Alexsey [then eighteen] well understands all my needs, and more than satisfies all my demands.' At eighteen, Aloysha was sexually over the hill for Tchaikovsky of course, having 'lost his looks' but nevertheless remained 'as dear to my heart as ever . . . Whatever may befall us I will not let him go.' In the vast collection of the composer's letters, there are very few disparaging remarks about Aloysha. 'Between the two poles of passionate emotion for a lover and son and irritation with an inferior,' writes Poznansky, 'the strange affair between gentleman and servant steadily grew and developed.' Occasional contretemps arose through such annoyances as Alexsey's frolics with a French maid, catching syphilis, and twice getting married.

Devoted as he was to his master, Alexsey made sure he had a top whack cut from Tchaikovsky's estate after his death, wresting from Modest an exorbitant 5,000 roubles for the furniture bequeathed from master to servant. Alexsey showed even more nerve by buying very cheaply, for 8,500 roubles, the Maidanovo house which Tchaikovsky had only rented, and then offering to rent it back to Modest for a steep 50 roubles a month.

None of this would have caused Tchaikovsky to turn in his newly dug grave, however. One of his most bereft times in his adult life was when his beloved Aloysha was called up for military service in 1880. This crisis of deprivation made the composer 'sick at heart' and drove him to nervous fits, 'continual dinners and suppers with drink' and to love-lorn hoverings outside the Moscow barracks housing his 'little soldier'. In an attempt to secure favours for Aloysha, Tchaikovsky even bore the painful drudgery of cultivating his regimental commander and, worse still, the commander's wife, spending 'entire evenings accompanying her singing and engaging in society talk'. Greater love hath no man!

Throwing all caution to the winds, Tchaikovsky risked the derision of the military censors at the Moscow barracks by sending Aloysha such truly abandoned declarations of longing as this:

> Each evening, after undressing, I pine for you. I sit at my desk sobbing, once I remember that you are not here beside me ... No-one could ever replace you ... Ah, dear sweet Lyona! If you were to stay in the army a hundred years I would never grow out of the habit of you.

Alexsey's absence virtually paralysed his master's creativity for many months of 1881, his only real work being the editing of a collection of sacred music by the eighteenth-century composer Bortnyansky.

When Aloysha informed his master that his military service was to be reduced to three years the creative juices began to flow again. Tchaikovsky was further bucked up when Aloysha was granted a year's sick leave in 1882 to recover from pneumonia. 'He is so perfectly sweet and caring towards me that I find no words to express my pleasure at sensing his nearness to me,' wrote Tchaikovsky to Modest. Aloysha was finally discharged from the army in March 1884. It is ironic that a storm in a teacup involving Alexsey resolved Tchaikovsky to accept no further hospitality from Mme von Meck (of whom much more, anon) at her new home in Pleshcheevo. He was livid when the father of one of Meck's retainer-protégés, the would-be composer Wladyslaw Pachulski – whom she had long foisted as a pupil on the reluctant composer – summarily forbade Alexsey to sleep in his master's boudoir. Alexsey also was a cause of friction between Tchaikovsky and his in-laws the Davidovs who resented the servant's presumption.

Boarding-school Love: Sergey Kireev

Tchaikovsky had a love life long before he took on his servant Alexsey. Said to be 'girlishly pretty' in his early years at his boarding school, the School of Jurisprudence in St Petersburg, he had a number of crushes there. When he was a senior he appears to have first lost his heart to a considerably younger lad named Sergey ('Seryozha') Kireev. Kireev seems to have received visits from his admirer in the out-of-bounds junior dorm and was the possible dedicatee of a song from the late 1850s entitled 'My genius, my angel, my friend'. Modest writes of this ten-year love affair that it was:

> the strongest, most durable, and purest amorous infatuation of Tchaikovsky's life. It possessed all the charms, all the sufferings, all the depth and force of love, most luminous and sublime . . . Anyone who doubts the beauty and high poetry of this 'cult' should be pointed to the best pages of Tchaikovsky's musical oeuvre . . . he never experienced later in life such powerful, lasting and painful emotion . . .

Except, of course, for his nephew Bob, as we shall later see.

Alexsey Apukhtin, Lyric Poet

In about 1853 the pubescent Tchaikovsky also became deeply attached to his school classmate Alexsey ('Lyola') Apukhtin, later to become an important lyric poet, flamboyant, hedonistic, and openly gay. In the words of one contemporary, Apukhtin 'mingled with the gilded youth of St Petersburg and shared the passions of their "frenzied nights" '. Despite their subsequent lurches between 'violent row and emollient embrace', Apukhtin, said Tchaikovsky, was 'my court jester and best friend', while for the poet, the composer was 'like the dominant in the chords of my youth'.

According to a diary reminiscence recorded nearly 30 years later of Alexsey Suvorin, editor-in-chief of the *New Times*, the composer spent an autumn in his mid-twenties (probably 1865) living rent free with the poet-like husband and wife. When Tchaikovsky announced it was bedtime, Apukhtin, whose apartment was lined with photographs of pages and guardsmen, would kiss his hand and say 'Run along, my darling, I'll join you in a moment.'

Tchaikovsky set some six songs to texts of his friend including 'To forget too soon' (written shortly after the eternally popular 'None but the lonely heart'). Apukhtin dedicated to Tchaikovsky a poem centred round an amorous meeting, entitled 'Fate: on Beethoven's Fifth symphony', one snippet of which reads:

And then she [Fate] comes, and in an instant
Love, anxiety, expectation,
Bliss – all flow together for them
In one mad kiss.

Perhaps Apukhtin's most caring and supportive moment in his relations with Tchaikovsky came in the aftermath of the composer's disastrous marriage, when he retreated to Italy in a state of shame, 'moral illness' and 'monomania', dreading to return home for fear of public ridicule through the unavoidable exposure of his homosexuality. Apukhtin reminded his friend that he had many thousands of admirers, and true friends who

> do not care what sauce you prefer on your asparagus: sour, sweet, or oily . . . You have done nothing dishonest. The chief error in your life has been concession to this base thing called public opinion. Take a look at the history of art: people such as you have never known happiness, but without them mankind would be bereft of its finest pleasures.

Tchaikovsky would surely have envied Apukhtin his long-term live-in relationship with his young lover Sasha Zhedrinsky, an experience the composer never ever enjoyed. 'The firmness and strength of his attachment moves me deeply,' he wrote in one of his letters.

The plump-faced and double-chinned Apukhtin kept up his colourful and unorthodox life-style right up to his final years before his undignified death from dropsy at the age of 52. One hot and stifling summer afternoon a lawyer friend found him very subdued in his city apartment, seated

> on an enormous ottoman, in a light silk Chinese robe cut widely around his plump neck, looking as he sat there like the traditional figure of Buddha. But in his face there was none of the contemplative Buddhist tranquillity. It was pale, his eyes looked mournful. From all the furnishings emanated a frost of loneliness, and it seemed that death had already brushed with the tip of its wing the soul of the pensive poet.

Princes and Potentates

A key aristocratic figure in the composer's youth was the flamboyant and solicitous homosexual Prince Alexsey Golitsyn.

Tchaikovsky spent the summer of 1864 living it up in breath-takingly high style – like 'something out of a fairy tale' – at the prince's estate at Trostinet in the Ukraine. The festivities included a nameday celebration for the composer which featured a cere-monial breakfast, and, later, a ride through the forest 'where the whole road had been flanked by flaming pitch barrels' to a sumptuous supper for peasants and potentates alike.

Eight years older than Tchaikovsky, Golitsyn openly defied the prohibitions on *muzhelozhstvo* (buggery). Indeed, his appoint-ment as Tsar Alexandr II's chief at the Ministry of Spiritual Affairs surely testifies to the tolerance of homosexuals in later nineteenth-century Russia. Golitsyn turned up recurringly in the composer's life, most disagreeably with his grand passion, one Nikolay Masalitinov, in Rome in late 1879, and on another occasion, with 'a blonde Lyceum pupil'. By this time, in the wake of his marriage crisis, Tchaikovsky had no wish to be reminded of his youthful excesses, a phase which the prince had apparently not outgrown.

Another prince and patron in Tchaikovsky's life, going back to school-days where he was two classes ahead of the composer, was his friend Vladimir Meshchersky – dubbed by one leading enemy as the 'Prince of Sodom and citizen of Gomorrah'. Meshch-ersky, who became a prominent and much-hated reactionary journalist, and confidant of the last two tsars (Alexandr III and Nicholas II) crops up recurringly in Tchaikovsky's correspon-dence. An important link between the composer and royal circles, Meshchersky was sufficiently in royal favour to survive at least three scandals: one arising from his crush on a young bugler in the Imperial Guards battalion; another in which he was impli-cated with some two hundred other persons, including members of the Guards and actors from St Petersburg's Alexandrinsky theatre; and yet another in which his enemies turned over to Nicholas II his letters to his lover Burdukov.

Tchaikovsky's close contacts went even higher up the social scale. From 1880 he developed a close 'elective affinity' (rather than an affair) with the highly cultured Grand Duke Konstantin Konstantinovich, nephew of Tsar Alexandr II. Once Tchaikovsky had overcome his natural reticence in such exalted company, the two men became very firm friends to the point where the Grand Duke invited the composer to join him on a three-year cruise round the world. Tchaikovsky politely declined such a restriction on his freedom, but confessed to Modest that he was 'utterly charmed by this uncommonly likeable person'. Konstantin dedicated a poem to the composer, who features often in the princely diaries he kept from the age of nine – diaries which, says a Soviet commentator, 'it is customary not to mention'. Konstantin's first reference to Tchaikovsky, in 1880, describes how 'we were all intoxicated by this wonderful music' after the composer had played to the assembled company the chorus of prayers from his *Joan of Arc*. The two men continued to correspond until a month before the composer's death.

Camp Followers

An early camp and colourful companion of the composer was the rouged and hair-dyed voice coach Luigi Piccioli, aged apparently anywhere from fifty-plus to seventy, and sporting in his collar a contraption to stretch his skin and smooth out the wrinkles! His real claims to immortality lie in having fired Tchaikovsky's enthusiasm for Italian opera and in encouraging him to produce his first published work, a rather limp canzonetta, 'Mezza Notte'.

A surprisingly indispensable figure in the composer's life was one of his lodgers and full-time pimp from 1871, Nikolay Bochechkarov, of whom he became fond in spite of himself. The stout and moustached Bochechkarov was a freeloading, parasitic 'Auntie' or 'passive homosexual' who seems to have paid his rent more in kind than in cash. Feminised in his Christian name by the composer to 'Old Lyvovna', Bochechkarov relayed all the latest gossip from the homosexual underworld and procured for his landlord rent boys in their mid-teens – the point in adolescence which, as we know, sent the composer's nervous system into spasm. On one occasion Bochechkarov arranged a 'rendezvous' for his landlord with 'one very nice youth of peasant origin serving as a butler'. Tchaikovsky was overjoyed, writing to Modest:

> I immediately fell in love as Tatyana with Onegin. His face and body – *un rêve* [like a dream] – are the fulfilment of a sweet fantasy. After a walk, and utterly infatuated, I invite him and Bochechkarov to a pub. We take a private room.

Tchaikovsky never deserted Bochechkarov, whose role, says Poznansky, was something like 'the stock character of the parasite in ancient Roman comedy – a witty and unprincipled figure of secondary importance, but without whom the more exalted dramatis personae cannot succeed in furthering their intrigues and satisfying their desires'. He remained 'very sweet' to Tchaikovsky who, loyal as ever to his close friends, visited him when he was dying from dropsy (didn't they all?) at Nizy in 1879. The composer recorded his feelings to Modest:

> The remembrance of the great part he played during the whole course of my Moscow life cuts into my heart like a knife . . . He possessed an amazing faculty for reconciling oneself with life; his presence and his company were always an irreplaceable source of entertainment, calm, and consolation to me. What matter that he was a nonentity in terms of moral and intellectual power! He was pleasant always and to everyone, and this took the place in him of a great mind or great talents.

Another bizarre member of the *demi-monde* among whom Tchaikovsky moved during this period was the poet Sergey Donaurov, towards whom the composer seemed to have an ambivalent attitude, finding him to have 'insatiable amorous appetites', and to be 'somewhat difficult', but also 'a kind of nice fellow'.

More than Just a Fare

A young *droshky* driver (cabby) by the name of Vanya (a diminutive name for Ivan), who used to drive the composer from his new home at Maidanovo to Moscow, and around Moscow, undoubtedly set his fare's pulse racing when he was in his mid-forties. Entries in Tchaikovsky's diary and a letter to Modest in the summer and autumn of 1886 speak for themselves:

> [Diary, 14 September] Ivan, unexpectedly. Happy. Long walk in the woods . . . In love with V . . . Hesitation. Virtue triumphs.

> [26 September] My Vanya. Endless visits to pubs. Stinking [drunk].

> [27 September] Misunderstanding with Vanya. I find him at the entrance on my return. Very pleasant and happy moment of my life. But then a sleepless night, while the torment and anguish I felt in the morning – this I cannot express.

> [28 September] Sensation of anguish. Searching for Vanya near the hotel . . . Decrease in amorous feelings. A strange phenomenon, as one would think the reverse.

[Letter to Modest, 30 September] I could say something more about this stay in Moscow, but better when I see you. In a word, in my old age, I have fallen rather heavily into Cupid's net.

[Diary, 17 October] Home with Vanya . . . Vanya received money yesterday and today.

[10 December] On the way conversations with Vanya. Surge [of love] . . .

[14 December] Vanyusha. Hands.

[23 December] Drunken Vanka

[24 December] Yesterday Vanya made me angry. Today I melted.

An entry in early April 1887 suggests that by then the affair was fizzling out: 'Coolness towards Vanya. Want to get rid of him.' Half a year later, however, on 6 October, they may have got together again for old time's sake, to judge by the autumn entry, 'Met Vanya, the cabman. Happy.'

Vanya wasn't the only coachman in Tchaikovsky's life, as we shall see in the immediate aftermath of his disastrous marriage.

Landowner and Playboy

One indefatigable lecher in Tchaikovsky's life, older than him by three years, was the prominent landowner and playboy Nikolay Kondratyev. Kondratyev, whose relationship with the composer was often fraught and stormy although nevertheless enduring, 'embodied' says Poznansky, 'the far loftier level of the homosexual subculture, the real *demi-monde*' as opposed to people like the aforementioned 'Auntie' and hanger-on Bochechkarov. Kondratyev reportedly exercised *droits de seigneur* over both his male and female servants. (The days of Russian serfdom, when those in service accepted their obligation to accommodate the sexual needs of their masters and mistresses, had not long been abolished.) Kondratyev eventually married, but dossed down at Tchaikovsky's place for a while when his wife rumbled his affair with one servant, Aleksey Kiselev, in what was in effect a scandal-fraught *ménage à trois* – or maybe *à quatre, à cinq* . . .?

On more than one occasion, Tchaikovsky discovered that Aleksey had reversed the role of master and servant. In 1878 'like a totally independent lord', Aleksey created scandalous scenes of 'general drunkenness, shouts and noise all night long, vomiting, . . . in short, such insolence that Tolya and I did not sleep all night and had our nerves shattered by our fury.'

There is every reason, says Poznansky, to suppose that Tchaikovsky's agonising visit to Kondratyev on his deathbed in Aachen in 1887 found its outlet in the Fifth Symphony, composed during 'one of the darkest periods' of his life. Witnessing his friend wracked in syphilitic pain and clearly frightened to die, Tchaikovsky's own torment was unbearable:

[2 September 1887] Painful, terrible hours! Oh, never will I forget all that I have suffered here.

[4 September] All today has felt like a nightmare. Violent egoism has tormented me. My one thought: to leave!!! No more patience . . . Lord! will the time ever come when I shall no longer suffer such torments?

Several months were needed for these shattering experiences of 'the soul of a man in deep crisis' to be sublimated into art. Beginning intensive work on the symphony in mid-May 1888, Tchaikovsky was still thinking constantly of Kondratyev. Writing of a visit to the park near his home in Maidanovo, he lamented that

everything there seemed to me somehow melancholy and sad, and nowhere else have I experienced so vividly the grief of N.D. Kondratyev's departure from this world as there, especially along his little path. In Maidanovo, in general I painfully regretted the past, and it was awful to realise the precipitateness and irreversibility of the past.

The earliest sketchbooks actually contain a 'programme' for the work, although not one as copiously detailed as for the Fourth. It begins:

Intr. Complete submission before Fate, or, which is the same, before the inscrutable predestination of Providence. Allegro. (1) Murmur of doubt, complaints, reproaches to XXX. (2) To leap into the embrace of *Faith*??? A wonderful programme, if only it can be carried out.

It has to be said that the composer's grief at Kondratyev's squalid and painful death was assuaged somewhat by the attentions of the deceased's servant Sasha Legoshin, who, with his sleepy eyes, had, in earlier days, frequently slipped into the composer's bed before waking his master. Once again Tchaikovsky, like his well-to-do fellow homosexuals, was sniffing out his quarry from among the lower orders, whose sexual favours to their patrons often brought them rich returns socially as well as financially.

Pupils and Protégés

One pupil for whom Tchaikovsky developed a 'deep and strong' attachment was Vladimir ('Volodka') Shilovsky, a sickly and precocious pianist, and would-be composer from a wealthy background who didn't live up to his early promise. According to Modest, Shilovsky was an intimate of the composer from the age of fourteen (1866), revering his teacher 'with a love verging on adoration'. They were very possibly lovers. For once it seems that Tchaikovsky was more pursued than pursuing in an affair which was, says Poznansky, 'an archetypal example of a pupil's amorous infatuation with a teacher who in turn, not without pleasure, allows himself to be loved'.

The relationship between master and pupil endured, although not without 'ruptures and hysterics' partly due to an unruliness Shilovsky inherited from his wilful and scandal-prone mother who had a passion for treading the boards. Later, in 1870, Tchaikovsky became for Shilovsky 'an Argus, the saviour of his life' during a severe illness when the composer, again with characteristic loyalty, interrupted his work on *The Oprichnik* to tend to him in Paris. Tchaikovsky frequently enjoyed Shilovsky's hospitality at his home in Ussovo, and even a free month's holiday in Nice in 1871. This resulted in two pieces for piano, a Nocturne and a Humoresque (Op. 10, the latter one proving to be very popular) which Tchaikovsky dedicated to his sugar-boy. The relationship deteriorated, however, when Shilovsky, who was all too often drunk and disorderly, married at the age of 24.

The crucial rift with Shilovsky came over money. Tchaikovsky was forced over the years to borrow, by his own calculation, some 7,550 roubles from him, though Shilovsky reckoned it was nearly four times as much. What irked Tchaikovsky was that his former pupil broadcast his largesse to the world (in 1879), thereby exposing his master's incurable financial incontinence. Happily, the pair were reconciled before Shilovsky's death from dropsy (what else?) at the age of 41.

'My guilt about him is unbearable . . .'

One of the greatest, and musically most important passions of Tchaikovsky's life was his protégé Eduard Zak, whom he met through a conservatoire student when the lad was an irresistible fifteen. There is precious little documentation on their mystifying relationship, although one letter from Tchaikovsky to his elder brother Nikolay, then a provincial railway official who had signed on Zak for an exhausting job, gives the flavour of the composer's infatuation: 'I have missed him terribly and fear for his future: I fear lest physical activity should kill him in his loftier strivings . . . it is absolutely essential for me to see him. For God's sake work it out.'

Zak committed suicide at the age of nineteen, an event over which the composer was still grieving intensely and feeling guilty some fourteen years later during the early gestation of the Fifth Symphony. (Zak was probably also one of the fainter wraiths hovering over that work, with its haunting flow of intense, yearning melody in the slow movement.) The September diary entries for that year (1887), are the longest referring to any one friend, and speak for themselves. Although they give no clue as to the cause of the crisis, they have, of course, teased out endless speculation. Was Zak overburdened by the strength of his patron's love?

[16 September] Before going to sleep, thought much and long of Eduard. Wept much. Can it be that *he* is truly gone??? Don't believe it.

[17 September] How amazingly clearly I remember him . . . the sound of his voice, the way he moved, but above all the way he used to look at me . . . The death of this boy, the fact that he no longer exists, is beyond my understanding. I believe I have never loved anyone as much as him. My God! no matter what they told me then and how I try to console myself, my guilt about him is unbearable . . . [I] love him still, and his memory is sacred to me.

How misguided one's youth can be! As a starry-eyed adolescent I used to drool over *Romeo and Juliet* as the supreme expression of heterosexual passion, and now I discover it was very possibly Zak who was the prime inspiration behind the work.

Certainly the *Romeo and Juliet* Overture – 'the best work I have ever done' said Tchaikovsky after its completion – gives passionate vent to feelings which would pour forth many more times in his music: the agonies and despair of unfulfilled and frustrated love. No wonder Rimsky-Korsakov responded so enthusiastically: 'What ineffable beauty, what burning passion! It is one of the finest themes of all Russian music!' And the Overture's dedicatee, Balakirev, after successfully insisting that its beginning and end needed 'completely rewriting', wrote of its 'fantastic and passionate anguish'.

Censors at Work

Another Tchaikovsky heart-throb, on references to whom the censors got to work with a vengeance, was a minor courtier named Vladimir Bibikov. One line which escaped the blue pencil was 'Bibikov sends you a kiss', in a letter of 1869 from Tchaikovsky to Modest, full of details of the lovers' nights on the tiles in Moscow. They became intimate some time before 1870, although relations had grown strained by 1872.

Sultan and Concubine

One very exotic-sounding lover of the composer was the young architect and dilettante Ivan Klimenko who, in his own words, 'succumbed to Pyotr Ilyich's seductive invitation and lived with him for some time'. 'Klimenko' became feminised in the composer's correspondence to 'Klimenka' and to the even more affectionate diminutive 'Klimenochka'. (Such progressive endearments were hallmarks of Tchaikovsky's infatuations.) In a highly suggestive letter of September 1871 to Klimenko – too long to explain or quote in full here – Tchaikovsky plays the role of Sultan, issuing a provocative invitation to his 'concubine' and ending with a threat of 'impalement':

> But can you, the most beloved of the concubines of my harem, you, the beautiful and at the same time young Klimenka, doubt for even a single moment my love for you? No, my silence can be explained merely by the laziness of your voluptuous Sultan; ever postponing a moment of voluptuous conversation with you, in the end he has brought this almost, I think, to the point of a rendezvous with you . . . I took pen in hand at the relentless request of my divan, which, having been reupholstered with new fabric on the occasion of my move, is drooping out of longing for you and prays, on your arrival in Moscow, to soothe your tired limbs on its resilient

shoulders newly furnished with fresh springs. To its request I add my own as well. If you wish to give us both considerable pleasure, stay at my place and live with us as long as you like . . . I hope you will not force me . . . to turn our requests into commands, disobedience of which entails the penalty of death by impalement . . . So I await you! Truly, it grows dull without Klimenka.

'A lovely, naive, sincere, tender creature'

From the moment Tchaikovsky first met the talented sixteen-year-old young violinist Yosif Kotek – 'a charming creature in every sense of the word' – master and pupil were a mutual admiration society. Tchaikovsky loved his Kotik (tom cat) 'to distraction' and frequently invited him to his recently acquired apartment. Although 'primarily heterosexual', Kotek unquestionably became Tchaikovsky's lover for a time, apparently being overwhelmed by his master's music. Here is Tchaikovsky writing to Modest on 31 January 1877:

I am *in love* as I have not been for so long . . . I have known him already for six years. I always liked him and a couple of times came close to falling in love with him. Those were rehearsals of love. Now I have made a leap and have surrendered to it most irrevocably. When for hours I hold his hand and with anguish fight a temptation to fall at his feet . . . passion storms me with an unimaginable force, my voice trembles like that of a youth, and I speak some kind of nonsense.

And in a later letter:

My love for you know who sparks with new and unprecedented strength! The reason for it is my jealousy . . . later I got accustomed to this horrible situation, but my love burned even stronger than ever before. I see him every day, and he has never been so affectionate with me as now.

But for fear of scandal and gossip, Tchaikovsky would have definitely dedicated his violin concerto to Kotek. The young man had, after all, not only revitalised the composer's morale and creative instincts in the aftermath of his marriage crisis, but had also helped him with the scoring and generally immersed himself 'lovingly' in the work. Instead, Tchaikovsky played safe by dedicating the concerto to the much better-known Hungarian violinist, Leopold Auer.

Although Tchaikovsky and Kotek sometimes fell out (partly due to the young man's sponging on his father, and to his constant womanising which resulted in syphilis), Kotek remained for the composer 'a lovely, naive, sincere, tender creature'. And it must never be forgotten that Kotek it was who, while he was resident solo violinist to Mme von Meck, first introduced Tchaikovsky to her in 1877.

In 1884 Tchaikovsky didn't hesitate to travel to visit the young man when, at the age of 29, he was dying of tuberculosis in Davos, Eastern Switzerland. After supplying 'moral and material aid' to his former pupil, the composer became too depressed to remain for long and left Davos after just six days 'knowing I had fulfilled the duty of friendship'.

A twist to this tale is that Auer protested that the Violin Concerto was 'almost impossible' to play and the première scheduled to take place in St Petersburg on 22 March 1879 was cancelled. Tchaikovsky later re-dedicated the work to Adolf Brodsky who performed it three years later with the Vienna Philharmonic Society under the baton of Hans Richter. As was often the case with Tchaikovsky's compositions, the Violin Concerto had flowed from his pen at breakneck speed: it was sketched within 11 days and scored within a fortnight.

Madly Ecstatic Blue Eyes

From Tchaikovsky's teaching days at St Petersburg emerges another probable student lover, the Englishman Joseph Ledger: 'small, very thin, blond, and pale, with the madly ecstatic blue eyes quite often found among the English', according to the composer's loyal friend and supporter Herman Laroche. Tchaikovsky's giveaway gayspeak euphemisms appear in a diary entry from the summer of 1886: 'Ledger (mysterious and enigmatic personality)'. Poznansky demonstrates fascinatingly how such coded language permeated the fabric of a taboo society in such that happened was literally unspeakable.

Exchanging Clothes

In 1886, whilst staying at the home of his younger brother Anatoly (in Tiflis in the Caucasus), Tchaikovsky met a young artillery officer named Ivan Verinovsky. Whether they became lovers is unclear, but Verinovsky certainly excited in the composer 'a sensation . . . of a special kind' and they dined together 'exchanging clothes'. Verinovsky became caught up in a very bizarre triangle completed by the composer and Anatoly's new and very coquettish wife Praskovya ('Panya') whom he had married in 1882. She appears to have competed with Tchaikovsky for the young man's attentions though it is not at all clear to whom the young man was more attracted. Whatever, he committed suicide soon afterwards. Tchaikovsky was predictably unable to work and 'wept so hard, sobbing almost hysterically, that [he] was not up to eating at all'. He certainly held Panya as partly to blame for the tragedy.

In fact, Tchaikovsky's unfortunate tally of suicide cases increased to three some two and a half years later when a third acquaintance mentioned in the diaries, Nikolay Svinkin, also killed himself. (The first had been Zak, of course.)

Boys

A bizarre blend of the erotic and avuncular surfaces in Tchaikovsky's obsession with the deaf-mute child Nikolay (Kolya) Konradi, the long-term tutee of Modest. The composer wrote to his brother of Kolya in ecstatic terms:

> Kiss that divine little boy's hands for me, and kiss his little feet too, but especially his divine little eyes. You've no idea how much I adore him. He is not out of my mind for a minute.

> I adore him passionately and think of him every second.

And to the lad himself he wrote: 'I kiss you warmly 1,000,000,000 times. Petya.'

Signed 'Petya', no less! Not even 'Uncle Petya'!

Tchaikovsky certainly worried about Modest's relationship with his tutee, fearing for the boy's abuse if the two of them lived outside Kolya's home, which had disintegrated with the defection of the boy's mother to a new man. 'I may rest easy concerning you only *while you and Kolya are in their home*,' he wrote to Modest, who parted company from his charge on less than cordial terms in 1890 when Kolya was 22.

Other objects of Tchaikovsky's (suppressed?) paedophiliac adoration included a young lad of ten or eleven, Vittorio, whom the composer heard singing 'in a wonderfully rich voice' which sounded 'uncommonly sweet on the lips of a child', in a street in Florence early in 1877. Two months later the composer even gave up an 'amorous rendezvous' to meet the boy again. When the lad sang, wrote Tchaikovsky, 'I wept, languished, melted with delight . . . Since that evening I have been utterly filled with one feeling [there is a cut here].' The boy visited Tchaikovsky in carnival costume and sang for him again, giving rise to another effusion: 'He is positively beautiful with his inexpressibly attractive gaze and smile.' As a memento of this infatuation Tchaikovsky made an arrangement of one of the boy's songs, 'Pimpinella', as the last of his *Six Songs*, Op. 38.

Tchaikovsky's renowned friendliness and largess with the local children who lived near the home he rented at Maidanovo (from 1885) were double-edged. During the summer of 1886, after his beloved Legoshin had departed with his master Kondratyev, the composer singled out one local urchin from the many 'ugly' ones who surrounded him on his obligatory two-hour constitutionals, scrounging for handouts in cash and kind. The favoured pretty lad was Egor Tabachok, from nearby Praslovo, who received double tips, lessons in kite flying, skates, a hat, and doubtless other goodies before growing out of the composer's preferred age range. In 1890 he surprised Tchaikovsky when he appeared from behind some bushes looking 'quite grown-up and very handsome'.

Just Good Friends

The Peresleni Brothers, nephews of his brother-in-law Lev Davidov, aroused 'poignant and lofty spiritualised emotion' in the composer – and also scrounged a good many roubles from him as well by way of subsidies. Tchaikovsky and Nikolay Peresleni ('What a precious person Kolya Peresleni is') seem to have been especially close, and on one occasion were fascinated by homosexual advances within the audience during the intervals of a visit to the theatre.

Tchaikovsky struck up one 'short-lived but tender friendship', during a boat journey in the spring of 1889, with a fourteen-year-old lad – an archetypal lily of the valley – named Volodya Sklifosovsky. Tchaikovsky was inevitably grief-stricken when Sklifosovsky died less than a year later, and immortalised the friendship with a dedication to the young man's memory of his 'Elegiac Song', one of the *Eighteen Pieces* Op. 72 for piano.

Unwanted Attentions?

Inevitably Tchaikovsky was the recipient of other men's infatuations which he may not always have reciprocated. One such ardent admirer was the elderly prominent actor in Moscow, Prov Sadovsky who on one occasion in 1866 lavished the bemused composer with repeated unsolicited plonkers:

> then, fixing, as it were, a greedy look on Petya, Sadovsky would quickly grab his shoulders, draw him near, and kiss the nape of his neck with a smack, and, pushing away, would exclaim, 'Who are you?' and again would draw him close, kiss his neck and push him away; one could not watch this amusing scene without laughing.

Tchaikovsky's Nephew: '100-Fold Divine' Bob (1871-1906)

> incomprehensible, wonderful, ideal, infinitely divine . . .
> 10 November 1886

> To see him, to hear him, and to feel him near to me will soon, it seems, become the paramount condition of my well-being.
> Tchaikovsky to Modest, 31 August 1890

> the most powerful and all-embracing passion of his life
> Poznansky: *Tchaikovsky's Last Days*

Tchaikovsky's most agonising and obsessive passion was undoubtedly that for his nephew Bob Davidov who had been his uncle's favourite since he was eight years old. By the time Bob was thirteen Tchaikovsky's feelings for him were overtly sexual and remained so, even though the poor lad quickly became abnormally overweight in his late teens after having been notably 'tall and good-looking' at the age of fifteen. Although Tchaikovsky had great hopes for the boy's creative talents as a 'writer-artist' or 'writer-philosopher', Bob's career went down the pan.

With so many tales ancient and modern written of incestuous passions, it doesn't really come as too much of a shock to discover just how bewitched Tchaikovsky was by his pubescent nephew. A selection of diary and letter entries, taken here from Holden and Poznansky respectively, speak very powerfully for themselves:

[Diary, May–June 1884] . . . feasted my eyes all day on Bob. How utterly ravishing he looks in his little white suit . . . A stroll with Bob . . . Ah, what a little darling he is! . . . I played piano duets with my darling, incomparable, wonderful, ideal Bob . . . Strange dreams last night, wandering around with Bob . . . In the end, Bob will drive me mad with his unspeakable charms . . . With Bob (the darling!) walked to the cliffs . . . As soon as I am not working or walking (which to me is also work), I start longing for Bob and missing him. I do love him terribly . . . inseparable from my wonderful, incomparable Bob . . . A strange thing. I'm *terribly* reluctant to leave here. I think it's entirely because of Bob.

Here is part of a letter to Bob written in July 1891:

Like a youth having received a letter from the girl he loves, I kissed over and over again, mercilessly, the traces of your wretched abominable hand. My dear wonderful fellow, I adore you.

Another extract written at Christmas 1891 reads:

Through every dark sensation, whether grief, melancholy or anguish, whatever the cloud on my mental horizon comes a piercing ray of light with the thought that you exist and that I shall soon see you again.

In 1892 he asked Bob for a family photograph in which

You are divinely enchanting . . . and recall to me one of the most delectable seasons (???) of your bloom. Thus, I want a big print, . . . enlarged twenty times, of you. This is my *idée fixe*.

In that same year he also composed a ditty for his nephew:

> No news from my darling,
> I can't take it anymore,
> If only he would write me
> Just an itty-bitty more.

And here is another desperate outburst from Berlin in the last year of his life, on 27 May:

This time, probably because I have been remembering too often our journey last year, I have pined and suffered and wept more than ever. It is simply some kind of psychopathy . . . It is absolutely essential that I know in London without fail: are you going to Grankino, and do you wish me to come? . . . I should like very badly to spend some time together with you in Grankino.

Tchaikovsky's guilt feelings over his passion for Bob appear to some scholars, including David Brown, to be coded in the references he made to sensations X and Z – the pressure of the latter 'overpowering, irresistible' – in his diary entries from 17 May (Gregorian Calendar) 1884. The likelihood, suggests Holden, is that Z is the sex-drive itself and X the composer's guilt at his methods of relieving it. Poznansky, however, has emphatically ruled out this interpretation in an e-mail to me dated 26 January 1998. 'In its context,' he writes, 'there is no room for wild speculations about X and Z. All those sensations directly related to card games and to nothing else.'

Bob was the dedicatee of the sixth and final symphony, the 'Pathétique', begun with a secret programme in February 1893 ('Let them guess,' Tchaikovsky wrote to Bob), and completed in August. There can be no doubt that the work expresses the anguish of the composer's unrequited passion for its dedicatee, of 'a conflict between platonic passion and the desires of the flesh, held forcibly in check so as not to profane the sublimity of passion'.

> For Tchaikovsky [continues Poznansky] there evidently arose an irresistible desire to retell in music the story of his life and his soul and to dedicate it to Bob so that his beloved nephew might be able to share and appreciate all that he himself had gone through.

The outer movements of the 'Pathétique' are a bottomless pit of despair, with the first movement even incorporating a quotation from the Russian Orthodox Requiem ('With Saints give rest'). The last movement, 'full of profoundly doleful music', is surely Tchaikovsky's most explicit personal confession to be found anywhere in his works, from its searing opening sequence with the interweaving violins to its obsessive clinging at the close to those two descending, heart-rending phrases, before the final fading into oblivion. No wonder Tchaikovsky rated it as the most sincere of all his works. 'I love it,' he wrote to Bob, 'as I've never loved a single one of my musical progeny.'

Bob appears to have been permanently traumatised by the

agonies of Tchaikovsky's drawn-out death. Far from fulfilling the composer's ambitions for him of a brilliant career, he ended up as a dopehead suffering from agonising headaches, before shooting himself at the age of 34 in his uncle's house at Klin.

Tchaikovsky and his Brothers

our triple union, to be broken only by death . . . I consciously regard you as the model of a human being.
Modest to Tchaikovsky, 29 October 1877

What to make of Tchaikovsky's relationship with his two adoring younger twin brothers on whom he lavished so much affection and who when young looked up to him as a father-figure, mother-figure, playmate and trusted friend? Certainly it is a very far cry from the stiff-upper lip kind of Anglo-Saxon brotherhood. Poznansky is in no doubt that 'the relationship of the three Tchaikovsky brothers was saturated with eroticism, including its physical manifestations, to an extraordinary degree'.

Modest became a playwright of no great distinction but was the composer's first very important, if protectively biased biographer, and so left his mark. He was less fortunate than his composer-brother in having, at one stage of his life, to endure a series of nasty operations for an abscess near his anus, which caused him to scream 'like a calf'. Perhaps his strolling sprees were to blame.

Anatoly (Tolya) was apparently 'an entirely average person', and a rakish, venereally infected heterosexual before he married and made a successful career for himself in local government in the Caucasus. For many years he was Tchaikovsky's prime confidant and first recourse in distress, although later Modest took on the same role.

Here are one or two telling extracts of letters from Tchaikovsky to his brothers dating from his middle twenties:

[To sixteen-year-old Tolya, 1866] I kiss you passionately every place . . . My little dove.
[To Modest, 1 February 1869] Soon I shall send a very large sum of money for Tolya, whom I commission you to smother with kisses. And are you pleased at this opportunity to spoon a bit with your brother?
[Winter 1872, to Tolya, then 22] My heart is aflame for you as always . . . Tolya, I kiss your little hands warmly . . . I smother you

with kisses . . . I kiss both your little cheeks and the wart on your ear . . . Farewell, you fickle, weak-willed but very loveable scamp . . . I kiss you everywhere.

Some of the most passionate and committed exchanges between Tchaikovsky and his brothers came in the aftermath of his traumatic marriage. He leaned on them very heavily for emotional and moral support while torturing himself over the humiliating gossip that had inevitably arisen from his hasty departure from St Petersburg for Clarens, Paris and Italy.

Here is Tchaikovsky writing from Florence to Anatoly, who had just departed thence after having been with his brother since the collapse of the marriage:

[13 December 1877] When we [i.e. Tchaikovsky and his servant Aleksey] came home and your room was empty, my heart was wrung with pain, and this heartache continued crescendo until evening . . . I . . . at once, as was to be expected, suffered a powerful hysterical fit . . . I lost the power to control myself . . . My love for you is a bottomless pit . . . Farewell my joy, my dear . . .

The very next day, he wrote again saying how after being left alone he downed two bottles of cognac, fell asleep, and drunk again to excess:

Farewell, my darling, my dear. I kiss you a million times. What would I not give to kiss you in actual fact.

On 2 January 1878 from Venice, he was even more effusive:

When I came home, I lay on the bed and lolled about right up to dinner, pondering, thinking, dreaming, longing, covering you in my mind with kisses (ah, how I love you Tolya!).

And a few months later, on 27 April:

I have come to the fourth page and now but for the fact that I love you passionately, I have absolutely no idea what to write to you . . . I kiss you, my pet . . . I kiss your neck. I kiss your eyes. I kiss your lips.

Anatoly reciprocated his brother's feelings. 'You cannot imagine how much I love you,' he wrote in one reply. There were also passionate exchanges with Modest, who wrote to assure his elder brother that his 'jumping into marriage' made no difference to a brotherly love that was truly unconditional:

> [29 October 1877] I love you more than anything in the world, never has anyone held a greater place in my heart, no-one ever will. . . . I live for you, yes positively for you, because all my life I have submitted and shall submit to your influence. . . . I . . . always lived and shall live to please you, because now I consciously regard you as the model of a human being.

One batch of correspondence between the brothers, known as the Petrolina Letters (1872), is notable for its homosexual word-play. During reams of detail about *demi-monde* characters and activities, Tchaikovsky becomes 'young Tchaichika' and 'your devoted and loving sister'. Modest becomes 'amiable Modestina' and 'dear sister'.

Nature and Nurture: Mother, Governess, Sister

I knew from experience what an indelible mark is left in a child's soul by motherly tenderness and motherly affection.
Tchaikovsky to Mme von Meck

It hardly needs stressing that men's and women's love lives are crucially determined by their relationships with their parents, and most researchers now believe that a child's sexuality is usually established even before puberty. The consensus in Tchaikovsky's case seems to be that his homosexuality, possibly evident as early as his mid-teens when he is seen in a school photograph in affectionate contact with his current favourite, may in some measure have been due to his partly dysfunctional and cruelly aborted relationship with his mother, Aleksandra Andreevna Tchaikovskya, who died suddenly from cholera when he was only fourteen.

Rather self-centred, and half-French, she was some eighteen years younger than her husband Ilya, and was his second wife. Although 'Petya' was her favourite of the five children, she was sometimes reluctant, for example, to accept his hugs for fear of crumpling her dresses; but that only made the emotionally fragile 'child of glass' ever more clinging. Tchaikovsky himself admitted that he loved her 'with a morbidly passionate kind of love'.

Herbert Weinstock suggests that this revealed 'a subconscious desire to leave [the world] by re-entering the womb from which he had issued'. Whatever, he certainly sought a mother-substitute for the rest of his days, and homosexuality is, according to Edward Garden, a 'rather usual corollary' of such fixations. Tchaikovsky certainly inherited his mother's morbid sensitivity and she may well also account for his strong attachment to French music: Massenet moved him to tears; he adored the ballets of Delibes, considering them to be superior to Wagner's 'boring' *Götterdämmerung*; and he regarded Bizet's *Carmen* as the greatest work of his era.

There is certainly no doubt that one of the most crucially wounding experiences of his life dates from the age of ten when his mother left her 'porcelain child' behind in St Petersburg to begin his boarding school life at the prep department of the Imperial School of Jurisprudence:

> he lost all his boyish self-control and sobbed uncontrollably. At the moment of final farewell, as the carriage door was closed upon her, he refused to let go the handle. Screaming, he had to be hauled off by force, and dragged away. As the coachman whipped the horses, and the carriage started to move off, he broke free of his captors and chased after it, flinging himself towards the rear wheels. Catching hold of the backboard, in a forlorn attempt to prevent his mother's departure, he was dragged along the muddied, cobbled street until the carriage's increased speed shook him off. The ten-year-old boy was dumped in the dirt as his mother's carriage sped away.

He could never, said Modest in his monumental biography of the composer, forget 'the burning feeling of resentment' as the carriage bearing his beloved mother disappeared from view. It was 'one of the most terrible days of his life' and he could never thereafter pass the turnpike where the incident took place without reliving the 'mad despair' of that occasion.

Tchaikovsky seems to have acquired some kind of hand-fetishism from his early mother-centred experiences. Aleksandra's hands seem to have symbolised his unfulfilled longing for her, and after her death he wrote that 'such hands do not exist nowadays, and never will again'. There were to be several later pointed references to hands. He craved to be slapped by those of the actor Boucher on whom he developed a crush at the Comédie-Française in 1878, and, as we saw with the cabby Vanya, he paid constant attention to the hands of boys and young men he fancied or loved. He also often felt an urge, so he wrote to Modest in February 1882, to lay his head on the laps of *middle-aged* ladies and kiss their hands.

His effusive, frequently gushing father, a mining engineer, was something of a ladies' man, which may, says Poznansky, 'have provoked in the boy, possibly at a subconscious level, a reverse reaction'. Holden suggests that his mother's disappearance from his life four years after he was sent to boarding school 'left him open to schoolboy practices which became the norm – and, as they diversified into an exotic range of homosexual tastes, supplied the subtext of a lifetime of psycho-sexual torment, expiable only in his music'. Certainly even at the age of fourteen when he lost his mother he was turning seriously to composition as an outlet for unfulfilled yearnings.

Tchaikovsky's latent homosexuality was perhaps also reinforced by the communal naked bathing, dancing lessons, mutual masturbation, buggery – and even rape – which were part and parcel of life at the Imperial School of Jurisprudence proper while he was there from the age of twelve to nineteen. So also were bullying, fagging, and public floggings which were administered with '[squealing], huge, supple birches' – and which may conceivably have induced buttock fixation in the impressionable young composer. Being markedly pretty, with feminine features, and pliant, Tchaikovsky must in his early teens have been the lover or 'bitch' of many older boys.

Sasha

Although we live a long way from each other, you play a very important part in my life. In difficulty my thoughts automatically turn to you. I always think: 'If things get really bad I will go to her', or 'I am sure I shall do what Sasha would tell me to do'...
Letter to Sasha, 1871

Tchaikovsky's beloved sister Sasha became in part a mother-substitute, ever supportive and non-judgemental about his sexuality, and ever ready to welcome him for as long as he wished into the bosom of her household at Kamenka, near Kiev in the Ukraine, where her husband Lev Davidov owned a large estate. Tchaikovsky's greatest need for her was probably immediately after the trauma of his marriage to Antonina Milyukova, when he fled to Kamenka to escape from the nightmare threat of conjugal sex.

After the marriage collapsed and Tchaikovsky had taken flight, Sasha actually provided a temporary home for the abandoned Antonina, realising, as she said to Modest, that her brother 'does not possess the slightest capacity to become even a bearable husband'. However, she soon realised that although Tchaikovsky had married Antonina 'to make her a screen against [his] own debauchery', Antonina, in turn, had married him purely for marital status rather than for love.

Alas, Sasha's support for her brother gradually collapsed to the point where by 1882 Tchaikovsky was more protector than protected, as his sister slid into morphine and alcohol addiction, and obesity. (Lev Davidov also suffered from deep depressions.) Tchaikovsky undertook his responsibilities uncomplainingly, although eventually reducing his summer visits to Kamenka. It was, he said, 'as if some ancestral curse were consigning them all to eternal gloom', not least because Sasha's daughter Tanya also became a drug addict with violent mood-swings. Tanya became pregnant by a waster named Blumenfeld and Tchaikovsky picked up the pieces – and the tab – in 1883 by adopting his grand-nephew Georges Léon and providing for him. Tanya collapsed and died suddenly at the age of 45 while attending a masked ball.

Fanny Dürbach

Before leaving the immediate family circle, we mustn't forget Tchaikovsky's French governess Fanny Dürbach. He never forgot her care and kindness to him over four years from the time he was four. He called on her in Basle in 1892 after a 40-year period of separation.

> She greeted me as though it was only a year since we'd seen each other – with joy, tenderness and great simplicity... I seemed to breathe the air of our Votkinsk home and hear the voice of Mama and others... She gave me as a present one wonderful letter from Mama.

Marriage to Antonina Milyukova, 18 July 1877

*'spawn of hell . . . reptile . . . serpent . . . lunatic . . . bitch . . .
madwoman . . . the most vile creation of nature'*

I should like by my marriage or, in general, an open affair with a
woman to shut the mouths of various contemptible creatures whose
opinion I do not value in the least but who can cause pain to the
people close to me . . . I shall not enter into any lawful or illicit
union with a woman without having fully ensured my own peace
and my own freedom.

Letter to Modest, 10 October 1876

he does not possess the slightest capacity to become even a bearable
husband.

Tchaikovsky's sister Sasha, to Modest, 1 October 1877

The blackest comedy in the Tchaikovsky love saga is undoubtedly
his rash and hasty strategic marriage to Antonina Milyukova
and its devastating aftermath. Described by Poznansky as an
'incarnation of the commonplace', Antonina at least had the
excuse of a limited intelligence allied to mental instability, while
the composer merely reinforced the truism that intelligence, education and the talents of a genius are no protection against idiocy
in affairs of the heart. Although there were moments when he
was able to view the fiasco in a perspective sympathetic to his
wife, for the most part Tchaikovsky simply reviled her *ad nauseam*
after fleeing from her less than three months after marrying her.
Personal abuse litters his correspondence over thirteen years to
his brothers and to his publisher, Pyotr Yurgenson, who at times
acted as an intermediary between husband and wife. 'That certain
individual' was a 'spawn of hell . . . a reptile . . . serpent . . .
lunatic . . . bitch . . . madwoman . . . the most vile creation of
nature' who was 'hateful to the point of insanity'. Only occasionally do more balanced comments appear, as when he wrote to
Mme von Meck that '[O]ne must be fair. She behaved honestly
and sincerely. She mistook her desire to marry me for love.'

Tchaikovsky's reasons for getting married are clear enough.
'Perched on the edge of disgrace' because of increasing gossip
about his sexual preferences, particularly following that insinuating remark in the Moscow *New Times* about 'affairs of another
kind' at the Conservatoire, Tchaikovsky decided to marry; both

as a front for respectability and to please his family, especially his sentimental father who had long wished for him to settle down. Believing that Antonina loved him 'like a cat', he may have even had in mind some kind of open marriage. Like his friends Kondratyev and the brothers Vladimir and Konstantin Shilovsky, he could play the field as a serial lover with various young men while his wife might turn a blind eye and keep house. In October of the year before his marriage he assured Modest that marriage would not be a yoke, that he 'would not enter any lawful or illicit union with a woman without having fully ensured my own peace and my own freedom'.

The story is pantomime-tragedy. In late April or early May 1877, while deeply immersed in painful composition of the Fourth Symphony, he received a letter, which is lost, from Antonina, in which, claiming to be a former pupil, she made a declaration of love. Tchaikovsky's reply is also lost, but its apparently evasive and negative response provoked two more letters from her, the second of which, after intense avowals of love, ended with a desperate suicide threat:

> Do you take me, perhaps, for a tease, or a gullible young thing, that you attach no weight to your words? . . .
>
> Since your letter I love you twice as much. What you may think to be your faults mean nothing to me. If you were perfect, I would perhaps not be so in love with you. As it is, I am dying of longing for you. I burn with desire to see you, to sit and talk with you, though I am also terrified that I would be struck dumb. There is no human failing that would cause me to fall out of love with you.
>
> All day I stay at home, pacing the room from corner to corner like a lunatic, thinking only of the moment I shall see you, and throw myself on your neck, smothering you with kisses . . . Let me assure you I am a respectable and honest woman in all senses of the word . . . My first kiss will be the one I give to you, and to no-one else in this world.
>
> Farewell, my beloved! Do not try any more to put me off you, because you are wasting your time. I cannot live without you, so perhaps I shall soon kill myself. Let me see you and kiss you so that I can remember that kiss in the other world.
>
> Farewell. Yours forever, A.M.

Tchaikovsky visited Antonina on 1 June and told her that however grateful he was for her love, he could not return it.

Nevertheless, having by then become deeply absorbed in the potential of Pushkin's *Eugene Onegin* as an opera subject, to the extent of writing a scenario, he began to merge life and art in his mind. He came to identify himself, so he later told his friend Kashkin, as the heartless Eugene Onegin brusquely rejecting Tatyana. Within a week of their first meeting he had visited Antonina again and foolishly proposed to her, trying, unsuccessfully, to hint that he could only offer her 'the love of a brother'. Although she accepted his terms immediately, Antonina never for a moment doubted that her powers of seduction, of which she was wont to brag, could turn his brotherly feelings into erotic conjugal passion. During this period he completed the short score of the finale of the Fourth Symphony. There is surely no doubting that its turbulent emotions were triggered partly by these cataclysmic events.

Having thus become engaged, and experiencing 'appalling horrors' in consequence, he promptly disappeared to spend several days with his devoted violinist protégé Kotek, and then some time at the estate of his intimate friend Shilovsky at Glebovo. Here he worked in earnest on *Eugene Onegin*, noting the striking parallel between Tatyana's letter scene and Antonina's first declaration of love. 'With his extraordinary engagement still a secret between himself and his fiancée,' writes Edward Garden, 'he retired mentally into the fairy-tale world of Tatyana's story, identifying himself with her to an exceptional degree.'

Returning to Moscow, he married Antonina on 18 July 1877, having informed Sasha only the previous day, as well as Modest whom he urged to follow his example. Only Anatoly and his father had been privy to his plans since the last week in June. He also informed Mme von Meck three days before the wedding in a letter in which he made it clear he did not love Antonina and attributed his betrothal to Fate. 'No man can escape his destiny. What is to be, will be.' With typically Russian fatalism, and perhaps also morbidly influenced by *Carmen*, he was plunging headlong into a maelstrom, enacting a self-imposed script of doom.

Much, although definitely not all of the rest is fairly familiar, harrowing history, however much overblown in biopics. In brief, he took Antonina to meet his father, and subsequently met Antonina's 'narrow-minded bickering family'. Then, immediately after the wedding the couple went to St Petersburg where (he told Modest) 'the night passed very quietly' and 'defloration did not happen'. On the following night (20 July) he seems to have made an attempt at consummation when he made what he called 'the first attack':

> The attack [he told Anatoly] proved weak; it is true it met with no resistance, but in itself it was very weak. However, this first step accomplished a lot. It brought me closer to my wife, since I resorted to various manipulations which established intimacy between us. Today I feel in her regard incomparably freer.

His confidence quickly evaporated. With the marriage unconsummated and Antonina 'discomfited' ('physically, my wife has become *totally repulsive* to me . . . the crisis was *terrible, terrible, terrible*', he wrote in his next two letters to Anatoly), Tchaikovsky fled once again. With funds of 1,000 roubles obtained from Mme von Meck, he pretended to Antonina that he needed to take a cure in the Caucasus, and escaped to the comfort and care of Sasha's hearth at Kamenka. In spite of his 'unbearable mental torments', which he poured out to Mme von Meck in a letter of 9 August, he was there able to score some of the Fourth Symphony and resume work on *Eugene Onegin*! Perhaps his torrid affair with the family's servant Evstafy had something to do with his recovery:

> [To Modest, 21 September 1877] As regards my source of delight, about whom I cannot even think without being sexually aroused and whose *boots I would feel happy to clean all my life long*, whose chamber pots I would take out and [for whom] I am generally ready to lower myself anyhow, provided that I could kiss, *even if only rarely*, his hands and feet.

The start of the Conservatoire term towards the end of September forced his return to Moscow and the 'unbearable mental torments' of marriage, not helped by Antonina's recital of all her fantasy conquests. Imaginary generals, nephews of famous bankers, well-known artists, even members of the Imperial family itself had all been enslaved by her irresistible charms. Within days, Tchaikovsky is reported to have botched a half-hearted attempt at suicide when he waded into the River Moscva 'almost up to the waist' in the hope of catching pneumonia. His general state was, he told Mme von Meck, a deep and interminable melancholy . . . In the end, death is truly the greatest of blessings, and I call to it with all the powers of my soul . . . my one thought is to find an opportunity to escape somewhere. But how and where? It is impossible, impossible, impossible!

Furthermore, the Conservatoire, with its school desks and clapped-out, untuned piano with yellowing keyboard was 'some loathsome, stinking, suffocating dungeon'. His laments did not fall on deaf ears, as we shall shortly see.

Soon afterwards, in a state of unremitting distress in which he spent his evenings wandering 'for hours through the far-flung, little-known streets of obscure Moscow', he manufactured, with Anatoly's co-operation, a pretext for going to St Petersburg. There he succumbed to a prolonged bout of nervous hysteria followed by a coma lasting 48 hours – rather than the fortnight of legend. He was examined by a specialist who prescribed a complete change and also advised that he should never see his wife again. In October, Anatoly took him for a month's recuperation to Clarens, on Lake Geneva, whence the brothers travelled to Paris and Italy. Meanwhile, Mme von Meck had settled a pension of 6,000 roubles a year on her idol, thus paving the way for his departure a year later from the Conservatoire to devote all his time to composition.

Thus was the marriage over in less than three months, during which he had been apart from his wife for more than half the time. Back in Moscow, Antonina received the news of their separation with astonishing equanimity, being more impressed by having entertained Nikolay Rubinstein, one of the bearers of bad tidings, to tea, than by her husband's disappearance.

The couple's incompatibility had not been merely sexual, of course. Like Haydn's wife Maria Anna, Antonina didn't know a single note of her husband's music, in spite of having claimed to have loved him from afar for four years. 'Never once,' the composer wrote to von Meck, 'did she show the least interest in my work, what I was writing, what my plans were, what I was reading, or my artistic or intellectual tastes.' But then, to be fair, what could he really expect?

Antonina was to remain a re-erupting and painful boil in her husband's neck for many years to come. Not until she gave birth to a love-child by one Bolkov, in 1881, did she pose less of a threat. (She was to produce three more children, one named Pyotr.) Throughout, she alternately cajoled and issued dire threats, referring openly to his 'terrible vice' for the first time in June 1880. Yurgenson reported that trying to negotiate with her was a continuously circular process like 'a squirrel on a wheel'. Altogether divorce was mooted and laid to rest four times, partly because Tchaikovsky, while desperately wanting to be rid of her, dreaded what she might drag up in court.

In one swing of the pendulum in 1879, for instance, when Tchaikovsky was staying with Anatoly in St Petersburg, 'his wife flung her arms around his neck and smothered him in tearful kisses'. After enduring more sobbing and protestations of undying love, he gave her 100 roubles to pack her off. Alas, she hovered around, accosted him in the street and even rented the flat above his. No wonder that merely seeing her handwriting on an envelope made him retch.

More than once she seemed to go on thinking they could live together. 'If you cannot love me as I love you, at least show me some compassion. Come to me. I am yours, body and soul. Do with me what you wish,' she wrote dementedly in 1879. Some seven years later Tchaikovsky wrote to Modest that she was still confident she could arouse him sexually!

> The gist of her letters is that she hopes I won't now doubt her love for me, that this love is passionate, and that I should hasten to enjoy its ecstasies with her. *Her letters are completely deranged* . . . She is so mad that in reply to my first letter, in which I told her to abandon all thoughts of living with me, she sent me a summons to visit her, to confirm with the hotel servant that she had indeed thrown over her last lover (who is still in love with her and might nevertheless turn up at any minute) and then to make passionate love to her. She says she knows how to arouse passion in me . . . She is now ready to be, as she puts it, 'all mine'.

She plagued him with a final round of letters in 1889, asking for her 100 roubles a month to be doubled. She also taunted him with the threat of exposure, via intermediaries, to the police. 'If I so wished, even now I could do you harm, though that will never happen', she wrote. In reality Tchaikovsky had little to worry about, since, in the words of one homophobic contemporary jurist, 'as a rule the filthy affairs never made it to court.' Furthermore, Tchaikovsky enjoyed a degree of royal favour, symbolised by the tsar's award to him of a handsome pension of 3,000 silver roubles in 1888, that would have made him immune to any official ostracism. Indeed there was a cluster of Grand Dukes with known homosexual preferences who were Tchaikovsky's friends – including the tsar's sons Sergey Alekandrovich and Pavel, and his nephew Konstantin Konstantinovich whom we have already met. This, however, was no lasting consolation to a man who seems to have lived in recurring dread of the humiliation of being outed.

In despair Tchaikovsky finally silenced Antonina by threatening to cut her allowance by a third. This did the trick and he heard no more from her. In fact, in 1890, he even instructed Jurgenson to cut her pension to 100 roubles, without in fact inducing a protest. From this time onwards, Tchaikovsky seems in general to have avoided contact with anyone except his family and a few close friends, spending much of his time conducting abroad or living in the country.

Antonina spent the last twenty or so years of her life in an asylum and died in 1917.

Edward Garden and David Brown have demonstrated how, in its traumatic aftermath, Tchaikovsky's marital crisis created a barrier between himself and his own music. There was a problem of personal commitment. The only 'superlative and completely successful compositions' between his completion of the Violin Concerto in March 1878 and his beginning of the 'Manfred' Symphony in April 1885 were the *Serenade for Strings* and the *Capriccio Italien*, both of 1880.

Other Women

Like other homosexuals, Tchaikovsky appealed to many women. While working at the Ministry of Justice in his early twenties he wrote to Sasha of many passing fancies and admirers, though these comments may have been purely diversionary tactics. When he went to the Conservatoire in Moscow he was surrounded by adoring women, confessing to his stepmother, in a letter of 15 January 1866, his horror at the sight of so many 'crinolines, chignon etc'. Any flirtations he initiated for reasons of propriety became 'tedious', 'less interesting', even 'nightmarish', and were soon aborted.

His brother-in-law's sister Vera Davidova fell seriously in love with him when he was 27, she being some eight years younger – obviously to no avail although she was reluctant to take no for an answer. However, even though her distressing attentions, encouraged for a time by the whole family, helped to induce 'fits' in the composer while he was working on his first symphony, 'Winter Daydreams' (whose gestation and birth drove him to a nervous breakdown and near-insanity), she became the dedicatee of his *Souvenir de Hapsal*. This comprised a group of slight piano pieces, the third being his very well known 'Chanson sans paroles', which Vera kept adoringly in a special folder. Incredibly, Vera, for whom the composer had never felt anything other than 'brotherly feelings', even had another fruitless go at interesting him after becoming widowed in 1884. She alarmed him greatly when she suggested that it would be 'nice to take a stroll'.

Another woman who distressed him with her attentions, in 1886, was Emma Genton, governess to the aforementioned lecherous playboy Kondratyev. Her floods of secret love letters, showers of 'compliments and artificial playfulness', 'sugary sweetnesses', 'tender feelings more passionate than I would have wished' induced a characteristic reaction of irritation and pity.

A much stranger relationship was the infatuation Tchaikovsky developed much earlier, at the age of 28, with a 'goddess of opera', the 33-year-old Belgian soprano Desirée Artôt, after meeting her in September 1868. Inevitably more enraptured by her stunning singing – 'tender, passionate and soul stirring' – than by her person, Tchaikovsky retreated into pure fantasy. (She was said to be putting on weight and to have a 'plain and passionate face' with a broad nose and thick lips.) Totally incapable of separating the diva on stage from the woman off it, he made a dotty proposal of marriage and was accepted. The betrothed couple, so Tchaikovsky wrote to his father, were 'inflamed with feelings of great affection for one another'. According to Tchaikovsky's friend Konstantin de Lazari they 'gazed at one another with shining eyes, blushing with mutual embarrassment as they talked'.

Fortunately, Tchaikovsky's boss at the Moscow Conservatoire, that formidable cradle-snatcher Nikolay Rubinstein, wisely came forward to pointedly inform the singer's mother that Tchaikovsky 'was not fitted for the part of husband'. Mother had been none too keen anyway and was also put off her putative son-in-law by the calumnies of a rich Armenian rival who sat on the front row for all Desirée's performances and showered her with costly gifts.

After Desirée went off to sing in Warsaw, Tchaikovsky predictably dithered over the wisdom of forever trailing around in the shadow of a travelling diva. The matter was resolved for good when news came via a letter to Rubinstein that the singer had married a Spanish baritone by the name of Mariano Padilla y Ramos early in 1869. Even so, the composer wept when he heard her sing. When the two sweethearts spent some time together twice in one week almost 20 years later, in Berlin, 'not one word touched on the past'.

Some lasting good came out of this freakish relationship. At the peak of their affair in 1868, Tchaikovsky dedicated his *Romance in F minor* (Op. 5) to Artôt; then after their amicable reunion she became the dedicatee of his *Six Romances on French Texts* (Op. 65).

How wide of the mark Balakirev was regarding this episode when he wrote to Tchaikovsky of his newly completed *Romeo and Juliet* Overture: 'When I play this I visualise you wallowing in your bath with Artôt-Padilla herself rubbing your tummy ardently with fragrant soap-suds.'

We have already seen that in spite of his dread of female predators, Tchaikovsky had a great fondness for women as mother-figures, as his envious response to the prospect of Anatoly's marriage makes clear:

> I think I can understand all you are feeling, though I have never experienced it myself. It is a certain kind of longing for tenderness and consolation that only a wife can provide. Sometimes I am overcome by an intense craving for a woman's caress. Sometimes I see attractive women – not young women, though – in whose lap I could lay my head, while smothering their hands with kisses.

Hands, again!

Tchaikovsky's Heroines

It is impossible to do justice to Tchaikovsky's love life without mentioning his heroines, with whom he conducted innocent affairs between the sheets of his operatic and ballet scores. David Brown demonstrates in detail how often Tchaikovsky's heroines are basically the same young, vulnerable, suffering and doomed woman, innocent or at least suffering far beyond her deserts. This female prototype was a 'natural wellspring' from which he drew bucketfuls of inspiration, invariably resulting in the best music of his operas. Tchaikovsky himself admitted that he could only write well when he had a character and a situation close to his own. Hence the many puppet figures in his operas for whom his music was never more than competent. We have already seen how Tatyana, in *Eugene Onegin*, is a supreme example of his blueprint heroine, a woman whose outpouring of love in the 'Letter Scene' is rejected by the heartless, blasé aristocrat Onegin. And we have seen also how Tchaikovsky's involvement with her spilled over into his real life with such disastrous results.

Mme Nadezhda Filaretovna von Meck

*'dear . . . beloved . . . priceless . . . incomparable friend . . . my
guardian angel . . . Benign Providence . . . I owe you everything . . .
I love you with all the strength of my soul.'*

' . . . perhaps the most attractive chapter in Tchaikovsky's life.'
Poznansky

. . . you do indeed personify my ideal, and can make up for all the
feelings of disenchantment, regret and melancholy that I endure.
Mme von Meck to Tchaikovsky, 30 March 1877

. . . I should feel that when you are near me, nothing bad can come
to me. Think about it, my dear, good darling, . . . and let us live all
summer together. . . . My dear, do come.
Ditto, May 1879

I love you as no-one else does, and I value you above all else in this
world. . . . I don't want any change in our relationship. I simply want
to be sure that nothing will change as my life draws to its close, that
nobody . . . but this I have no right to say.
Ditto, 26 September 1879

Ultimately, he failed to understand the woman with whom he conducted for thirteen years so intimate a correspondence and who had been his partner in arguably one of the most extraordinary unions between a man and a woman to known modern history.
Poznansky

'Incandescent' passion without sex, without even shaking hands, let alone holding them! Such was the essence of this extraordinary relationship between a very wealthy widow and a homosexual composer. Poznansky draws attention to fascinating parallels from Ancient Greece: Diotima's role (according to Plato) as confidante to the Greek philosopher Socrates, who was ever scanning his rows of male pupils for a responsive gleam in the eye; and the platonic affair between the Renaissance genius Michelangelo and Vittoria Colonna, marchesa and mature widow. Michelangelo and Colonna sent reams of passionate sonnets to one another.

Having married when she was only sixteen, Mme von Meck gave birth to eighteen children, eleven (or twelve) of whom survived – experiences which seem to have left her frigid, because she made it clear in her correspondence with Tchaikovsky that she derived no pleasure at all from marital sex. She would, she said, have preferred humans to reproduce by mitosis like amoebas and avoid marriage altogether! A tough, go-getting business woman, she pushed her husband into a spectacularly successful career in the railways during the period of massive expansion in the 1860s. After his death as a multimillionaire tycoon in 1876, Mme von Meck, then 46, took over the management of the vast family empire and, as a fanatical music lover, channelled substantial funds towards commissions and personal patronage.

Mme von Meck's connection with Tchaikovsky started in 1876 through the young Kotek, who, while acting as her resident soloist, put some commissions Tchaikovsky's way for arrangements of his music for violin and piano. The rest, as they say, is history, but it began with this thank-you letter on 15 February 1877 (nearly three months before his first letter from Antonina):

Gracious Sir, Pyotr Ilyich,
...To tell you into what ecstasies your composition sent me would be unnecessary and unfitting, because you are accustomed to the compliments and homage of those much better qualified to speak than a creature so musically insignificant as me... I shall content myself with asking you to believe absolutely that your music makes my life easier and pleasanter to live.

As soon as Tchaikovsky encouraged her to speak openly and freely, she responded with a flash-flood of love and admiration. In asking for his photograph, she declared on 19 March 1877:

I want to search your face for clues as to those sources of inspiration, those feelings which inspire you to compose music which transports me into a realm of sensations, aspirations and desires that life itself can never satisfy.

. . . I must tell you that I cannot separate the musician from the man; and in that man, the servant of such high art, even more than in others, I hope and expect to find all the human qualities I adore. . . . It is my opinion, you see, that it is not only friendship which draws people together, but even more a similarity of outlook, a shared capacity for depth of feeling, and a common range of sympathies, so it becomes possible to be close although far distant.

Then came the crux of the matter. It was possible to love intensely at a distance:

There was a time when I was desperate to meet you. But now, the more enamoured I become of you, the more an acquaintanceship frightens me – I am sure I would be in no fit state to make sense as we began a conversation . . . In short, I prefer to think of you from a distance, to hear you in your music, and to feel at one with you in your work.

In a reply of 28 March Tchaikovsky expressed his fear that she might be disappointed in the reality of him, that 'you would not find that balance, that perfect harmony between the musician and the man, of which your imagination dreams'. In this same letter he also realised that they both suffered from the same 'sickness' of 'misanthropy'; not so much a hatred of mankind, though, as 'the disappointment, the yearning for the ideal, that every intimate acquaintance entails'. If anything, her passion for seclusion exceeded his own.

In her reply two days later, Mme Meck assured him that nothing could destroy her image of his perfection both as a man and musician, that 'this is no longer a question for me'. She was almost certainly relieved to be freed in their relationship from what she considered to be the 'vulgar, shameful and humiliating aspects of sexual love'.

Some weeks later she commissioned a *Reproach* for violin and piano, revealing more of her mindset and what she sought from music:

My *Reproach* must embody an impression of sadness beyond endurance, of suffering which can be no further endured – of death itself, if possible, so as to find in music, at least, the solace and relief that life itself rarely grants when most they are needed . . .

The relationship developed rapidly and inexorably, particularly once she had solved his 'ticklish' problems of recurring cash shortage. After one-off payments of 3,000 roubles and 1,000 roubles in May and July of 1877, in the autumn of that year, when his disastrous marriage had collapsed, she settled on him an annuity of 6,000 roubles, thus paving the way for his departure as 'a free man' from the Conservatoire, where he gave his last lesson on 18 October 1878. She subsequently provided many further emoluments, not to mention (in 1880) such extravagant presents as a 'subtle, extraordinarily exquisite' watch costing several thousand francs and bearing the image of Joan of Arc on one side and Apollo on the other.

The allowance continued for nearly fourteen years. Mme von Meck provided not only cash and presents, but also rent-free accommodation at her various properties and estates, and also in palatial rented residencies outside Russia.

> Every note that henceforth flows from my pen [responded the com-
> poser after she confirmed his allowance] will be dedicated to you!
> To you I shall owe the love of labour returning to me with redoubled
> force, and never, not for a single second, shall I ever forget while
> working that you have given me the opportunity to carry on with
> my artistic vocation.

During the aftermath of his marriage, Mme von Meck also played a vital therapeutic role in helping her idol regain some kind of mental equilibrium. 'She [Antonina] won't suffer in the least from the separation,' she wrote to him at the end of October 1877. 'Don't be upset if you're told that she is in tears . . . Be assured she only does it for show.' Well might his patron write in such a vein. She now had him all to herself!

This unique relationship cannot be played out in full here. Suffice it to strike one or two motifs. A letter Tchaikovsky wrote to Sasha from his patron's estate at Brailov, (south-west of Kiev) in May 1878 is brimful of delight in his good fortune:

> I am in clover here . . . I live in a palace in the literal sense of the
> word; the furnishings are luxurious, apart from polite and affection-
> ately obliging servants I see no human figures and no-one comes to

make my acquaintance, the strolls are charming, and at my disposal I have carriages, horses, a library, several pianos, a harmonium, a mass of sheet music – in a word, what could be better.

Alexsey was likewise effusive in his comments: 'What a house, what a garden, what people, what food, and you can ride in the woods too, and it's peaceful and pleasant etc.'

As the relationship between patron and protégé intensified they shared their thoughts about almost everything – religion, idealism, politics, music, family, relationships . . . For Nadezhda Filaretovna, the mere sight of a letter from her beloved (for such he most certainly had become) was 'rose-coloured, aromatic . . . like ether, for inhaling its scent will ease my pain'. Their compatibility was infinite. 'I have long been amazed,' she wrote, 'by the remarkable empathy and almost supernatural affinity of ideas and feelings evident in almost every single one of our letters.' Rooms in her home at Brailov, she told him in May 1878, had been turned into a shrine and she literally worshipped the ground he had walked on:

Now more than ever, and here more than anywhere, I feel our spiritual closeness and I revel in it. The rooms you used have already been renamed 'Pyotr Ilyich's bedroom' and 'Pyotr Ilyich's sitting room'. The trees in the woods where we have both sipped tea, the benches on the crag where both of us have lingered, those same nightingales we have both heard – all of them, all, *belong to both of us*. My God, what ecstasy this brings.

On one occasion only, in 1879, Tchaikovsky miscalculated and they met by accident in a 'nose to nose' encounter in the woods near Simaki, her smaller house, close to Brailov, where he was staying. After receiving his abject apology she replied gushingly:

It was thrilling. I can't tell you how sweet and enchanting a moment that was . . . I do not want any personal contact between us, but silently, passively, to be around you, to be near you . . . to perceive you not as a phantom but as a living, breathing person whom I so adore, from whom I receive so many blessings, all of which fill me with rapture.

The relationship peaked with Mme von Meck's abandoned declaration of passion – ostensibly platonic, but surely erotically charged – on 26 September 1879. By then privy to all Tchaikovsky's post-marital woes, including, surely, the root cause of them, and intoxicated by 'their' Fourth Symphony she let herself go in this extraordinary outburst:

> I doubt if you could ever realise how jealous I am of you, despite the lack of personal contact between us. Do you know that I am jealous in the most unforgivable way, as a woman is jealous of the man she loves? Do you realise that when you got married I was in utter despair? I felt as if part of my heart had been torn away. In my agony, I became bitter. The thought of your intimacy with that woman was unbearable. And do you know the full extent of my unworthiness? When you proved to be unhappy with her, I rejoiced. I was full of self-reproach, and hid my feelings from you, but I was powerless to control them. No-one can hide her true feelings. I hated this woman because she made you unhappy, but I would have hated her a hundred times more if she had made you *happy*. As I saw it, she had stolen from me someone who was mine by right, mine and mine alone, because I love you as no-one else does, and I value you above all else in this world. . . . I don't want any change in our relationship. I simply want to be sure that nothing will change as my life draws to its close, that nobody . . . but this I have no right to say. Forgive me and forget everything I have said. My head is not right.

The supreme creative memorial to their relationship – what she called 'the phantom child of our spiritual union' – was the Fourth Symphony, which he dedicated to her (anonymously, at her request), 'as I think you will find it reflects your innermost feelings and thoughts.' (Their 'marriage' was later to be vicariously 'consummated' when her second son Nikolay married Tchaikovsky's third niece Anna Davidova in 1884.)

In a letter to Mme von Meck written well over a year after finishing the symphony in January 1878, Tchaikovsky made clear its role in his life as spiritual autobiography – as a 'faithful echo' of the torments he had endured. It was, he said,

> a *memorial* to a time when, after a long-evolving spiritual illness and after a whole series of unbearable agonies and despair that had all but driven me to utter madness and ruin, there suddenly shone a dawn of rebirth and happiness in the person of her to whom the symphony is dedicated.
>
> 29 September 1879

Her reaction to the work was that of a besotted acolyte. The first movement in particular was 'the last word in art, the summit of genius, the crowning triumph, the meaning of God ... There is nowhere else for music to go. For the sake of this music, one could surrender one's soul or lose one's mind without a moment's regret'.

Scholars warn us that the Fourth Symphony must not be associated too directly with Tchaikovsky's marital crisis, as it was conceived and mainly written before it. Nevertheless, he orchestrated and made changes to the work afterwards. Embodying his emotional and creative anguish of the autumn and winter of 1877, the symphony released, writes Edward Garden, 'all the frustrations of his endemic homosexuality and bottled-up emotions, further engendered rather than released by the fiasco of his marriage'.

There can be little doubt that the opening theme of the symphony, with those devastating blasts from the French horns, symbolises Fate. In David Brown's words, the theme then intrudes 'peremptorily and inexorably' throughout the movement, 'sweeping aside all other material'. Man, Tchaikovsky told von Meck, was totally governed by this

fateful force which impedes the impulse toward the happiness of reaching one's goal, which jealously ensures that prosperity and peace are never complete and cloudless, which hangs overhead like a sword of Damocles and steadily and continually poisons the soul. It is invincible, and you will never overpower it.

'There is never a barrel of honey without a spoonful of tar'

Inevitably the relationship was not all sweetness and light. Tchaikovsky came to resent the restrictions on his freedom when his patron summoned him to be near her in Paris, Clarens, Brailov, Simaki or wherever. And even their most idyllic time 'together', during the November and December of 1878 when they lived in adjacent houses on the viale dei Colli in Florence and exchanged some 50 letters, was not problem free.

Every morning [the composer wrote to Modest] I see her stop while passing my villa and try to catch sight of me. How am I to act? Go to the window and bow? But, in that case, why not also shout from the window, 'Good Morning'?

'There is never a barrel of honey without a spoonful of tar' wrote the composer to Anatoly in the summer of the following year. The tar in this case was not only the restrictions on his freedom but also the irksome duty Mme von Meck imposed on him of assessing and supervising the compositions of her seriously talentless young protégé Wladyslaw Pachulski, who later became her indispensable factotum. Resentful of Tchaikovsky's low opinion of his work, Pachulski was almost certainly a key player in the ultimate collapse of the relationship.

Another temporary source of friction between them was Tchaikovsky's conducting, a career he pursued very actively and successfully at home and abroad from 1887. Like Marie d'Agoult with her protégé Liszt, Mme von Meck was none too keen for her god to descend to the podium in the mortal clothing of white tie and tails:

> In my view it is not merely unnecessary, but positively profane to mount the podium and submit yourself to the gaze and criticism of *hoi polloi*. I consider a composer too sacred a figure to exhibit himself like that before the mob.

> 27 October 1886

'Oh, Nadezhda Filaretovna, you treacherous woman, why did you betray me?!!'

By 1883, Mme von Meck's fortunes had changed. She had lost a great deal of money in her business ventures and had been compelled in 1881 to move to a smaller property at Pleshcheevo. She was also shattered by the death of her youngest twelve-year-old son Mikhail. However, although her flow of letters to Tchaikovsky had slowed down markedly from the summer of 1882 because of pains in her hand, the allowance still continued because it was a mere drop in the ocean of her losses.

Totally out of the blue, on 6 October 1890, came a bombshell, 'the most mysterious incident in his life', in the form of her last letter to him, unfortunately lost. She was weighed down with problems and the allowance would have to stop. But he must never forget that the bad news came 'from one whose love for you knows no bounds'. After nearly fourteen years and some 1,200 letters, it all ended as abruptly as it had begun. The probable reasons for the sudden cut-off included the aforementioned Pachulski's jealousy of his teacher's hold over his employer, and the resentment of the von Meck family and relations at the diversion of funds away from themselves. In addition, her children must have played heavily on her guilt feelings, especially as her eldest son Vladimir had become a mental and physical wreck and was slowly withering before her eyes.

There may also have been elements of blackmail. The family could have threatened the frail old lady, now in her sixtieth year and probably in a tubercular condition, with the exposure of Tchaikovsky's homosexuality. A further hold they had over her was the existence of a love-child, living within the family, whom she had borne by her husband's secretary. Her husband's discovery of this had precipitated his fatal heart attack in 1876.

All the indications are that Mme von Meck herself had no wish to stop the allowance. According to her daughter-in-law Anna 'his loving patron never bore him any ill will.' She had, though, foreseen the end and had even prepared for it as far as possible by sending him his allowance secretly and in advance before it was finally stopped.

Alas, Tchaikovsky was permanently disgusted and ashamed by what he considered to be a betrayal of love and friendship. It wasn't really the money that mattered – he had, after all, his substantial royalties, conducting fees and the pension of 3,000 silver roubles already mentioned. 'I could not imagine inconstancy in such a demigoddess,' he wrote to the evasive Pachulski after his return from America in 1891. 'It seemed to me the globe of the world might crumble to bits before NM ever became different towards me.'

His mother figure had shattered him by suddenly cutting the umbilical cord which sustained him spiritually and emotionally. His paroxysm of anger in a letter to Jurgenson of 15 August 1893, shows he was incapable of viewing the matter in perspective, forgetting all she had given him:

> Oh Nadezhda Filaretovna, you treacherous woman, why did you betray me?!! I am amazed at the fickleness of female infatuations. One might think, rereading these letters, that fire would sooner turn to water than her subsidy cease . . . Then, suddenly, farewell! Above all, I almost believed, really believed, that she had been ruined. But it turns out to have been something else altogether: merely female inconstancy.

It is not really surprising that within six days of receiving von

Meck's letter Tchaikovsky mentioned for the first time his work on the symphonic ballad *The Voyevoda*. With its eerie string effects and cascading harp it contains, in Edward Garden's words, 'quite the most spine-chilling music Tchaikovsky ever produced', Sibelius-like in its evocation of the 'snowy landscapes and icy finger of death'.

Mme von Meck outlived Tchaikovsky by only a few months, dying in Nice on 13 January 1894.

The Guilt Question and the Suicide Theory

... it is true that my damned pederasty does form an unbridgeable abyss between me and most people ... I often dwell for hours now on the thought of a monastery or the like.
Tchaikovsky to Modest, 21 January 1875

I think of nothing but ridding myself of all pernicious passions.
To Modest, 22 September 1876

The teasing question about Tchaikovsky's homosexuality is the extent of his guilt feelings about it. Unlike most other scholars and biographers, Poznansky is in no doubt on the matter, asserting that '[N]owhere in any of his written texts known to us is there the slightest hint that he thought of himself as sexually pathological.' Poznansky stresses also that the legal prohibitions against sodomy were never enforced in Russia, and that official-dom's tolerant approach to it resulted in a moral climate generally more permissive than that which prevailed in England, France or Germany.

There is certainly no doubt that Tchaikovsky came fully to terms with his sexuality:

[10 October 1876, to Modest] I am so set in my ways – and my *tastes* – that it is simply impossible just to cast them off like an old glove. Besides, willpower is not one of my stronger points. Since my last letters to you [i.e. in less than a month] I have already given way three times to my natural compulsions. Would you imagine! One of these days I even went to Bulatov's country estate, and his house is nothing but a pederastic bordello ... I fell in love as a cat with his coachman!!! So you are perfectly right when you say that whatever vows one may make, it is impossible to resist one's weaknesses.

[13 February 1878, to Anatoly] there is nothing more fruitless than wanting to be other than what I am by nature.

Nevertheless, in the wake of the humiliating 'Chautemps scandal' in his youth (quoted earlier), Tchaikovsky 'experienced a growth of anxiety in regard to his sexual tastes' that contributed to his fits of hypochondria and was also the key factor in his decision to marry. However innocent of blame he believed himself to be for his condition, he felt stigmatised by it. Unlike so many of his more flamboyant fellow homosexuals, he was forever unable to carry it off, take it in his stride.

This letter of 1876 to Modest clearly betrays Tchaikovsky's sense of shame and guilt about his sexuality, even if, as Poznansky emphasises, he was primarily trying, fruitlessly, to persuade his brother to cultivate heterosexual habits and avoid the tempting embraces of any 'passing trash':

[22 September 1876] It seems to me that our *inclinations* are the biggest and most insurmountable obstacle to our happiness, and that we must fight against our natures with all our strength . . . not just to silence the gossips [but] for you yourself, for your peace of mind . . . I shall abandon for ever my previous habits, and shall endeavour to be numbered no more among the company Gruzinsky and Co [homosexuals] . . . I think of nothing but ridding myself of all pernicious passions

Even masturbation, for Tchaikovsky, was a shameful abomination. 'In general,' he wrote to Modest at school, 'masturbation should be seen as an abominable habit that can become very deep-rooted, and therefore, it is better to endure some slight discomfort, and preserve your self-esteem, than to slide towards ruin.' He gave advice in the same vein to his 'wild and strange' acolyte Leonty Tkachenko who periodically latched on to the composer in the early 1880s. 'The point is this,' wrote the composer: 'to be able to rise above one's bodily desires and thus control them. This comes only with training.'

Holden quotes many Tchaikovsky experts and some performers who challenge Poznansky's firm view that 'homosexual anxiety' ceased to be a dominant feature of the composer's inner life. The senior archivist at the Tchaikovsky Museum in Klin, Polina Vaidman, acknowledges that Tchaikovsky's references to his one-night stands are 'filled with remorse and self-loathing'. The scholars Henry Zajaczkowski and Boris Nikitin, the writer Yuri Nagibin, and the star performers Vladimir Ashkenazy and Peter Donohoe all reportedly veer towards a scenario in which the composer remained guilt-ridden about his sexuality.

Tchaikovsky's Death

Of the unending controversy surrounding the composer's death very little need be said here. The exhaustive case for Tchaikovsky's death by suicide at the behest of a Court of Honour appears in Anthony Holden's *Tchaikovsky*, and its withering refutation in Poznansky's *Tchaikovsky's Last Days*.

In my opinion, for what it is worth, having read both books carefully, Poznansky demonstrates conclusively that the planks of circumstantial evidence on which the suicide lobby bases its case turn out to be riddled with dry rot. His conclusion about the causes of the composer's death seems to be unassailable:

> On the balance of evidence . . . it seems likely that the composer, despite protestations of the less informed sources, failed to survive the algid stage of cholera, which was diagnosed too late for any effective treatment, and died from uraemic blood-poisoning, caused by the eventual paralysis of the kidneys.

The possibility – no more – that Tchaikovsky contracted cholera from one of his seedier 'rimming' encounters rather than by drinking polluted water has already been mentioned. But one fact is certain in all this: the composer was honoured with what was, in effect, a state funeral funded by the deeply admiring Tsar Alexandr III.

Sir Arthur Sullivan

Born: London, 13 May 1842
Died: London, 22 November 1900

It may be that Death's bright Angel,
Will speak in that chord again;
It may be that only in Heav'n,
I shall hear that grand Amen.
'The Lost Chord', music by Sullivan (1877), words by Adelaide A. Procter

[27 May, 1881] To Cad. Place: accès!
Secret diary entry

[Kassel, 5 September 1881] Found my friends there. Our rooms are 5,
6, 7 . . . Nothing to do in the evening. L.W. (2).
[6 September] L.W. (1) straight up! . . . Himmelische [sic] Nacht (1)
[Heavenly Night]
Secret diary entries

The dominant principle was not the cultivation of virtue but the
avoidance of scandal.
Diplomate Etranger, pseudonymous author of La Société de Londres, 1885

Sullivan's most active sexual period coincides with his busiest and most
fruitful creative period, and the two activities decline together.
Arthur Jacob: The Secret Diaries of Sir Arthur Sullivan, High Fidelity, 1977

if not one of the world's major composers, then one who has a special
place in the uniting of sophisticated and popular taste.
ibid.

Dear Miss Violet [age 20],
What do you and yours propose doing? Shall we sit under the trees or
lie on the grass, or saunter on the promenade? Or shall I write a
joint letter to your sister. What time do you wish to see me today? I
will of course obey any order you may give.
Yours sincerely

A.S. [age 54]

Even though we are nowadays largely inured to endless revelations of blatant hypocrisy among the movers and shakers of our society – especially sanctimonious politicians and royals who publicly preach but privately flout the Decalogue of 'family values' – it can still come as a shock to discover how often and how far Sir Arthur Sullivan, highly revered Victorian composer of 'The Lost Chord', 'Onward Christian Soldiers' and the G&S canon, fell from grace. (Knock 'The Lost Chord' if you must for its maudlin sentimentality, but it nevertheless reportedly sold 25,000 copies a year for 25 years, while the splendid hymn is still going strong for The Salvation Army and, presumably, the more die-hard remnants of Christian worship.)

Certainly, Queen Victoria, strait-laced, though impressionable, as she was, would never have invited Sir Arthur to tea at Windsor Castle had she had any inkling of his history of rabbit-like sexual behaviour. She exemplified and promulgated the concept of clean and respectable living, notwithstanding her bizarrely flirtatious relationship with Prime Minister Disraeli, and her infatuated dependence, in grieving widowhood, on her highland ghillie 'best friend' and bit of rough, the crofter's son John Brown, a lock of whose hair she carried with her to the grave.

What on earth would Her Gracious Majesty have made of all the orgasm counts Sullivan logged so scrupulously in his locked secret diaries? The plethora of ticks or bracketed (1)s, (2)s, and sometimes, alas, (0)s, after various initials were related either to his 'Heavenly Nights' in a long-term relationship with his American-born divorcee mistress, or to his encounters with any number of other mistresses and passing fancies, including the prostitutes of Paris. He certainly had plenty of whores to choose from in his dozens of visits to the French capital, because it was estimated in 1888 that there were more than 15,000 of them in the swelling number of unlicensed brothels.

Maybe Sullivan's randiness came from the non-standard mix of Irish and Italian blood flowing through his veins: although both his parents were Irish there was Italian blood in his mother's lineage. Whatever, thanks to the watertight conspiracies of concealment in the corridors of power – the only real rule then, as now, in contemporary cabinet government, being 'Don't get caught' – Sullivan's social standing remained such that the long-widowed Queen *did* indeed invite him to tea in 1896. Having met him on the Easter Sunday of that year in Cimiez on the French Riviera, where he played the organ for her morning service in a makeshift chapel in her hotel, the 77-year-old monarch renewed the acquaintance later that same year. 'I have spent most of my time lately at Windsor,' he wrote to Richard D'Oyly Carte, 'and have had three long and pleasant chats with the Queen (bless her, she is so kind and gracious). We are beginning to be talked about!'

Although Mendelssohn seems to have been the Queen's favourite composer, Sir Arthur had long since been a blue-eyed boy and was in effect her Poet Laureate in Music. In 1872 she had even accorded him the very rare privilege of consenting to be the dedicatee of his *Te Deum*, composed to celebrate the Prince of Wales's recovery from typhoid.

It is, incidentally, through the scholarly researches of Arthur Jacobs, recorded in his richly detailed biography *Arthur Sullivan: A Victorian Musician*, that Sullivan's recorded encounters between the sheets have been most widely disseminated. This chapter is greatly indebted to Jacobs' book. Most of Sullivan's diaries which Jacobs quotes from and interprets at length are now housed in the Beinecke Libraries at Yale University.

Sullivan, of course, was by no means the only pillar of Victorian society to lead a life of immorality kept well under wraps. In spite of his ten children, the moral and social crusading novelist Charles Dickens, seeming exemplar of middle-aged Victorian respectability, found little happiness in his marriage to Catherine Hogarth and separated from her in 1858 to enjoy a long-term clandestine relationship with his mistress Ellen 'Nelly' Ternan, 27 years younger than himself. Interestingly, a recently surfaced miniature water-colour by the London portraitist Mary Millington of Dickens at the age of fifteen brings out his raffish side, with his sensual, elfin face and curly hair combed down over his high forehead. Even more interesting, if rather hard to swallow, are the Dickensian interpretations of Professor William A. Cohen, who reportedly detects coded homosexual obsessions in *Great Expectations, David Copperfield* and *Oliver Twist*, with passages 'open to a masturbatory reading'.

Sullivan's successfully maintained public profile reflected the guiding principle of 'absolute propriety' which he and his renowned partner William Schwenk Gilbert embraced in their celebrated cornucopia of comic operettas stretching over some 20 years. In Gilbert's words:

> Sullivan and I . . . resolved that our plots, however ridiculous, should be coherent; that our dialogue should be void of offence; . . . Finally we agreed that no lady of the company should be required to wear a dress that she could not wear with absolute propriety at a private fancy-dress ball.

Curiously enough, Gilbert, who married a kittenish girl eleven years his junior, penned some mysterious Xs in *his* diary, although his latest biographer Jane W. Stedman doubts that they refer to women. Altogether, he wrote 71 stage works of which 69 were produced. It has often been noticed that the women in his G&S libretti are either pretty pubescents (Three Little Maids from School) or elderly man-eating harridans.

For an 'umble musician, Sullivan's climb up the social ladder was mind-boggling. The son of a comparatively lowly military bandmaster who later became 'chief professor of the clarinet' at the Royal Military School of Music, Arthur Sullivan surely goes down in British history as the most solid-ever musical pillar of the Establishment. He was knighted by the Queen in 1883 when he was 40, and before that made an Officer of the Légion d'honneur, after attending the Paris International Exhibition as British Commissioner for Music in 1878. He was also awarded the Order of Saxe-Coburg-Gotha. Holder of doctorates from Oxford and Cambridge Universities, first Principal of the National Training School for Music (later the Royal College of Music), composer of at least 45 hymns (including 'Onward Christian Soldiers'), editor of a collection of *Church Hymns with Tunes* published by the Society for the Promotion of Christian Knowledge, Sullivan had a ready entrée into the very topmost circles. In 1881 more than one-sixth of the 500 names appearing in his diary were titled. He was a particular friend and close intimate of Queen Victoria's violin-playing second son Alfred, Duke of Edinburgh, who proposed his membership of the Marlborough Club and in whose flagship he once cruised as a guest to northern Europe and Russia.

Sullivan built up a guest-list which speaks for itself. Take the following invitees to a Sunday night dinner party and soirée he gave in July 1884:

> Dined here: Duke of Edinburgh, Count and Countess de Florian, Lord and Lady Wharncliffe, Lady Hothfield, Lady Sykes, Mr and Mrs W. Oppenheim, Mrs Ronalds, Mrs Grant Corrêa [a Brazilian diplomat], Sir Al[gernon] Borthwick, and self . . . [After dinner seven famous musicians – five singers and two instrumentalists – and a 'marvellous' conjuror performed] . . . Supper, and everyone went about a quarter to three.

As Arthur Jacobs points out, there can have been few gatherings to rival his in mixing royal and noble guests with leading artists of the day.

Sullivan also hobnobbed more or less regularly with – just to name one more handful – the Prince of Wales (later Edward VII), Prince Christian of Denmark, Princess Victoria and Princess Louise (two of the Queen's daughters, the former becoming Crown Princess of Germany and remaining a devoted groupie), Prince William and Prince Henry (sons of the Crown Princess), Prince Leopold (Duke of Albany), Duke Ernst II of Coburg, the Duke of Connaught, the Duchess of Westminster, the Marquis d'Aoust, Lord and Lady Stafford, Baron Meyer Rothschild, Baron Ferdinand de Rothschild, Lord Rosebery, Lady Molesworth, Sir Edward Malet, Sir Auckland Colum, and dozens more including two Lord Chief Justices of England and Prime Minister Gladstone. When residing in Leeds as Chief Conductor for the triennial choral festival he was invariably offered the hospitality of the Judges' Lodgings.

Sullivan didn't just socialise with the aristocracy in Britain: Cairo, Algiers, St Moritz, Lucerne, wherever he sojourned he seems invariably to have been on ready visiting terms with the *crème de la crème*.

For the benefit of fellow foodies everywhere, here is one sample menu from the mammoth junketings in these circles. What a dinner and a half this was! – given by the Prince of Wales at Marlborough House on 14 June 1885:

Consommé printanière
Purée de pois verts
Whitebait
Saumon à l'épluche
Filets de turbot au vin blanc
Côtelettes d'agneau
Chaux-froix [should be chauds-froids] de cailles
Boeuf rôti
Poulet nouveaux [sic]
Asperges
Plum pudding
Timbale gauffres à la crème
Pailles au fromage
Glaces de fraises

Perhaps the very ease and frequency with which Sullivan moved among such endemically inartistic, not to say philistine circles as the British aristocracy explain or accord with the lack of real depth in even his serious music. Although considered the leading British composer of his day, it is only as the composer of the ever popular comic operas in uniquely symbiotic partnership with Gilbert that Sullivan has achieved enduring renown. But to say 'only' is not in any sense to belittle his truly amazing genius as the much-loved tunesmith of pitter-patter songs, graceful airs, pastiche madrigals and very clever double choruses. There is surely something *almost* Mozartian about the effortless grace and simplicity of this music, notwithstanding its indebtedness to Mendelssohn, Schumann, Rossini and Donizetti. Sullivan himself, of course, regarded most of this output as essentially hackwork and craved in vain for international recognition as a great composer of serious masterpieces. He went to the grave with guilt-feelings of having prostituted his art.

Perhaps it is not by chance that a good many of the greatest composers and musicians were often abrasive and/or ill at ease in posh company: Mozart, Beethoven, Schubert, Paganini, Berlioz, Wagner, Brahms, Puccini . . . Sullivan was seemingly often unmoved by the greatness of his contemporaries. Meetings he noted with Liszt, Dvořák and Saint-Saëns elicited little apparent excitement and he is certainly the blandest of the famous composers in this volume. He seems, indeed, to have been jealous of the furor created by his greatest rival in the populist market, Charles Gounod.

A Ladies' Man

As early as his twentieth year when he completed his incidental music to *The Tempest*, Sullivan was a very handsome lady-killer, a darling of the drawing rooms. In his late teens he was, according to one reminiscing admirer Clara Barnett, 'a smiling youth with an oval, olive-tinted face, dark eyes, a large generous mouth, and a thick crop of dark curly hair which overhung his low forehead'. A later portrait in his forties shows him looking very suave, with designer eyebrows, moustache and sideburns, and his hair parted in the middle. A thumbnail sketch unwittingly suggesting his woman-appeal appeared in the *New York Herald* in 1879, during a tour of *HMS Pinafore* in the States, where 100,000 barrel organs were built to turn out his tunes:

> In his appearance gentle feeling and tender emotion are as strongly expressed as cold, glittering keen intellect is in that of Mr Gilbert. He is short, round and plump, with a very fleshy neck, and as dark as his *collaborateur* is fair, with a face of wonderful mobility and sensitiveness, [on] which the slightest emotion plays with unmistakable feeling, with eyes which only the Germanic adjective of 'soulful' would fitly describe and the full, sensuous lips of a man of impassioned nature. With all this Mr Sullivan, who keeps a monocle dangling over one eye while the other twinkles merrily at you, and whose dark whiskers and hair have an ambrosial curl, is also something of a polished man of fashion.

A tribute after Sullivan's death from François Cellier, son of Alfred Cellier who was the composer's maestro in the theatre pits for many years, also suggests the qualities of a ladies' man:

> I do not remember ever hearing a harsh word from Sir Arthur Sullivan. His wonderful tact steered him through all the shoals of dispute and controversy, which with most men would have provoked hostility. His every suggestion came with such grace and courtesy as to still all idle argument.

Libido and Creativity

One wonders, idly, when Sullivan first lost his virginity; certainly not in his mid-teens, when he was first let loose in London as a student at the Royal Academy; nor in his late teens, as the first holder of the Mendelssohn scholarship in Leipzig, where he was loth even to go to concerts on the Sabbath! In London, nevertheless, he would no doubt have been solicited by the many ladies – and children – of easy virtue with their standard come-on of 'Are you good-natured, dear?' and their standard asking price of five bob. (The age of consent was then only twelve.) Sullivan more likely 'completed his education' in his twenties in a Parisian brothel.

The marked correlation between Sullivan's sex drive and his work rate, so neatly summarised by Arthur Jacobs in a piece he wrote in *High Fidelity* magazine in May 1977, is fascinating. The accelerando and ritardando of the sexual encounters recorded in his diaries more or less peak and subside with the intensity of his composing and many other musical activities in the late 70s and through the 80s. Here is another case, most definitely, of high creativity linked to a high libido.

Sullivan's enormously successful collaboration with Gilbert ran from the immediate hit *Trial by Jury* in 1875 (a curtain-raiser for Offenbach's *La Périchole*) through ten more of the comic operettas to *The Gondoliers* in 1889 (*Utopia Limited* in 1893 and *The Grand Duke* in 1896 were never in the same league) and 1886 was the year of his then hugely popular cantata *The Golden Legend*, based on a text by Longfellow.

Also during various parts of this period Sullivan was heavily occupied by non-composing activities: as principal of the aforementioned National Training School for Music (1876 to 1881), as conductor of the Philharmonic Society in London (1885 to 1887) and as visiting conductor of many choirs and orchestras. In particular he was Chief Conductor of the highly prestigious Leeds triennial choral festival from 1880, a post he deeply valued and held on to until he was edged out three years before his relatively early death at the age of 58.

There was also his demanding trip to the States in 1879–80, touring *HMS Pinafore* (pirated and produced everywhere) and *The Pirates of Penzance*.

By 1890, however, Sullivan was in physical and creative

decline, due to a persistent kidney-related urinary problem which had been causing painful discharges from 1877. He regularly took the waters in geriatric fashion at French and German spas, and was subjected to all manner of ghastly cures including, latterly, the application of hot potato poultices. By the 1890s there is, Jacobs tells us, a remarkable change in the diaries.

> They are not only much more sparsely filled, but contain hardly any indications of sexual activity. Moreover, Mrs Ronalds, [his long-term American divorcee mistress] has become 'Auntie'! . . . A remarkable indication of a change of role, it would seem – all passion spent. Here the correlation between Sullivan the man and Sullivan the composer suggests itself.

Rachel Scott Russell – 'Chenny'

By the time Sullivan's and A.C. Burnand's successful comic 'trium-viretta in one act' *Cox and Box* was publicly premièred in the orchestral version in May 1867, Sullivan, then 25, and Rachel Scott Russell, the 22-year-old second daughter of John Scott Russell, a famous Scottish engineer and naval architect, were passionately in love. They had developed a serious interest in each other during the previous two years, Sullivan being a regular guest at the family's house parties held after the famed Saturday symphony concerts conducted by August Manns at Crystal Palace. (They were later to be attended by the young Elgar on his strenuous seventeen-hour day-return trips from Worcester.) The Russell circle included the highly sought-after painter John Millais, a founder of the Pre-Raphaelite Brotherhood and a personal friend of Sullivan; and also the composer's much loved (and loving) mentor and champion Sir George Grove, 22 years his senior. Although he was a distinguished Biblical scholar, Grove is, of course, best known to posterity as founder-editor of the *Dictionary of Music and Musicians*, still every musician's Bible in its updated versions. Later that year, Grove and Sullivan were to embark on a Schubert-foraging expedition to Vienna where they discovered some important *Rosamunde* music, two symphonies and other bits and pieces.

Alas, the intense ardour of the lovers was intolerable to Mrs Russell, who, even though Sullivan had dedicated one of his songs to her – 'If doughty deeds my lady please' – did not wish her daughter to marry a musician, for goodness' sake, the son of a military bandmaster with no real money behind him and as yet no firm 'prospects'. True, the charming young man's reputation as a composer was already beyond question: he had been the overjoyed holder of the first Mendelssohn Scholarship, and had had several works performed professionally including the highly acclaimed incidental music to *The Tempest*, a ballet *L'êsle enchantée*, the masque *Kenilworth* (in collaboration with Henry Chorley), the 'Irish' Symphony, a Cello Concerto and many anthems and drawing-room songs . . . But none of this added up to real money in the bank, and Sullivan's only regular income was from teaching, and an organist's post at St Michael's, Chester Square, worth £80 a year. Barely enough to feed a couple of horses for a year, let alone keep Mrs Russell's precious daughter in the style to which she was accustomed.

In a stern letter grieving that Sullivan had abused her trust, Mrs Russell forbade him entrance to the family home and from engaging in any correspondence with Rachel until he could guarantee that his passion had subsided into friendship only. Rachel herself dutifully realised that her lover was in no position to propose marriage, writing thus:

> Do you not see that, even if everything befell so that I could say tomorrow 'Take me', you would have to answer, 'I cannot, you must wait'?

Nevertheless, she gave her all to Sullivan in her role as muse and mentor, suggesting an opera libretto and touchingly urging him on to great things:

> Do it with your whole soul and your strength – working at it intensely and religiously as the old masters worked, like dear old Bach – and it *must* be a great work, for you have the power in you.

She also helped him with the hasty last-minute copying (as was to be his wont) of *Cox and Box*. As dedicatee of his song 'O fair dove, O fond dove', Rachel sometimes signed her letters as 'Fond Dove', or 'Passion Flower', in rather little-girl letters like this one, urging him to wear a certain jacket when he was allowed to visit her in Zurich in 1868:

You looked so sweet in it . . . I like that better than anything else and so oo does it to please oo's bird – please do darling . . . I always liked that coat – so oo gives up oo's will to oo's bird . . . your little Passion Flower.

But she was not so innocent as might be imagined, since it seems clear that on at least one occasion the sweethearts went 'all the way'. Mrs Russell would have been apoplectic had she known:

Ah me! when I think of those days when cooing and purring was enough for us, till we tried the utmost – and that is why I fancy *marriage* spoils love. When you can drink *brandy*, water tastes sickly afterwards.

Rachel would not have been at all amused had she known that her randy lover was also almost certainly bedding her elder sister Louise, who signed off her letters to him as 'your truly loving' or 'your own devoted Little Woman' and who on one occasion declared: 'you have taken as your right the only thing I have to give'. Yet another of the many, many cases (today's tabloids are full of them) of men everywhere locked in lust with the sister of a wife or lover!

Sullivan's ardour seems to have cooled down before Rachel's, although he remained very fond of her, giving her a camellia on Christmas Day, 1869. The next month she left for a prolonged stay in St Petersburg, bidding her sweetheart to 'Spread your wings, my beautiful eagle and show how you can soar!'. She married one William Holmes in 1872 and they didn't meet again until June 1881 when by chance they were both attending a ball at the house of John Millais. 'We sat on the stairs talking for three hours!' wrote Sullivan in his diary. 'She is as handsome as ever.' Sullivan's last rather wistful mention of her comes in a further diary entry four months later: '[5 October] Chenny came at 4.30 – stayed till 6.15. Had a long talk. She is very little changed.'

Mrs Russell needn't have worried about young Arthur's prospects, of course. By the time of these reunions when Sullivan was 38 and Chenny 35 Sullivan had been known as the 'favourite young composer' of one of the greatest coloraturas ever, Jenny Lind ('The Swedish nightingale') and had been described in *The Orchestra* as 'the most conspicuous composer we have'. (This was to remain the case until Elgar's rise to fame in the late 1890s.) More significantly from the point of view of eligibility for marriage, 'Gilbert and Sullivan' had become an institution. In the wake of *HMS Pinafore, The Pirates of Penzance* and, especially, *Patience*, and 'The Lost Chord' Sullivan was earning a good deal more than Prime Minister Gladstone. The latter's salary of £7,500 in 1881 compared with the composer's top-whack gross earnings of £9,988 12s 6d. Phenomenal sums indeed, if not quite in the league of Rossini, Verdi, Puccini, Gounod and even Ambroise Thomas. By 1885 when he was at the zenith of his fame and earning power, Sullivan was able to demand the incredible sum of £700 outright for the sale of the copyright of one song 'Sweetheart'. In this country, only mega-star singers like Adelina Patti and his revered and revering Jenny Lind (one of his few real goddesses) could command higher fees for their services.

It is tempting to speculate whether, had Sullivan been allowed to marry Chenny, the union would have lasted. Would all her ardent caring and watchfulness have kept her dear Arthur on the rails, or would he anyway have broken loose and indulged his taste to the full for continental travel, racing, casinos, drinking and women? Because of his assiduously pursued hedonism, the gross value of his estate at his death – £56,536 13s 10d – was comparatively small compared to Gilbert's £120,000 and D'Oyly Carte's £240,000. Sullivan also maintained summer homes in the country in addition to his elegant London flat in Albert Mansions, Victoria Street. Here, at one stage, there was a resident engineer to maintain the electricity generator as well as a team of domestics headed by his highly temperamental housekeeper (and confidante) Clotilde Raquet. Sullivan and Raquet seem to have developed a somewhat bizarre relationship in which the master, not for the first or last time, became emotionally dependent on the servant. The diaries are littered with references to her 'storms' and their aftermath.

Mary Frances Ronalds (Fanny, L.W., D.H., Cad. Pl.) – and her rivals

'Himmelische Nacht!' (misspelling for Himmlische)

Three years older than the composer, the high-spirited Bostonian beauty Fanny Ronalds was to be Sullivan's companion until the end of his life – and also his mistress until his declining health metamorphosed her role into that of 'Auntie'. In about 1867, some four or more years before she established a close friendship with Sullivan, Fanny Ronalds had separated from her husband, thirteen years older than herself, after having borne three children. Before her marriage she had reportedly been the object of rivalry between two of New York's wealthiest men: the high-living womaniser Leonard Jerome, who for a time was a patron and intimate of the dazzling 'Home Sweet Home' superstar soprano Adelina Patti, and one August Belmont. No wonder they fought over her, with her oval face, high forehead, and abundant, deep-chestnut brown hair falling in ringlets at the back of her head; 'a lovely woman', noted one male New Yorker, 'with the most generous smile one could possibly imagine, and the most beautiful teeth'.

Not only was she a stunner to look at, she was also a dashing skater and a fine amateur singer who could not, of course, demean her social status by turning professional. Nevertheless, the admiring Prince of Wales was reportedly prepared to travel the length of the realm to hear her sing 'The Lost Chord'. She certainly looked handsome and charismatic in her early fifties, full bosomed, hair thickly coifed atop, in an ornamented after-noon gown and fur-lined coat in a portrait of 1881.

Fanny set up house with two of her children in Chelsea, eventually settling at 7, Cadogan Place, the setting for many of those secretly recorded trysts with her dear Arthur. She could never divorce her husband and marry Arthur, for to do so would have caused both of them to be excluded from the royal circles to which each was separately invited. But certainly by the end of 1878 she regarded her destiny as being secretly linked with Sullivan's. His graphically vivid diaries, which he actually started keeping in 1879 while working in North America, show that they successfully maintained a double life of public propriety and private passion. He made substantial maintenance payments to her all his life.

The first batch of constant references to Fanny date from May 1881, a year in which he travelled extensively. By then his output of serious works had dwindled in favour of the comic operas, with the G&S partnership having produced *Trial by Jury*, *The Sorcerer* (175 performances), *HMS Pinafore*, *The Pirates of Penzance* and *Patience*.

After careful and thorough analysis, Arthur Jacobs is now

certain that the formerly baffling initials 'L.W.' (perhaps standing for Little Woman) refer to Fanny in her secret role of mistress, sometimes almost alongside references to 'Mrs Ronalds' or 'Mrs R.' in connection with the above-board dinner parties, house parties and musical gatherings which they both attended.

It is also very likely that 'D.H.' (Dear Heart?) also refers to Fanny, as do, obviously, mentions of 'Cad. Pl.'. By now Sullivan was making Fanny a regular allowance from his whopping income.

[8 May 1881] Got up late, stayed at home all afternoon. Called at Cad. Pl. en route for Fulham [visiting his mother]. Came home 10 [p.m.]. D.H. came in for a few minutes at 11.30.

[12 May] D.H. breakfasted with me . . .

[13 May] Formally gave up office of Principal. Called at Cadogan Place on my way home. Mrs R. not very well. Dined at the Marlborough with the Duke of Edinburgh . . . Gave L.W. share of earnings £300.

Alas, love Fanny as he did, he was unable to resist other women as the following entries make clear:

[17 May] L.W. to breakfast 1.30. A telegram on my table was seen – painful scene in consequence. At 4, went to Gloucester Place – another painful interview – confirmed what I had said the night before. Came home – sent a bouquet. Dined at Millais' – only men: [guests included] Anthony Trollope . . . [Thomas] Hardy . . . Sir Henry Thompson [an eminent surgeon]

Presumably the 'other woman' lived at Gloucester Place and received the bouquet for being ditched! Whatever, Fanny was obviously soon placated:

[18 May] L.W. came at 12.30, stayed till 2. Storm over . . . Sent the brougham for Mrs R. and Fanny [daughter] – called later at no 7 [Cadogan Place] . . . Add metronome marks in proof of *Patience* . . .

Near the end of the month, after a few days in Paris, where he doubtless visited a brothel or two, Sullivan makes one of his dual entries, the first triumphantly unambiguous:

[27 May] ... To Cad. Place: accès! Dined at Hall's ... Ran away to play Lost Chord at St James's Hall for Mrs Ronalds: sang well, great success.

From this point, after each of his amorous visits, Sullivan began to log his number of orgasms in brackets after the lady's initials. Thus on 2 June 'L.W. (2)' appears and on 3 June 'L.W. tea (1)'.

After a trip to Russia in July Sullivan was clearly anxious to make up for lost time with Fanny!

[1 August] ... Afterwards Cad. Pl. (1)

[2 August] ... Dined at home. D.H. (2)

[4 August] ... Home L.W. (1)

[5 August] ... Dined at Cad. Pl. (2), then home.

Soon afterwards he and Fanny visited different Spa towns in Germany, doubtless because he had been prescribed a period of sexual abstinence. When the enforced period of celibacy was over – 'a miserably dull existence' was how he described it – he joined Fanny and her mother in Kassel, and was soon back in action with a new soundbite, frequently misspelled in the German:

[Kassel, 5 September 1881] Found my friends there. Our rooms are 5, 6, 7. Very comfortable. Mrs R. looking much better. Mrs C. [Fanny's mother] also better. After lunch drove out to Wilhelmshöhe. Visited park and castle. Drove back and shopped ... Nothing to do in the evening. L.W. (2).

[6 September] L.W. (1) *straight up*! Coffee at the restaurant. Shopped a little. V.S. Stayed at home and played poker all evening. Beautiful moon. Himmelische Nacht! (1)

[7 September] After dinner went to Dreike's Circus with L.W. So cold we came in again at nine. Himmelische Nacht (2).

Jacobs cannot account for the 'V.S.' on 6 September. May I suggest that it stands for 'very sore'?

The good times went on and on as they travelled with Fanny's mother (Mrs Carter) to north-eastern France, staying with the Marquis d'Aoust, an amateur composer, at his chateau of Cuincy near Douai. As well as displaying his unflagging libido, Sullivan shows his keen judgement of church organs.

[15 September] *Cuincy.* Wet. Played besique [i.e. bezique] the greater part of the day.

[16 September] *Cuincy.* Fine day. After breakfast drove into Douai to try the organ at St Jacques. New organ by a Belgian builder – three manuals, pedals etc. Good mechanism but poor tone – diapason work thin and reedy – reeds too powerful. Introduced to the organist, M. Delahaye. Accompd. Mrs Ronalds in 'The Lost Chord' [just for a change!] and [Mendelssohn's] *Oh for the wings.* Him. N. (2).

And so back, via Paris, to London, where the D'Oyly Carte's new Savoy Theatre was ready, the first London theatre to be lit entirely by electricity and seating just under 1,300 (including eighteen private boxes). The thrill of the inaugural night, featuring *Patience*, was evidently boosted by the stimulus of a tea-time quickie as the public Mrs R. doffed – let us imagine – her long, fur-trimmed coat, large veiled hat or velvet bonnet, and bustled and bodiced afternoon satin gown with its high neck-line, to reveal the now very familiar private world of 'L.W.' beneath: rustling, flounced, starched outer and under petticoats, the outermost probably of silk, the innermost one of flannel; heavily boned corset; white drawers and chemise both probably lace-edged; and suspenders, maybe by this time, attached to silk stockings, black, white or coloured. Given that time was pressing, did the gallant Arthur help her pull off her boots, one wonders? Or maybe he liked her to keep them on for these tea-time surges?

[10 October] Rehearsal at Savoy at 11 – lasted till 4.30. Lady K[atherine] Coke, Mrs R. etc. there. L.W. tea (1) ... Went to conduct ... Great house, enthusiastic reception for all ... returned home at 3 a.m., changed my clothes, had coffee and drove to Liverpool Street to take the 5.10 a.m. train to Norwich [where there was a rehearsal that morning of *The Martyr of Antioch*.]

In the winter of 1881–2 Sullivan undertook a long trip to Egypt and Italy during which he received 'nasty' letters from Fanny for being so long absent, but the two lovers were again reunited in Paris in the spring. Sullivan, however, was clearly not content to sate his passion in the arms of his beloved, as we find him warming himself up for her, as it were, with two encounters (possibly with two different ladies?) in a five-and-a-half-hour stint in a favoured brothel:

[10 April 1882] arr. at 6 a.m. Descended at Grand Hotel – rooms 197–199. Adèle [a servant] came at 9. Breakfasted at Voisin's at 11. At 12 went to keep appointment at no. 4, rue M.T. Stayed till 5.30. Dined with Dicey and D.H. at Restaurant Poissonnière. Took Dicey home, then D.H. (1). Then home myself, very tired.

No wonder!

There were other visits to 'No. 4' during this trip to Paris – a trip which nowadays has its nearest equivalent in the sex holidays taken by those who go on tacky package trips to the Pacific rim for the same purpose (and worse, of course). Presumably Fanny had no inkling of how Sullivan spent his time before he took her out for the evening or after he had dropped her off afterwards.

[11 April] Dined at Véfours [a celebrated restaurant] with D.H. Then went on to no. 4 till midnight (2).

[13 April] Spent a couple of hours at no. 4 (1). Dined at Véfours with Mrs R. and Fan.

[15 April] Spent an hour at no. 4 till 12.30 (2)

[16 April] Spent an hour and a half at no. 4

[17 April] Spent a couple of hours at no. 4 (1)

Now almost 40 years old, Sullivan's insatiable sexual appetite was matched by the breathtaking recklessness of his gambling, on this occasion perhaps topping all his other losses:

[14 April] Spent an hour and a half at no. 4. Then called on the Duke of Edinburgh and had a chat; dined at Voisin's, and spent the evening at Prince Leopold's with Mrs R. and Fan. Went to the club. Chemin-de-fer, minus £720.

It is indeed very sobering to consider that the £720 he lost in one evening represented something like seven or eight years' income for the chorus members singing in his shows at the Savoy at a weekly rate of perhaps £1 10s 0d to £2 0s 0d. And as to his own live-in maids, whom, as one would expect, he treated with consideration, such a sum blown in one evening would have kept them going for about 36 years!

No sooner had he crossed the channel than he continued in like fashion, maintaining contact with a mysterious lady 'Rem', and again losing enormous sums of money. Gambling remained a life-long obsession, most often in London being indulged at the Portland Club in St James's Square.

[20 April] Dined at Cad. Pl. (1).

[24 April] Called at Clarence House [residence of Duke of Edinburgh]. L.W. came (1). Wrote to Rem. Conducted 366th performance of Patience – fine house, splendid performance. Afterwards walked with George Lewis to Argus – minus [£]500.

'Rem' probably doubled up as a 'Charlotte C' in the diaries who had visited him in Cairo with a certain 'Tootsie'. The pair dined with him on 9 June when their relationship seems to have been terminated with great chagrin on both sides:

[9 June] Long talk with Rem . . . Settled 'all off'.

[13 June] Sent letter to L.W. telling her to be happy . . . All over about Miss C. Awful letter back – completely staggered and upset me. Couldn't do any work all day.

Clearly Fanny, now middle-aged, must have been understandably distressed when naively told to be happy against the threat of a younger rival! Sullivan, although a ladies' man and attentive lover, was clearly a very self-centred, blinkered bachelor, more concerned about not getting any work done than about upsetting Fanny. However, the usual whiskery Sullivan charm worked its magic and she was soon pacified and bedded (or maybe bedded and pacified) once more:

[June 14] L.W. dined here (1). Left much better than when she came.

During this year it seems that Fanny became pregnant and that Sullivan therefore had recourse to a certain 'M.' who was either a doctor who performed abortions or an unlicensed abortionist.

[25 May] Important business with Mrs R. Drove after dinner with D.H. to M., who advised a delay in taking action until 20 June. Submitted to this advice (fee £1 1s), returned home (2).

[2 June 1882] L.W. came. Had seen A.C. [Dr Alfred Cooper] Symptoms beginning [of induced miscarriage, presumably].

[3 June] L.W. suffering a good deal, but thankful for the cause.

[5 June] Things going well

Sullivan was clearly overdoing things when on yet another occasion, during work on *Iolanthe* in the summer of 1882 in the German resort of Bertrich, he had to admit to scoring a zero:

[25 August] D.H. (1). L.W. (0! disappointed ambition!)

However, he was soon back on form with another Heavenly Night and similar ecstasies:

[30 August] Him. Nt! (2) 11.30–1.30
[5 September] Long, Circassian

Another pregnancy scare erupted in 1884 while he was in the intensive throes of working on *The Mikado* (of which, by the way, Tchaikovsky could 'hardly endure two thirds of one act'). This diary sequence concludes with a riveting mesh of his working and intimate life:

[11 December 1884] Uncertainty changed to conviction.

[12 December] Went to M. alone

[13 December] Things very bad. Took D.H. to M. Usual course advised.

[16 December] Dined Cad. Pl.

[19 December] Signals of safety began. Attended performance of Prodigal Son by R.A.M. [Royal Academy of Music]. Very well done. Walked home with Mrs R. *L.W. to see A.C., important.*

[20 December] Signals of safety. Things going well. Dined at Cad. Pl.

[21 December] Worked at home all day. Wrote two numbers, Three Little Maids and quintet [*Mikado*, latter probably converted to quartet No. 8]. Called at C[adogan] P[lace]: Mrs R. told me about Louise. Dined at Ferdinand Rothschild's: Prince of Wales and Princess Louise there. Portland [Club]. Out of the wood.

Several ticks, rather than numbers, appear in the diary against Fanny's name, or the word 'shrubbery' during August 1884 while he was working feverishly on *Princess Ida* and also on an anthem for Novello Co., at his country house Stoneham. (His creative routine was always, with the operettas, to wait until the last possible moment before blitzing through the numbers every night for a week or so. *Trial by Jury* was composed from start to finish in three weeks.)

The clandestine lovers were separated for several months when Sullivan crossed North America to see his family in 1885. Their reunion in Philadelphia where Fanny was staying was duly recorded with a tick against a graphic entry in October: 'Went to 78'.

Auntie

By 1889, when Fanny was 50 and Sullivan had ten G&S operas under his belt, their relationship had fundamentally changed. Whilst still cherishing her – as evidenced in his support for her at the time of her father's death – his sexual passion for her was clearly subsiding into familial affection and dependence. 'Bertie [his nephew who lived with him after the death of his brother Frederick in 1877, commemorated in 'The Lost Chord'], Auntie and I went to the Surrey Theatre,' he wrote on 12 January 1889. The lovers metamorphosed into extended family, taking in her parents, her children, and his own nephew. In April 1890 he was taking 'Grandma' – Fanny's mother – to the gaming rooms in his favourite winter gambling resort of Monte Carlo, where the old lady was convinced she was being cheated! Although, from 1890, 'Auntie' occurs with ever-increasing frequency in the diaries, there is no knowing how Fanny herself reacted to the change from mistress to mother-figure:

[5 September 1890] Wonderful little woman is Auntie.

[22 September] Went up to town in the afternoon to meet Auntie.

[27 September] Went to Westgate at 5.15 with Bertie and Auntie. Dined with Gdma and Auntie, then ?? joined us.

Final Flings

Although no orgasmic scores are notched against Fanny's name from this point onwards, Sullivan's parts were still in working order. At the age of 47 he entered a prominent tick against the entry in his diary of 'ABC' – 'a pretty young thing' – with whom he drove down to Richmond on 7 June 1889, and to Greenwich on 9 July.

Still other women surface in his diaries after the launch of *The Gondoliers* in December 1889. In January 1890, when he lost more colossal sums gambling ('Tables very hostile – am now minus 10,000 [francs – just over £1,000]'), he recorded receiving two letters from a certain 'R'. Later, in March, he logged a meeting with yet another lady in Brussels:

[22 March] Saw E.W. Long conversation. A little bit 'touched'. Arranged for future.

In 1890 he was sending this same lady a £5 note in a registered letter.

To judge by the repeated ticks in his diary during yet another trip to Monte Carlo in February 1891 (after the launch of his failed operatic magnum opus *Ivanhoe* in which he had invested so much time and emotion), Sullivan was still performing with yet another lady. He was also in correspondence with a certain 'O'. In August his letters to a certain P.C. from Contrexéville, where he was taking the cure, suggests a *further* apparent love affair.

Although these flings and forays never seriously undermined his changed relationship with Fanny, in August 1896, after an unsuccessful *Grand Duke* in London and the failure of *Ivanhoe* in Berlin, he messed up with her birthday while holidaying in Switzerland. She forgave him thus with a very touching poem on the correct day, 23rd (he had thought it was the 29th):

> If I have ever made you glad
> Have ever made one single hour
> Pass brightlier than else it had,
> Have planted in your life one flower –

If I have ever had such power,
I cannot now be wholly sad.

Mary Frances Ronalds [writes Arthur Jacob] was not, in a formal sense, separated from Arthur Sullivan – since, in a formal sense, she had never been united with him. Nor did he ever cease to maintain a solicitous responsibility for her. But the close companionship was over, and since it was she who had basked in *his* sun it must have been she that felt the cold.

Even so, the value to Sullivan of Fanny's emotional support as muse, lover and 'Auntie' was surely incalculable.

If they could have married, would Sullivan have actually given up his convivial bachelor club life for her, gambling at the Argus or the Portland well into the small hours, dining at the Beefsteak and frequenting the Fielding Club and the Marlborough Club whose most illustrious member was the Prince of Wales? One clue to the answer, admittedly written in jest, is in a letter he wrote from Turkey, when he was almost 40, to his ever-solicitous and much-loved mother on the aggravations of deficient servants:

My treasure of a servant that I brought with me (Finch) is a failure . . . lazy, light-headed and worst of all a tendency to drink. This last is quite enough so we part when we reach English soil again.

Oh, the bother of servants! – and I shall have to get a cook also, besides a man. It is enough to make one marry – but the cure would be more awful than the disease. I can get rid of servants but not of a wife – especially if she is *my* wife.

In the final analysis, although he needed plenty of club company, Sullivan was emotionally self-sufficient. Fanny was perhaps a bonus rather than a necessity in his life.

Sullivan continued to be a concerned and caring friend to Fanny within the constraints of his pursuit of pleasure at the gambling tables. Writing to Bertie in 1896 from yet another villa he was renting on his beloved Riviera, he expressed relief that his nephew was making regular visits to no. 7 and continued, movingly:

You see, my dear Bertie, it is a very trying period of life for her . . . In spite of misfortune, imprudence and jealousy, she kept [her social] influence for many years. Now, the years will tell, although her mind and spirits remain young, and this is a terrible time for any woman to go through. And so all of us who are really fond of her must be gentle and considerate.

After attending the Bayreuth festival in 1896 – where he dismissed the characters in *Das Rheingold* as 'a lying, thieving, blackguardly set of low creatures' and Wagner's operas as a whole as 'a curious mixture of sublimity and absolute puerile drivel' – Sullivan entertained Fanny in the Alps with visits to Splügen, Thusis and Disentis. In March 1897 in a letter from the Riviera he instructed his secretary Bendall to tell No. 7 'that she may rely upon hearing from me on Wednesday'. She was also with him in Paris in the April of 1898, doubtless for consolation and company after the recent death of her mother and a bout of poor health.

Thereafter they were very likely frequent companions, for he recorded that Auntie visited him at his favourite club, the Portland, in May 1899 and shortly afterwards accompanied him to a performance of his ballet *Victoria and Merrie England* at the Alhambra Theatre. The last mention of her in his diaries, entries for which were now very spasmodic, records his visit to her daughter's for a family dinner on Christmas day, and then dinner at Auntie's on 29 December.

On Sullivan's death on 22 November 1900 – the result of the kidney troubles which had plagued him for well over 20 years – Fanny received many letters of condolence from those who no longer had to pretend they didn't know about the relationship, including Lady Randolph Churchill (Winston Churchill's mother, formerly Jennie Jerome, and one of Fanny's New York set), Leopold de Rothschild, the renowned émigré composer Sir Paolo Tosti and other colleagues. Fanny's reply to an enquiry shortly before the end from Princess Louise makes a fitting epitaph:

Dear Princess,
In the communion of friendship he was so gentle, so tender, so thoughtful that the sweetness of his disposition endeared him to all.

Although he had made regular maintenance payments to Fanny during their long association, Sullivan left her no money as such in his will. His bequests 'to my old and dear friend Mary Frances Ronalds' probably meant more to her than any amount of cash.

In addition to a valuable dinner and dessert service and other objects, he left her:

> the original manuscript of 'The Lost Chord' and any other autograph score she may like to have; also any other musical and vocal scores she may care to have.

The 'Lost Chord' went with her into her grave after she died at the age of 77 in 1916.

1896 Proposal of Marriage – and Rejection

Sullivan seems to have totally lost his head over a young girl of 20 when he was 54, and to have gone so far as to propose marriage and make her his heiress. While staying in the tranquil surroundings of Lake Lucerne at the Hotel National in September he met a Miss Violet and wrote to her thus:

> Dear Miss Violet,
> What do you and yours propose doing? Shall we sit under the trees or lie on the grass, or saunter on the promenade? Or shall I write a joint letter to your sister. What time do you wish to see me today? I will of course obey any order you may give.
>
> Yours sincerely
A.S.

According to an informant of the G&S specialist Leslie Baily, Jacobs tells us, 'the composer offered her "a secret marriage" at a register office and told her he thought he had only two years to live: she would be the inheritor of all he possessed'.

Her refusal caused him great pain:

> I am off in half an hour. It *was* painful last night. I couldn't stand it any longer, so I left. Yesterday was the most miserable day I ever spent.

Miss Violet has been reliably identified as Violet Beddington, one of whose sisters was Sybil Seligman, wife of the rich banker David Seligman, and briefly lover and long-time muse and soul-mate of Puccini. Wheels within wheels!

This rather bizarre episode, and also Sullivan's relationship with Fanny Ronalds, were to emerge in fictional guise in a novel by the man whom Violet Beddington married, Sydney Schiff. Schiff, writing pseudonymously as Stephen Hudson, includes a chapter in his novel *Myrtle* which describes the relationship of a famous musical knight with an older woman 'Leonora'; and also his rejected proposal of marriage, in Switzerland, to a much younger woman.

After conducting, in obvious pain, his last Leeds Festival in 1898, Sullivan was taken ill in November 1900 and died of a heart attack a few days later. Richard D'Oyly Carte survived him by less than six months, while Gilbert lived on to be knighted, eventually, in 1907 by Edward VII. Gilbert died at the age of 74 while attempting to rescue a young female swimmer. Sullivan's unfinished *The Emerald Isle* was completed by Edward German for a posthumous première in 1901.

$\mathcal{P}$UCCINI

'Il maestro cuccumeggiante' (Composer of Harlot Music)

Born: Lucca, 22 December 1858
Died: Brussels, 29 November 1924

a mighty hunter of wild fowl, opera librettos and attractive women.
Puccini on himself

his amours were rarely anything but brief, explicit and uncomplicated by deep emotion.
Stanley Jackson: *Monsieur Butterfly*

'Archimede Rossi, merchant of Milan, with cousin.'
Puccini's self-registered alias at 'a quiet hotel', Bayreuth, 1912

You imagine immense affairs. In reality, it is nothing but a sport to which all men more or less dedicate a fleeting thought without, however, giving up that which is serious and sacred; that is, the family . . . See to it that my house be not odious to me and burdensome, that I find here a cupful of jollity and calm instead of this continuous and discouraging aggravation . . . The wife of an artist has a mission different from that of wives of ordinary men.
Puccini to his wife Elvira on his infidelities, 30 August 1915

Oh, people of Lucca, if you love farts, I send you one: Merry Christmas.
Letter from Puccini to his sister Ramelda

The short answer to Puccini's enduring popularity with the punters, if not the critics and musicologists, is – sex! At least that's according to the journalist and opera critic Tom Sutcliffe in his review (*Guardian*, 16 April 1994) of a revival of *La Rondine* (The Swallow), the least known of Puccini's mature operas. After pointing out how such teary-eyed heroines as Magda (Rambaldo's mistress in *La Rondine*), Manon Lescaut (the doomed tart-with-a-heart who comes to a sticky end in the Louisiana desert), Mimì (the poor seamstress in *La Bohème*), and the little geisha Madama Butterfly were working girls who wanted true love after a career in the trade of love, Sutcliffe continues:

> Puccini's philandering made him particularly sympathetic to the woman's viewpoint in these cases. His compositional style, which consists of endless foreplay leading up to intensely orgasmic but brief melodic climaxes, mimics sexuality – and that explains his undying popularity.

He was undoubtedly the most successful opera composer after Verdi that Italy has produced, and the fact that not long before his death *Tosca* was playing concurrently in 73 cities around the world goes some way towards proving the point. So does the estimated 4 million dollars he was worth at his death. That figure would, indeed, have been much larger if he had collected royalties due from many early pirated recordings, not to mention a bootlegged full score of *La Bohème*. *Turandot* (1926) is the last opera written to remain a steady repertoire piece, and today only Wagner, apparently, has as high a percentage of his work currently active.

Tom Sutcliffe might also have added melody as the other crucial explanation of Puccini's undying popularity. 'I am an Italian and I love melody. Melody must always be the queen in music,' he told the New York *Times* in 1910. Had he not possessed such stunning gifts as a tunesmith, as a purveyor of melting, sensuous, incandescent melodies, it is doubtful whether all his other skills – his film-score craftsmanship, and particularly his extraordinary instinct for theatrical effect – would have been so spectacularly exploited. It is certainly the melodies that lift him above his contemporaries Mascagni, Leoncavallo, Giordano, Cilea and others. And what a joy they are to scrape, blow or bang to in the theatre pit or concert hall, even for the most hard-bitten professional musician.

Puccini's ability to jerk tears and to deliver blows to the solar plexus is unequalled. The very 'emotionalism', the 'all-pervasive eroticism and sentimentality' for which eggheads have derided him is the siren call that lures in the crowds. Womb music. We can all have a glorious weepy wallow, just as Puccini sometimes did as he actually composed, and as he so often did in his letters bewailing his creative and personal problems.

To put it in the more academic language of *Grove's Dictionary of Music and Musicians*, on 'the level where erotic passion, sensuality, tenderness, pathos and despair meet and fuse, he was an unrivalled master.'

'The theatre has its fixed laws: it must interest, surprise, touch, or move to laughter,' Puccini once said. He knew how to operate these laws with consummate skill. The action 'must move forward to the close without interruption, rapid, effective, terrible'. It must also be evident even to those who cannot understand the words in what the French call *l'optique du théâtre*. 'Be sparing with words. Try to make the incidents clear and brilliant to the eye rather than the ear,' he wrote to his librettist Giuseppe Adami about *Turandot*. (Had he lived half a century later he would undoubtedly have been a Hitchcock fanatic.) His supreme stage instincts could repeatedly spot and exploit the theatrical potential in given storylines by expanding or adding to them: he developed, for instance, the unique Embarkation Act of *Manon Lescaut*, added a manhunt to the final act of *La Fanciulla del West* and invented the character of Liù and her suicide in *Turandot*. Conversely, he removed any sub-plots and historical details that threatened to congest the action.

Puccini knew his limitations as well as his strengths as a composer. In another letter to Adami he leads up to this oft-quoted apologia: 'the Almighty touched me with His little finger and said: "Write for the theatre – mind well, only for the theatre!" And I have obeyed the supreme command.' Interestingly, although perhaps not surprisingly, unlike Verdi or Mendelssohn or Berlioz or Wagner, for example, Puccini's artistic interests did not extend beyond his work. He read little outside of his endless search for librettos resonant with his erotic obsessions, and, writes Stanley Jackson, was 'almost completely immune to the glories of art and architecture'. He was, however, spellbound by technology and gadgets: cars, motorboats, sailing paraphernalia, guns, combination locks, garden watering systems, electric clocks, the wireless, interior light fittings, 'everlasting' matches, balloons, aeroplanes invented by Wilbur and Orville Wright . . . He also greatly admired mechanical geniuses of the calibre of Edison and, especially, Marconi.

' . . . who lived for love, died for love . . . '

Puccini's true loves were not, with the exception of Baroness Josephine von Stängel and, most crucially, his cultured Italiophile friend Sybil Seligman, to be found in his 'real' life at all. His scores of casual encounters with mainly 'insignificant, obscure and socially inferior creatures' – starting from his mid-teens when he lost his virginity to a certain Lola whom he met in a Lucchese brothel where he occasionally played the piano – were driven essentially by a high libido and also, suggests his unabashedly Freudian biographer Mosco Carner, 'by an irresistible need to suppress irrational doubts about his virility and to assert himself'. He picked up 'chorus girls, waitresses and other readily available admirers . . . with as little emotion as the wildfowl on Lake Massaciùccoli'. In all the circumstances, it is remarkable that he never contracted syphilis nor sired a cluster of love-children. Sex with more upmarket leading actresses and aristocratic nymphomaniacs held no allure for him, although he no doubt fulfilled his obligations as a gentleman from time to time.

Puccini's real loves were his doomed and hapless heroines, his fantasy women, over whom he self-confessedly wept with 'nostalgia, tenderness and pain' during their birth on staves of near-illegible manuscript: Manon, Mimì, Musetta, Tosca, Cio-Cio-San, Angelica and Liù. Cio-Cio-San most of all, he told us, 'for whom I wrote music in the night', closely followed by Angelica.

Wherein lies the phenomenal appeal of women loving but doomed – in Carner's words, of 'love as tragic guilt to be atoned for by suffering and death' – that Puccini tapped in to? So many of his heroines finally perish for offering men true and unbounded love, in a process triggered off, except in *Suor Angelica* and *Turandot*, by men 'in their roles of either catalyst or persecutor'. 'Who lived for love, died for love,' as the street song vendor has it in *Il Tabarro*'. Only in his late works *Suor Angelica* and *Turandot* did Puccini begin to move beyond the idea of love-as-guilt into love-as-a-redemption. He himself felt he was breaking new ground as a creative artist. 'All the music I have written so far seems to me just a farce in comparison with the music I now write,' he wrote, as he was giving such painful birth to *Turandot*.

It wasn't only Puccini who exploited the love-as-tragic-guilt theme. The till-busting, eccentric French playwright Victorien Sardou, whose *La Tosca* formed the basis for Puccini's opera (for a 15 per cent cut of the gross takings!), made the same point about his own heroines: 'Women in love all belong to the same family. I have created Marcella and I have created Fedora, Theodora, and Cleopatra. They are all the same woman.' At the other extreme, perhaps this perennial theme of 'eroto-nihilism' finds its most profound and ecstatic enactment in Wagner's *Tristan und Isolde*.

According to Carner, Puccini's *idée fixe* derives ultimately from a mother-fixation. Puccini's was a 'splintered neurotic personality, feminine in many ways, and rooted in man's strongest biological urge – sexuality'. His quiet, gentle, wistful-looking father Michele (also a musician, and descended from a line of four generations of musical Puccinis) died when he was five, and he was brought up 'in a wholly feminine environment' of five sisters controlled by a relatively young, wilful and energetic mother, Albina, whose favourite he was. Puccini missed her intensely when he left home for the Conservatoire in Milan. He wept hysterically when she died, and wore her wedding ring for the rest of his life. 'I shall never be very happy again without my darling mother,' he wrote soon afterwards to his younger, and favourite sister Ramelde. His woman nearest to becoming a mother-substitute in his life was Sybil Seligman.

All the flawed women in his operas, says Carner, 'stand at the bottom of the height on which [he] enthroned the mother'. So, as a sort of operatic Bluebeard, he is compelled to murder them. There are those who discount such theories by declaring that given the opportunity Puccini would also have chosen other storylines by Zola and Daudet, for instance, and that he later set about making his audiences laugh instead of weep in such a miniature masterpiece as *Gianni Schicchi*. But in the final analysis, the intense eroticism in the music of Puccini's 'doomed heroine' stories surely speaks for itself.

To repeat the earlier question, however. Why are we all so drawn to this preoccupation with female suffering? Are all men mother-fixated misogynists deep down, sublimating unconscious urges when they witness the destruction of bimbos, or working girls? Whatever the answer, it is certainly interesting to note that even today Italy appears to be a land of whopping Oedipus complexes. According to a piece originating in *Süddeutsche Zeitung*, 'South German Times', what is known as the 'mammismo syndrome' is still very much alive and kicking, with the 'mamma' apparently being a more important institution than the prime minister or the Pope. Here, a prominent 57-year-old 'mammista' politician like Sig. Francesco D'Onofrio lives with his 85-year-old mother who waits up for him every night. There, a star like the skier Alberto Tomba says 'I dream of finding a wife like my mother.' Forty per cent of men in the 25–34 age group still live at home as opposed to only 25.9 per cent of women. Marriages founder in cases such as that of Sig. D'Onofrio whose wife could not tolerate her mother-in-law so frequently dropping by 'with newspapers or cheese'. It's a safe bet that had she lived longer, Albina Puccini would have been ruling the roost in her dear Giacomo's household.

Widening the operatic net, it is also interesting and relevant to note a fascinating point once made by the *Guardian* journalist Martin Kettle: how so many operas besides those of Puccini end up with the climactic and often violent death of a woman on stage: Traviata, Carmen, Tristan, Salome ... Wagner's misogyny is overwhelming: barely a woman is ever left standing at the end of his very long music-dramas. Are composers giving vent, asks Kettle, to feelings about women they can't express in real life?

> It is as though men require opera to convey to them an inherently impossible vision of women. Women appear on the operatic stage as brilliant singers, glamorous stars, and icons of passion. And, since women aren't like that, and can't in the end be like that, the men then kill them. And since so many of these women die at the very end of the opera, it seems that there is a ritualistic quality about the serving up of this vengeance.

Only Mozart seems to manage without the need for such seemingly ritualistic annihilation.

I report only a few bare observations and invite you, dear

reader, to speculate endlessly while the kettle is boiling or the red wine is coming up to room temperature (if you can wait that long). It is also noteworthy that Strindberg, whose personal life was tumultuous, with three disastrous marriages as well as 70-odd plays on his C.V., created patterns obverse to Puccini's, showing men being 'persecuted like hunted animals by women of pathological cruelty'. Phew!

'Mrs Elvira Gemignani and child' move in with Puccini

Following his many romps as an adolescent and young man with a bevy of women, including a girl from the tobacco factory in his home town of Lucca and a chorus girl from La Scala, Puccini's first and most decisive romantic involvement climaxed towards the end of 1884 when he spirited away the young wife of an acquaintance. He was just getting himself established after the triumph of his first opera *Le Villi* (based on the beautiful witching legend set in the Black Forest that Adolphe Adam also used for his ballet *Giselle*) in May 1884, in Milan. ('Clamorous success. Eighteen curtain calls. First Finale repeated three times. I am happy,' wired Puccini to his mother.) He had graduated at the Milan Conservatoire in the previous year, having been inspired in his studies especially by Amilcare Ponchielli of *La Gioconda* fame, but having suffered all the privations of student life, just like Rodolfo in *La Bohème*. *Le Villi* led to his first publication contract worth 1,000 lire (paid in cash and substantially blued-in on a good night out with close friends), and a monthly-payable advance of 300 lire for another opera from the leading firm of Ricordi.

It was in the year before the triumph of *Le Villi* that the 24-year-old Giacomo had fallen in love with his 22-year-old pupil back home in Lucca. She was Signora Elvira Gemignani, a tolerable singer and pianist erstwhile tolerably married, it seems, to a local wholesale grocer Narcisco Gemignani to whom she bore two children.

It is little wonder that the feelings of the charismatic and struggling, though increasingly successful young composer were encouraged way beyond the bounds of conjugal propriety. The 'Doge', as Giulio Ricordi had already dubbed Puccini, reportedly because of his habit of standing apart at drawing-room gatherings, was certainly by now a heart-throb. He was tall, slim, long-legged and soft-voiced. He had, Carner and Jackson tell us, sensitive features, dreamy, grey, heavily lidded eyes with a slight droop of the left eyelid, thick and curly chestnut hair, a long flowing moustache, sensual lips, and he dressed with studied elegance. All through his life – certainly from the time of his visit to Madrid in 1892 – he was to be beckoned and chased by women, or readily accepted by those willing wenches to whom he gave the eye. After *La Bohème* he would receive photographs of young women through the post signed 'Your Mimì', but perhaps his most spectacular known offer was to be made in Vienna after the première of *Butterfly* there in the fall of 1907. His bosom pal Tita Ruffo, a Pisan baritone and gifted raconteur, relates how a pretty young lady, accompanied by a small boy clutching a violin, arrived at Puccini's apartment in the Hotel Bristol one morning, while he was still in his dressing-gown, for an 'interview'. Naturally, the maestro feared he would be subjected to the scrapings of a putative Paganini, but the *fräulein* explained that the boy was her brother and was to be despatched for his violin lesson. When the composer returned from his bedroom after dressing he was amazed to find the young minx standing there stark naked. As might be expected, his gallant response was as if to the manner born. 'I felt too sorry for the lunatic to send her away,' he told Ruffo, himself a notorious womaniser.

Returning to Puccini and Elvira, she was also tall, and statuesque, elegant, full-bosomed, and classically beautiful, with dark, velvety shining eyes, and rich dark blonde hair piled up in plaits atop her head. She fell passionately in love with her teacher who was, it seems, a former schoolmate of her husband. It was poor Gemignani, indeed, who had introduced teacher and pupil to each other in the first place and snored in his armchair while they played post-prandial duets. His frequent forays from Lucca to Turin or Florence to buy and sell all manner of wholesome and mouth-watering goodies – cheese, Parma ham, olives, sun-dried tomatoes, salami, beans, polenta, pasta, coffee, spices, wine, spirits – gave pupil and teacher opportunities for ecstatic music lessons and outdoor strolls which didn't go unnoticed. Inevitably, they created a colossal scandal when, in November 1884, Elvira walked out on her husband and baby son to live in sin with her lover and her elder child Fosca. Puccini was then in Milan, about to depart for a production of a revised version of *Le Villi* in Turin. Since all parties in the triangle were, of course, professing if not practising Catholics, neither the lovers' union nor the birth of their son Antonio in December 1886 could be legitimised until after the death of Narcisco Gemignani in 1904. Not surprisingly, before his death Gemignani would have none of Elvira's desperate pleas for forgiveness and had her turned away from his house as a 'faithless whore'.

Although – not without severe provocation – Elvira was later to become a sullen, stubborn and possessive wife with little interest in Puccini's music, she showed astonishing courage at this stage in her life to walk out of a secure marriage and brave the colossal stigma and the discomforts of living over the brush with an archetypally impecunious musician. Even today, 'living in sin' in Italy attracts relentless disapproval from the families of the sinners. In a country of nearly 60 million people, there are only about 6,000 couples living out of wedlock. Even more astonishing is the statistic (also from ISTAT, the state statistical bureau) that at least once a month on average, somewhere in the country an illegitimate baby is murdered or abandoned.

The extended Puccini family and all the *petite bourgeoisie* of Lucca were deeply distressed by the behaviour of the young man who as a boy had, with the help of his discerning teacher Carlo Angeloni, done all the right things. He had sung in the choirs of San Martino and San Michele and later played the organ in various churches. If Puccini's poor mother hadn't already died in July of that fateful year (1884), such a scandal created by her darling Giacomo may in any case have seen her off. Her outraged benevolent bachelor uncle Dr Nicolao Cerù was soon to demand back the advance he had given to his great-nephew to help see him through the Conservatoire, although Puccini had as yet no chance of repaying it. His indulgent younger sister Ramelde, however, more tolerant than his elder sister Iginia who took the veil, saw him as a victim ensnared by 'an unprincipled Delilah'.

Alas, the gleam slowly wore off their chalice of love. Puccini had severe money worries, and although 'Papa Giulio' Ricordi (grandson of the founder of the music publishing firm and then in his late forties) was sympathetic in stretching Puccini's advance on his next opera beyond the contract date, Puccini struggled to maintain his lover, their son Tonio, and Fosca. Puccini's drifting younger brother Michele was also a source of worry until he emigrated to Argentina.

Puccini and Elvira had to move through a succession of grotty attic digs in and around Milan, and Elvira even had to make her own shoes with stitched felt soles, and her blouses from Puccini's old shirts. Puccini was reduced to making his own envelopes from sheets of paper, and Fosca often had to stay in bed while her one dress was washed, dried and ironed. Elvira's obsessive possessiveness began to surface when she harangued Puccini for leaving her alone even for a few hours. She also locked him in the room containing his piano in an attempt to get him to finish his next opera. However, it comes as no surprise to discover (in Stanley Jackson's *Monsieur Butterfly*) that in time-honoured traditions of sacrificial wifehood, Elvira went without food so that Puccini could have his daily fix of fags and sugar-laced aqua vitae. (Puccini was also addicted to coffee, sweetmeats and sugary food.) She and the children sometimes had to stay in Florence with her sister, whilst Puccini wailed that he was reduced to living on bundles of onions and had to beg Ricordi for his bus fares and free manuscript paper.

These were hardly circumstances conducive to the long drawn-out creation of *Edgar*, which Puccini later described as 'a blunder'. To make matters worse, he had a lousy, cliché-ridden libretto set in medieval Flanders from Ferdinando Fontana who had already written the words for *Le Villi*. After the indifferently received première at La Scala on Easter Sunday 1889, Giulio Ricordi was attacked by his directors for chucking 18,000 lire down the drain on his disappointing protégé. Ricordi's faith, however, was not seriously shaken and he took endless pains to find the right librettists for Puccini's next opera *Manon Lescaut*. Puccini had been drawn to the story of this love-doomed heroine who dies in the Louisiana desert via Massenet's score and the novel on which it is based by Abbé Prévost, which he read with great excitement. (In the event the libretto for *Manon* was fathered by no less than five different authors: Luigi Illica, Giuseppe Giacosa, Giulio Ricordi, Marco Praga and Domenico Oliva. And no wonder, with Puccini disputing almost every line, changing verses, and ditching entire scenes after agreements had been reached during the burning of gallons of midnight oil.)

During this long gestation – deeply frustrating to Elvira who yearned for her husband to achieve the astounding success of his then friend Pietro Mascagni (with *Cavalleria Rusticana*, 1890), and of Ruggero Leoncavallo (*I Pagliacci*, 1892) – Puccini stayed with Ramelde in Lucca, in the spring of 1891, to search for an idyllic spot where he could live and eventually build a house. He found just what he wanted at the nearby fishing village of Torre del Lago (later to be renamed Torre del Lago Puccini), where he would be able to compose and indulge to excess, just like so many of his fellow countrymen even today, his life-long mania for hunting. Kitted out in his corduroy breeches, fisherman's jersey and heavy boots, he would creep out of the house at the crack of dawn with his gun dogs (Lea, Schaunard and Nello, at one stage) and join his cronies to shoot almost any dumb creature that took wing: wild ducks, moorhens, coots, quails, snipe . . .

Having occupied rented accommodation in Torre from September 1891, Puccini finally moved with his family into his newly built villa in the early summer of 1900. Complete with its gun room and studio, Torre became an idyllic home, a spiritual base and refuge, for composing, most often in the small hours, all his operas except *Turandot*. Overlooking green valleys, ringed by deep pine forests and rejoicing in pure air, it was, in his own words, 'supreme bliss, paradise, Eden, Emphrean [whatever that means], ivory tower, spiritual vessel, and royal palace'. 'Ah, to be out shooting where there is really some prey!' he once wrote to his friend Father Panichelli. 'It is the supreme moment when the spirit is at rest.'

Or he could slop around in his stetson hat, canvas trousers and rope-soled shoes and enjoy the rough local wine over card games with his cronies in his beloved Club La Bohème (formerly Stinchi's tavern shack), and then relish Elvira's simply baked lake fish, the local oysters, the succulent watermelons and the regional cheeses. (Stories abound of Elvira's superb cooking of such dishes as barbecued birds, and wild boar with tomatoes, herbs and cheese.) Or he could go boating on the lake in his posh motorboat *Butterfly*, sometimes with a pretty local girl smuggled on board. He also acquired a yacht, *Mimì I*, later replaced by the 15-metre *Minnie* with a 100hp Volpi engine and aerial propeller.

When forced to travel to distant parts he longed to be back and, unlike Tchaikovsky, he didn't immediately become restless until he was on the move again. 'I cry out – as the snow does for the sun, as coffee does for sugar – for the peace of the mountains, the valleys, the greenery, and red sunset,' he had written in 1898 from Paris to his bohemian painter friend Ferrucio Pagni, a trusted accomplice in some of his amorous escapades. And to his friend Alfredo Caselli:

'I yearn for the scented woods, with their fragrance, for the undulation of my paunch within loose trousers, without a vest. I yearn for the free and fragrant wind that reaches me from the sea. I savour its salty air with dilated nostrils and wide-open lungs . . . I love the green expanse of the cool shelter of the woods – old and young. I love the blackbird, the blackcap, the woodpecker. I hate the horse, the cat, the tame sparrow, the house dog. I hate the steamer, the top hat, the tails. . . .'

His yearnings were further satisfied when he also acquired an idyllic mountain villa at Abetone, 1,550 metres up the lower slopes of Monte Cimone in the Apennines, surrounded by firs, chestnut and beechwood.

Meanwhile the money that started to pay for all this had come from the success of *Manon* – what the famous tenor Beniamino Gigli called 'a supreme musical expression of youthful passion and ardour'. Perhaps there is no Puccini hero more enslaved by his penis than des Grieux. *Manon* was to become a smash hit in places as far apart as Moscow, Odessa, Warsaw, Prague, Montevideo, Alexandria, Malta, Mexico City and Covent Garden, and was the only unqualified triumph of Puccini's life. At the première in Turin on 1 February 1893, he was bowing an estimated 25 times during the actual performance, starting after des Grieux's very first aria! After the show ended in near-hysteria, he acknowledged a further 40 calls. Less than a week later he received the honour of Cavaliere dell'Ordine della Corona d'Italia and was characteristically tongue-tied when obliged to stand up to make a speech of thanks. Puccini's money worries were over and Ricordi's faith in him as the firm's worthy successor to Verdi (and money-spinner) vindicated. Nevertheless, it took Puccini time to become used to affluence: he continued to spend hours bottling strawberries and cherries and insisted on buying a new cheap bicycle on the never-never.

His progress to international fame moved inexorably. *La Bohème*, over whose heroine he had wept buckets while completing the final bars – 'It was like seeing my own child die,' he said – was based on Henry Murger's autobiographical *Scènes de la vie Bohème* and first reached the boards in February 1896 in Turin, under the baton of Toscanini – although not without much blood, sweat, toil and tears on the part of Puccini's librettists, Illica and Giacosa.

I confess to you [wrote the hapless Giacosa] that I am exhausted from this continual redoing, retouching, adding, correcting, cutting, piecing together, blowing up on the one hand in order to thin out on the other . . . I've done this whole blessed libretto, from beginning to end, *three times*, and parts of it four and five. How can I go ahead at this pace?

Such travails were the result of Puccini's perfectionism and the results speak for themselves. 'That's the way libretti are made!' he told one of his later collaborators, Giuseppe Adami. 'By re-making them.'

Although not immediately popular with the critics (invariably a good sign!), *Bohème* is now considered by many to be his greatest masterpiece. The theatre was sold out for the rest of the month, and in Palermo in April the conductor had to encore the entire final act in the small hours of the morning. (Did the musicians who had not gone home receive any overtime, one wonders, or were such supreme feats of manual labouring simply part of the job?) Thousands of Italian babies were christened Mimì and municipal bands everywhere were blowing the big tunes.

A similar story of critical carpings (Verdi called them 'gnat-bites') and 20 nights of sold-out houses applied to the reception of *Tosca*, premièred in January 1900 in Rome. Based on Sardou's play of the same name, it was the composer's first venture into the world of blood-and-thunder *verismo* melodrama. There was also real life drama on the first night when the conductor Mugnone (later described by Puccini as having a 'flabby' beat) ran for cover to his dressing-room, thinking an anarchists' bomb had exploded as late punters battered the door to get into the theatre and find their seats.

During a visit for the première of *Tosca* in the summer of 1900 in London, where he was annoyed by the chattering opera audiences although overawed by their liveried attendants, boiled shirts, dress uniforms, and beautiful women wearing elegant gowns and glittering tiaras, Puccini saw David Belasco's play *Madam Butterfly*. Originating in a true-life incident in a magazine, its storyline and exotic oriental ambience, created in the first scene by a series of illuminated screens featuring rice fields, a garden of cherry blossom, and a snow-capped volcano in a sunset, intoxicated him. He homed in subliminally and unerringly on the fate of the spurned little geisha girl Cio-Cio-San. In Belasco's words, 'I never believe he did see *Madam Butterfly* that night. He only heard the music he was going to write'. Although he thought his own *Butterfly* his best work to date, its reception at La Scala in February 1904 was, in spite of record box-office receipts for the première there, a pandemonium rare in the history of opera, with growls, howls, shouts, groans, laughter, giggling, hisses, catcalls, obscene sneers, barking, braying, birdsong, mooing, whistling and constant parrot cries of 'Bohème' coming from the auditorium. (They may have been engineered by a nasty faction supporting Mascagni, who developed megalomaniac tendencies and became pathologically jealous of Puccini's success.) At the end of the show Puccini chain-smoked and his diva Rosina Storchio (Toscanini's current mistress) sobbed hysterically. There was also a Witches' Sabbath in the press, to wit: 'a diabetic opera, the result of a motor accident'.

Other comparable first-night flops in the annals of great opera include *The Barber of Seville, Tannhäuser* and Bellini's *Norma*.

Puccini took heart from the fact that Venice had first laughed *La Traviata* off stage as well. He made various changes (crucially by dividing the overlong second Act into two), and *Butterfly* reappeared with great acclaim the following May in Brescia, with 32 curtain calls and seven encores, especially of 'One Fine Day', the reading of the letter and the Flower Duet.

'So many years of bickering'
Corinna; the '*Affaire* Doria'

Meanwhile life on the home front had become fractious and sometimes turbulent. The gap of nearly six years between *Butterfly* and Puccini's next opera *La Fanciulla del West* (1910) was due primarily to repeated minor eruptions of a domestic volcano before it exploded violently in January 1909, with the suicide of Doria Manfredi, the Puccinis' servant girl.

In 1903 Puccini also suffered a compound fracture of the right shin and numerous contusions in a serious accident on a treacherous February night in his motor car – a powerful, evil-smelling Clement he bought after being deluged in a rainstorm of royalties from Tosca. (His later purchases included a 70hp Itala, a small Fiat, a Sizaire runabout, a motorcycle when petrol was scarce in World War I – and three Lancias, the last an eight-cylinder costing him 90,000 lire.) He was laid-up in a wheel-chair for several months in a condition he described as 'semi-nursery'. To make matters worse, his diabetic condition came to light and he was put on a punishing diet (for him) of 'five sugar-free meals a day with Karlsbad water and small doses of strychnine'. The one compensation in all this for Elvira was that, being KO'd, her husband was unable to philander and she tended him with unusual solicitude.

Eventually marrying in 1904, Puccini and Elvira were clearly never made for each other. Until they reached their sixties, their relationship tended to be mutually destructive, though Elvira came off infinitely worse because her life became so restricted. Puccini was utterly self-centred in his artistic preoccupations while Elvira was essentially an ordinary woman who, although proud of her husband's success, took little real interest in his creative problems. She found life at Torre boring, and filled their house with her relations, whose presence only drove him out of the house and into the arms of all-too-willing local hussies. A townie at heart, Elvira would have much preferred the razzle-dazzle of life in Milan where Puccini rented a barely furnished apartment in the via Verdi, near La Scala. She could have dressed up and spent his piles of royalties in the posh shops, stores and elegant cafés. (The Milan apartment served Puccini well for the 'auditions' he sometimes held there for work-hungry chorus ladies.)

Although Elvira sometimes accompanied Puccini on his trips abroad – for instance, to South America for a season of his operas in 1905 (where he was induced by a massive £2,000 fee), to Paris for the première of *Butterfly* in 1906, and to New York in 1907 (lured by a bait of $8,000) – she would not usually accompany him to obligatory receptions and other functions. In Puccini's words to Ramelde, 'she is happy when she can put her arse in bed and sleep for nine or ten hours'. By the same token, Puccini rarely made any real attempt to include her in his creative and professional life, infinitely preferring to depend, from 1904, on his beloved muse Sybil Seligman. In the words of one of Elvira's closest friends, 'she was always around and always absent'. As the marriage waned, he stopped addressing her by most of her pet names – 'Elviretta', 'Little Pea', 'Birdie', 'Piglet' and 'Little Mouse' – and rarely any longer signed himself as 'Topizio' (Little Mouse).

All in all, Puccini must have been an increasingly difficult man to live with: he was in constant need of reassurance, pathologically vulnerable to criticism, and highly prone to melancholia, depression, hypochondria (in later years) and whinging Italianate self-pity. His reaction to the ageing process was to consume vast quantities of lozenges, powders, tablets, hair dyes, lotions, and aphrodisiac elixirs. Towards the end of his life he became dysfunctional to the point where he seriously contemplated having an operation to restore his youthful vigour by grafting the reproductive glands of an ape onto his own! Only his diabetes apparently prevented him from going ahead. 'Give me back my youth and I will give you *Tosca*,' he once said to his valued priest friend Father Panichelli, who helped him substantially with the liturgical aspects of that opera and of *Suor Angelica*.

Elvira could not cope. To a woman with such limited horizons, Edwardian London, for example, was 'as remote as Tibet'. During Puccini's second trip to New York in 1910, when he was accompanied only by Tonio, she wrote to him sullenly, 'Now you are a great man and compared to you I am nothing but a pigmy'. In the manner of so many Mediterranean women, she aged prematurely, 'with deep lines round her eyes, her lips habitually tight, the corners of her mouth drawn', making her 'severe and bitter-looking'. She became increasingly dowdy, matronly, tense, gloomy and morose, rarely venturing out except in the company of family and relations.

Nevertheless, whether or not she was the 'right woman' for her husband, Elvira had cause for grievous complaint. At times, only humiliating dependency can have stopped her walking out on him. As early as six years after their elopement she was accusing him, when he was away, of infidelity in letters of violent protest and Puccini was trying to assure her that she was his 'only and true, holy love', at the same time winding her up with mention of their 'adored bed, the sheets with certain suspicious spots'. Writing from Madrid in 1892, he couldn't resist taunting her with mention of 'certain types' of women who were 'capable of raising one's trousers', following this with an assurance that he was her 'true Topizio. Do not worry'. But even before *La Bohème* was finished in 1895, he was cheating on Elvira on their own doorstep, grooming his moustache before being boated across Lake Massaciúccoli for various assignations (one of them for several days) in the pine forest. His standard get-out line to Elvira for his delayed returns was that he had been trying 'to reach the open sea from the canal'. On one occasion (in 1900), he was caught by a neighbour of one of his sisters waiting with a 'beautiful companion' on the station platform at Pisa for an express train to Genoa on which he had booked a double sleeper.

When confronted about the lady by Elvira (who had fortuitously rumbled the assignation), Puccini was contrite, but blamed her partly for not being her former self. 'You are no longer the same, your nerves dominate you . . . In my own house I feel myself more of a stranger than you do.' He made up to her by giving her a pair of diamond earrings on his return to Torre, and initiating a spell of passionate lovemaking. But he was soon at it again. In the summer of 1901, when word of his assignations in a hunting lodge, deep in the pine forests, with a pretty young schoolteacher from Turin reached Elvira's ears, she hunted out the adulterous pair. Alas, she found the hapless groupie but not her husband, whose arrival had been delayed. Beating her rival off with an umbrella, Elvira returned home and set about her other half with her fingernails, scratching him so violently that he 'carried the scars on his nose for several days'. These Latins! Puccini fled to Milan and this time averted terminal disaster by playing the sympathy card and bleating of a fever, probably malaria, which had kept him awake for three nights without a wife to nurse him. Alas, the ploy didn't work and there was no kiss-and-make-up this time. There was a sea change in their relationship. Elvira hardened and withdrew into herself. At the age of 42, suffering from a chronic bronchial cough, she now rarely left the house except for shopping. In Stanley Jackson's words:

Inevitably she put on flesh which added to her gloomy dissatis-faction. Puccini had become sprucer with affluence, while she already looked dowdy at forty-two and took to wearing black. Moreover, she had denied herself the social stimulus to dress more becomingly. In all their years at Torre she never accepted an invitation to Ginori's handsome villa, La Piagetta, across the lake. [The Marchese Carlo Ginore owned an adjacent estate and became an intimate friend of Puccini.] Apart from infrequent visits to La Scala or the Ricordi offices, she saw nobody in Milan and spent her days shopping or endlessly tidying the apartment. Acute middle-aged depression had accentuated the anomalies of her unmarried status, while Puccini's growing celebrity simply magnified her fears instead of bringing reassurance. She now found it difficult to face receptions where he might look twice at a younger and more attractive woman or make some remark to signal a new liaison. Instead she took refuge behind the walls of the villa, entertaining her relatives or occasional guests like Giulio Ricordi, who had always shown her respect and gentle sympathy. . . . As Fosca had stopped adoring Puccini and now warmed to men of her own generation, Tonio had automatically benefited but this shift in relationships left his mother feeling even more loveless and isolated.

By 1903 Puccini was openly admitting to his philandering and expecting Elvira to tolerate it: 'Mine is the guilt. But it is my destiny that I must be guilty.' Twelve years later he would even argue that a bit on the side was an artist's privilege – a necessity, no less, just as other creative artists needed alcohol or opium:

> 30 August 1915
>
> You have never looked at these matters as do other women who are more reasonable – Good God! The world is full of such things. And all artists cultivate these little gardens in order to delude themselves into thinking that they are not finished and old and torn by strife. You imagine immense affairs. In reality, it is nothing but a sport to which all men more or less dedicate a fleeting thought without, however, giving up that which is serious and sacred; that is, the family . . . See to it that my house be not odious to me and burdensome, that I find here a cupful of jollity and calm instead of this continuous and discouraging aggravation . . . The wife of an artist has a mission different from that of wives of ordinary men.

The double bind in their neurotic, demoralising relationship was that, although they could not live happily together, they could not bear to be apart. 'Within hours of parting', Jackson tells us, 'they would be exchanging telegrams, postcards and letters affirming their love and longing for each other.'

Corinna – 1901

Puccini's first really serious affair (that we know about) after cohabiting with Elvira was with an intelligent law student, Corinna, from Turin. It lasted nearly three years after he met her on a train in 1901, although of course his car accident caused a suspension of their passionate encounters. Her surname is not known and she is often referred to in the mountains of correspondence which the affair generated within Puccini's circle as 'the Piemontese'.

The affair flared up during his work on *Butterfly*. As Puccini enjoyed secret meetings with Corinna he was steeping himself in *japonaiserie*, reading intensively, collecting recordings of Japanese music, conferring with the wife of the Italian ambassador to

Japan who sang him native songs, and listening to a Japanese actress, Sada Jacco, speak her native language.

Corinna was far from being the whore that everyone, particularly Papa Giulio Ricordi, made her out to be. Given the rocky state of his marriage and his very flexible approach to monogamy it is no surprise that Puccini became addicted to a woman offering him prolonged and uninhibited passion. But for the combined and sustained pressure from Ricordi, Illica and his sisters, Puccini might well have abandoned his family altogether.

Although there are no intimate or steamy letters between the lovers to present for titillation, the reactions to the affair from within Puccini's circle reveal very fascinating glimpses of the individuals who voiced them.

Ricordi's foamings at the mouth are staggering. His despair, and rage even, at the prospect of the irreversible moral and physical decay of his beloved protégé, and its effect on his future creativity (and, of course, on his firm's balance sheets) resulted in a letter on 31 May 1903 which must have been the longest he ever wrote to his 'caro, amatissimo Puccini'. The horrifying, tragic prospect of another syphilitic Donizetti, who ended up as a pathetically gibbering onanistic idiot in a funny farm, seemed certain. Convinced that Puccini's slow recovery from his accident of 1903 was due to venereal disease caught from Corinna, Ricordi had already noted in a letter to Illica the 'flabbiness of the muscles in [Puccini's] jaw, the movements of his body, his sudden boredom . . .'.

Excerpts plucked from Ricordi's astonishing letter (taken from the biography by Howard Greenfeld, the first Puccini scholar to disseminate the details of this affair) speak for themselves:

> How is it possible that a man like Puccini, an artist who has made millions of people palpitate and cry with the strength and charm of his creations, can have become a faint-hearted and ridiculous toy in the meretricious hands of a vulgar and unworthy woman . . . Is it possible that sadistic lust has more of a grip on him than does his pride as an artist and as a man . . .? And doesn't this man understand the immense difference between love and the filthy obscenity which destroys the moral perception and physical vigour of a man? To think that a low creature, with whore-like instincts . . . by means of obscene sensual pleasures . . . can make him her toy . . . The lowest and most vile creature, I say, and I shout it out loud: vile, low . . .
>
> Oh, what painful blindness . . . a corrupt woman drives out this

marvellous individuality, by means of influence, and like a filthy vampire sucks from it all thought, all blood, all life.

Come on, my dear Giacomo, or rather our dear Giacomo . . . break this chain of lewd excitement and rise up to nobler and higher ideals . . .

Never more than now, is it the time to say 'Where there's a will, there's a way'.

And so it goes on for another few cajoling paragraphs. Although Puccini was upset by Ricordi's distorted portrait of Corinna, he nevertheless acknowledged, in a letter to Illica that 'what shines through his letter is his affection for me, and this is a great consolation for me.' When Ricordi died in 1912, Puccini was bereft, losing, writes Stanley Jackson, not only 'a sympathetic guide, impresario and banker, but also a second father [for close on 30 years], tolerant of his weaknesses yet resolute when others had yielded to flattery or self-interest'.

Although Puccini's sister Iginia (who became a Mother Superior) said his accident had been a combined act of Divine punishment and mercy, Ramelde was more practical. She proposed, unsuccessfully, to Illica that the answer was for him to try to pull strings and bring forward Puccini's marriage. Elvira's husband had died, but the ten-month period of mourning compulsory, in Italian law, before a widow could marry needed to be circumvented.

Illica, although much concerned about Puccini the fish being trapped in Corinna's net, was even more non-judgemental. In his view Elvira (who, inevitably scarred and enraged, started opening all Puccini's letters) was at least partly to blame:

I think that if Puccini acts in this way, it means that Elvira has been unable to inspire him to greater respect. People have the governments they deserve and so does Elvira.

Eventually, feeling weary and hounded, Puccini wanted out of the affair.

My life is a sea of sadness, in which I am immersed [he wrote to Illica in a characteristic outburst of histrionic self-pity]. I feel I am loved by no-one; understood by no-one, and so many people tell me I am to be envied. Something went wrong at birth . . . I spend my time in an atmosphere of complete darkness.

He finally broke his ties with Corinna in 1903, but not before she had squeezed an undisclosed legal settlement out of him after dangling the possibility that she would publicise his incriminating letters to her.

'Are you happy now?' wrote Puccini to Ramelde on the day after his wedding to Elvira on 3 January 1904. What a relief it must have been to all of them – but to no-one more than Giulio Ricordi.

The 'Affaire Doria'

Nothing remotely suggested that [Doria's] destiny would parallel that of Puccini's most tragic heroines.
Stanley Jackson: Monsieur Butterfly

I defy anyone to say that he ever saw me give Doria even the most innocent caress.
Puccini to Sybil Seligman, 1909

The saddest time of my life.
Puccini

'Jealousy is a passion which seeks with passion that which causes suffering.'
Old German proverb

The Doria tragedy shows that, however much cause Elvira had for complaint, her jealousy became a pathological illness 'near to lunacy' (as the baritone Titta Ruffo put it). She had already developed the habit of putting camphor (known to be a debilitating drug) in her husband's riding breeches, and, on her own admission, mixing his wine or coffee with an anaphrodisiac whenever an attractive woman came to dinner. And even after the crisis finally subsided, her paranoia was such that she once threatened with an umbrella a beautiful young singer who called in at Torre on business.

In the autumn of 1908 Elvira became convinced that Doria Manfredi, the family's strikingly attractive, gentle and modest 21-year-old servant girl was having an affair with her master. The couple had first engaged her at Torre five years earlier while Puccini was laid up after his motor accident. In her utter devotion to the Puccinis, Doria was 'a rare domestic pearl' whom Puccini regarded as a member of the family, almost a replacement for the departure of his devoted stepdaughter Fosca.

Ever a scourge to her servants, bursting into tantrums and making unfair demands on them, Elvira suddenly went berserk. Her time-bomb of hatred and suspicion exploded one night when she woke up and heard Puccini and Doria chatting by the open door leading to the garden. Battered by a torrent of abuse, Doria fled to her room and locked herself in while Elvira banged dementedly on the door.

After dismissing Doria, Elvira made the girl's life a living hell, demanding through the local priest that she leave the village, pursuing her down the street, vilifying her as a slut, a tart, a whore and much more, and threatening 'as sure as there was a Christ and a Madonna' that she would drown her in the lake. Early in the new year of 1909, plagued also by her own family who had swallowed Elvira's demented lies – in Puccini's words, 'faced with Hell in her own home and dishonour outside' – Doria poisoned herself with three tablets of corrosive sublimate [mercuric chloride] and died 'after five days of atrocious agony' on 28 January. According to the coroner's report based on an autopsy, she was *virgo intacta* (a virgin).

Elvira fled to Milan, and a distraught Puccini escaped temporarily to his friends the Tostis in Rome, but the Manfredis, hardly surprisingly, were bent on redress and sued Elvira for persecution and public defamation. To cut a long story short, on 5 July Elvira was sentenced to five months and five days in jail for 'defamation of character, libel, and menace to life and limb', and fined 700 lire plus costs. While an appeal was pending, Puccini finally made an out-of-court settlement of 12,000 lire on the Manfredis, who then dropped the case, erected a memorial to Doria and bought themselves a nice house with the proceeds.

No wonder Puccini had been 'lovingly fingering [his] revolver', taking doses of barbiturate and wanting 'to go far away and create a new life'. And no wonder either that the superstitious locals dubbed Elvira '*l'iettatura*' or 'the evil eye'. At least Puccini had the small consolation of knowing that in the end neither Doria ('my poor little butterfly') nor her family held the tragedy against him personally. Likewise the villagers, who not only adored his music but also had always appreciated his quixotic (although limited) acts of generosity. As to Elvira, she had veered uncontrollably between believing in and defending her accusations in court, and admitting her wrongdoing to the point where, if she had possessed the necessary courage, she would have thrown herself out of the window 'if it were a little higher'.

Naturally the press had a field day with the '*Affaire* Doria', which took its toll on Puccini's hypersensitive nerves, put years on his life, and left him with a feeling of severe public humiliation. His wounds were salted by his son Tonio, who sided with his mother throughout and even threatened to escape permanently to Africa.

It was some months before there was any kind of reconciliation between husband and wife. Their first two meetings in Milan ended acrimoniously and it wasn't until twenty days after the trial, on 26 July, that Elvira's defences broke down, the family became reunited, and Puccini felt at last able to get on with sustained work. As Stanley Jackson points out, although Puccini had no intention of ending his philandering, nor his friendship with Sybil Seligman, 'his home life was clearly the solid and indispensable base of the triangle'.

The Doria Tragedy and Puccini's Music

Mosco Carner believes that the Doria episode accounted for 'signs of an exhaustion in his inventive faculty' in both *La Fanciulla del West* (which had been neglected for almost eight months) and *La Rondine*, and 'a reduction in his powers of concentration'. Carner also suggests that 'the vision of that poor victim' and her suffering were at the back of Puccini's mind as he created so poignantly the Nun in *Suor Angelica*, and the little slave girl Liù who kills herself rather than betray her Prince and master, Calaf, in *Turandot*. 'Doria's tragedy,' continues Carner, 'is perhaps the only instance in Puccini's life when a profound experience in the world of reality was transmuted in the crucible of his imagination.'

More sinisterly, Carner also believes that Elvira's responsibility for the 'horrible things and atrocities' in the '*Affaire* Doria' influenced the roles of two persecutors in his operas: the sadistic Aunt in *Suor Angelica*, who causes her niece to take poison by brutally telling her that her illegitimate child is dead; and the Chinese Princess Turandot who drives little Liù to suicide after threatening to torture out of her the real name of her master, Calaf.

These two women may, according to Carner at his most Freudian, also be a projection of his mother:

not, of course of the real mother, who was anything but a monster, but of the *idea* formed of her in his unconscious, under the pressure of the conflict between a guilty longing for her and moral censorship.

Highly fascinating, however imponderable.

Josephine von Stängel, 1911

Puccini's second serious affair, lasting for several years (also disseminated for the first time by Henry Greenfeld), was with the German baroness Josephine von Stängel. Separated from her husband and some seventeen years younger than the maestro, she was 35 when they met and had two small daughters.

They met on the beach at Viareggio in the summer of 1911. In spite of the intense heat Puccini stayed in nearby Torre that year rather than retreat into the mountains to Abetone as was his wont. Josephine offered him everything Elvira didn't: passion, compassion, and, most importantly, adoration as a man and a musician. Not least of her attractions was that, like her lover, she hated Richard Strauss's *Ariadne auf Naxos* – although, also like her lover, she loved *Die Meistersinger*! (Puccini's attitude to 'new music' was curiously ambivalent. Although he was averse to atonality he was nevertheless fascinated by Schoenberg and Stravinsky, whose presence hovers over *Il Tabarro* and *Turandot*, as does that of Debussy and Strauss over *La Fanciulla*.)

The adulterers devised all sorts of subterfuges to arrange clandestine trysts. They were certainly serious enough about each other for Josephine to initiate a divorce from her husband (in 1915) and for Puccini to arrange to buy land for a house he would build for them to live in. (As we shall see, he ended up taking Elvira there instead!) He was her 'Giacomucci' or 'Mucci', while to him she was 'Josi' or 'Busci', whom he addressed in one letter with 'one thousand tender names'.

She was clearly passionately in love and very romantic to boot, declaring that 'I would like to have your dear mouth and your tender eyes now, but deep in your eyes I have you forever.' Later she wrote:

> I adore your art, your music, your great knowledge, and above all I love ... your modesty and your simplicity in everything you do. ... And your love for me is the most sacred of poems, and your goodness is so sweet that it makes me your slave.

The advent of World War I seems to have put an end to their affair, although it is doubtful whether Puccini would ever have had the bottle or the will to walk out on Elvira. He was also too obsessed with his physical and spiritual decay, and, at that time, very pained by a vicious musicological attack on him by Fausto Torrefranca and his followers.

'These Little Gardens'

The doom, gloom and mutual frostiness in the Puccinis' precarious marriage prevailed for many years. One letter from wife to husband in late 1909 suggests that her sexual appetite for him was not reciprocated. 'Perhaps,' she wrote, 'you miss me for the comfort of your life. But I miss you in quite another way.' His affairs continued, of course, as we have seen in his long, self-exonerating letter of 1915. One 'little garden' he cultivated around this time was a Hungarian woman called Blanka Lendki, with whom he corresponded secretly. Her brother had come to his aid at the time of the Doria tragedy. 'I kiss your beautiful mouth,' he wrote to her in October 1911 after warning her to stop sending letters to his secret postbox in Viareggio, and to send them care of his old friend Carlo Carignani instead.

Puccini had another adventure with an attractive tourist who agreed to accompany him to the Bayreuth festival in 1912, where he registered himself in a 'quiet hotel' as 'Archimede Rossi, merchant of Milan, with cousin'.

After the outbreak of World War I he tended another of his 'little gardens' just across the Swiss border, the wife of a German officer. He was visiting her so frequently that the border guards suspected him of espionage, and the Italian Ambassador had to intervene to avert a diplomatic incident. When the young lady's husband was killed in action on the Western Front, she moved to Bologna and dented Puccini's fragile ego by ditching him for a handsome young Italian officer. 'La Tedesca', as she became known, thereafter pestered Puccini for loans until he finally got her off his back with a gift of 5,000 lire.

While in Vienna for the première there of *Il Trittico* in 1920, he was as tacky and corrupt as so many other powerful figures in the music business when he went to considerable trouble to further the interests of a work-hungry young soprano in return for her favours. His efforts to get her work at the New York 'Met', however, met with a firm rebuff from the director there, Gatti-Casazza.

'Like two old family portraits . . .'

By about 1921, when they were in their early sixties, Puccini and Elvira were pulling through to a kind of mutual understanding and warmth. In April of that year he surprised her by inviting her to join him in Rome while he was attending rehearsals for performances of *Manon*. ('Come quickly and I will start to live again.') The Seligmans noticed an absence of tension between them after so many years of bickering, with Vincent recalling that age had given Elvira 'a new sweetness and a new serenity'. Puccini, likewise had never been more 'tender, gentle, affectionate, gay'. He took renewed pleasure in the company of Fosca's lively children.

That same year they moved from Torre, which had been ruined for Puccini by the erection of a smelly and noisy peat factory on the doorstep, to a new and luxurious villa with an oriental flavour at Viareggio, complete with a new Steinway grand as a gift from the makers.

Puccini summed up their new marital contentment to Adami in May 1923, some nineteen months before his death:

> Elvira and I are here, the two *ancêtres*, like two old family portraits, frowning from time to time at the cobwebs that tickle us. We sleep, eat, read the *Corriere*, and with a few notes in the evening, the old maestro makes ends meet.

On his deathbed his final words to Fosca were reportedly: 'Remember that your mother is a remarkable woman . . . My poor Elvira, my poor wife.' She died in 1934, a few months before Sybil Seligman.

On the work front, Puccini was keen to break away from the soft-centred mode of *Butterfly* to something tougher. In 1907, after seeing in New York another melodrama by David Belasco, *The Girl of the Golden West*, he was attracted to its blend of realism and romance in a storyline featuring miners at the time of the first California gold rush. The première of *Fanciulla* took place at the Met in New York in December 1910, under the baton of Toscanini with the legendary and fabulously wealthy Enrico Caruso (by then earning $100,000 a year) as Johnson. With those two megastars performing, and such on-stage spectacles as eight galloping horses, a blizzard on Cloudy Mountain and a showpiece poker game, it couldn't and didn't disappoint the public, although some critics were characteristically lukewarm. With its adventurous incorporation of elements of Debussy (in the harmonies) and Richard Strauss (in the orchestration), *Fanciulla* is a masterpiece, even though Puccini's brand of unforgettable, erotically charged melodies is less in evidence. Inevitably so, because the heroine Minnie is far tougher than any of Puccini's previous ones.

What did it really matter that about two years later a new generation of Italian composers (Casella, Pizzetti and Malpiero) and the critic and musicologist Fausto Torrefranca attacked Puccini viciously for being bourgeois, commercial and lacking in idealism, and called for a return to the heroic character and spirit of the ancient masters? (Their ideals were embodied in the work of the very colourful pre-fascist poet, novelist, dramatist, soldier and hideously toothed womaniser Gabriele d'Annunzio.) Puccini was deeply wounded by these volleys of venom and could not then console himself with the knowledge that his enemies now remain insignificant unknowns, whereas he is still, surely, the world's most popular opera composer. Interestingly, d'Annunzio, desperately short of cash, was quite prepared to sell his soul and write a libretto based on his film drama *The Children's Crusade* for Puccini when they met in 1912. The 'shapeless monstrosity' he produced, however, 'unable to walk or live', was totally unacceptable to Puccini.

A row in that same year with Tito Ricordi, the new descendant head of his long-standing publisher, prompted Puccini to accept a commission (worth £8,000 plus 50 per cent of royalties) for an operetta from the Vienna Karltheater. This resulted in *La Rondine*, for which his new, young and compliant librettist Adami submitted no fewer than sixteen acts! At the première at the Casino Theatre in Monte Carlo in March 1917, the audience of 'gamblers, war-bored sophisticates and profiteers' were enchanted by its waltzes and lilting duets. However, it took Puccini some time to extricate himself from a charge of being a traitor to the Allies after Léon Daudet, the editor of the French nationalist newspaper *L'Action française*, accused him of 'culpable commerce with the enemy', having sold his 'Austrian opera' to Monte Carlo.

In spite of such atrocities as the German invasion of Belgium, it seems that Puccini was ever more interested in his royalties and press cuttings – or even the short supply of shotgun cartridges, and petrol for his motor boat – than the rape of Belgian nuns or the cutting off of babies' hands. Unlike Toscanini, who made massive financial sacrifices for the war effort, Puccini seems not to have contemplated even a few benefit performances for the Italian Red Cross. Only after Daudet's attack did he belatedly offer to donate a year's royalties from his operas performed at the Opéra-Comique in Paris to a fund for disabled soldiers. On the other hand, he seems to have been more than willing to compose a song celebrating Italy's victorious arms, which became an official Fascist hymn under Mussolini's régime.

Because of the hostilities, Puccini's next works forming *Il Trittico*, a triple bill of three one-act operas (*Il Tabarro, Suor Angelica* and *Gianni Schicchi*) were premièred at the Met in December 1918. (They were conceived as a sequence in the French Grand Guignol tradition of a horrific episode, a sentimental tragedy and a comedy or farce.) The European première was given in Rome the following year. The comedy proved for a long while to be more popular than its partners, though *Il Trittico* is now performed in its entirety according to Puccini's wishes.

Determined in his last years to 'strike out on new paths', Puccini searched for a libretto that combined a fairy-tale atmosphere with characters of flesh and blood. He finally settled on Count Gozzi's *Turandotte*, believing that he was at last becoming a true, adventurous creative artist with an 'original and perhaps unique work in the making'.

The gestation of this opera was the most painful of all. In particular, he had never experienced such labour pains as when giving birth to the great love duet in Act 3. He was constantly urging his librettists to complete their work quickly.

> Hurry, [he wrote in November 1920 to Adami] because . . . without fever there is no creation; because emotional art is a kind of malady, an exceptional state of mind, over-excitation of every fibre and atom of one's being, and so on ad eternum.

He took as much trouble to assimilate the trappings of chinoiserie for this opera as he had done with *japonaiserie* for *Butterfly*.

Between times, he moved, as we have seen, to Viareggio in 1921. Towards the end of 1923 he began to experience severe throat pains, hardly surprising in view of his lifelong chain-smoking habit. In the autumn of 1924 cancer of the throat was diagnosed and Puccini, accompanied by his Tonio, went for X-ray treatment to a clinic in Brussels. (Elvira was too ill with bronchitis to accompany him.) Although the treatment seemed to be working, Puccini's heart couldn't stand the strain and he died on 29 November. His body was brought back to Milan and placed temporarily in Toscanini's family tomb. (Although Puccini's relationship with Toscanini had always been volatile, and hit rock bottom over their polarised responses to the horrors of World War I and Toscanini's rejection of *Il Trittico* as an entity, they became fully reconciled after Toscanini's conducting of *Manon* at a gala performance at La Scala in 1923.) Mussolini, of whom he had been a supporter, gave the funeral oration and Toscanini, heartbroken and near collapse, conducted the Requiem music from *Edgar*. Two years later Puccini's body was exhumed and buried in the villa chapel at Torre del Lago.

The final two scenes of *Turandot* existed only in three sets of sketches. One of these sets consisted of 36 pages in short score and was amplified and orchestrated for performance by Franco Alfano. At the première at La Scala on 25 April 1926 Toscanini stopped the performance at the point where Liù snatches a dagger to kill herself in the last scene that Puccini completed. The curtain fell to total silence, with many in the audience weeping freely. The next night they played the full opera with Alfano's ending.

'My Sybil of Cunae'
Sybil Seligman

the person who had come nearest to understanding my true nature
Puccini

She has the most beautiful voice ever possessed by an amateur.
New York *Herald*, September 1904

The spring of 1905 found Puccini in London for performances of *Butterfly*. Once again he splashed out on the trappings of upper-crust London life: the Savoy, Maxine's, silk cravats, dressing-gowns, lavender-coloured kid gloves, a scarf for Elvira, a tortoiseshell moustache-comb, Savile Row suits with ingeniously sewn-in lead weights to disguise his limp . . . Some five years later his English ensemble was further enhanced by the gift of an elegant diamond and ruby pin from Queen Victoria after she accepted the dedication of *La Fanciulla del West*.

Far more important than all this, however, was his introduction to the woman who became the best friend and truest love of his life, by his old friend Paulo Tosti (later Sir Paolo). Tosti had settled in London in 1880 as singing master to Queen Victoria's brood, and was the highly revered composer of such charming and very popular drawing-room ditties as 'Good-bye', 'Ideale', 'The Last Song' and 'La Serenata'.

The wife of the wealthy banker David Seligman, and one of Tosti's favourite former pupils, Sybil Seligman reportedly had a very fine contralto voice and was a passionate opera fan and Italiophile, paying frequent visits to Italy and keeping open house for Italian and other artists visiting their Georgian London home in South Street – Caruso, Adelina Patti, the Australian soprano Nellie Melba, Paderewski, Kreisler (who, with his similar moustache, was often mistaken for Puccini and once showered with hot kisses by a crowd of eager Roman signoras as a result) . . . It is no wonder that Puccini soon homed in on Sybil. She certainly looks ravishing in one unsigned sketch, perhaps from her late twenties, showing a sensitive smile with expressive Jewish eyes, delicate facial features and masses of dark chestnut hair gathered above her head. Slender-waisted (after bearing two sons), with an exquisite neck and shoulders, she demonstrated impeccable chic in her choice of elegant low-cut gowns, dazzling jewellery, matching hats and lacy parasols . . .

Thus it was that a communion of highly compatible and like-minded souls developed between this beautiful young lady and her revered idol, then 46. Initially, apparently, the communion was not confined to their souls. According to information given by Sybil's sister, Mrs Violet Schiff, to Mosco Carner, Sybil and Giacomo were passionate lovers before their blazing fire subsided into the embers of a deep platonic friendship. A rare achievement indeed. Several people noted a tender understanding between them when they were together. Puccini took to signing himself as 'Naughty Boy' or 'The Successor' (i.e. to Verdi) in his letters to her.

Sybil thus joined the string of compassionate platonic muses who were so crucial to their composer-devotees: Maria von Genzinger to Haydn; Clara Schumann and Elisabet von Herzogenberg to Brahms; Madame von Meck to Tchaikovsky; Lady Alice Stuart-Wortley to Elgar . . .

Sybil's role in Puccini's life was incalculable. Fortunately, her high-born tact and diplomacy ensured that even Elvira didn't regard her as a threat, except on one sole occasion in 1909 when he reported that 'Elvira has taken our friendship amiss.' This happened after he had sent Sybil a series of consoling letters in the wake of her severe family misfortunes, including that of a son, Esmond, who was developing incurable epilepsy. Sybil always sent Elvira presents – a handsome woollen stole, for example, flowers, a splendid cushion, tasteful trinkets – when Puccini had been to London. The two couples even holidayed together on the French Riviera and at the Puccinis' villa at Abetone. Sybil's presents to Puccini over the years included a fine walking stick, Turkish cigarettes, a casket for them, a set of green ties, socks, a pipe, recipes for new elixirs or cough medicines, and a picnic basket which he vowed would remain virginal until he had the chance to share its contents with her.

Puccini was enchanted by Sybil as by no other woman. She was forever balm to his vulnerable soul. Here he is writing with unreserved delight to her from Torre in November 1905 after returning from their first meetings in London:

> How I can remember everything – the sweetness of your character, the walks in the park, the melodiousness of your voice, and your radiant beauty.

She was the ready repository for all his Italianate woes. Here he is, for example, early in 1906 bewailing all the hassles before the première of *Butterfly* at the 'Met' in New York, especially the 'asinine, listless time-beating' of the conductor Arturo Vigna:

> rehearsals are going well but not too well, partly on account of the imbecility of the conductor, and partly on account of Butterfly's lack of souplesse . . . I'm so tired of this life; I've had to arrange the whole mise-en-scène – all the musical side of it – and my nerves are torn to shreds. How I long for a little calm. Believe me, our life is not to be envied – the texture of our nerves – or at any rate of mine – can no longer stand up to this drudgery, these anxieties and fatigues.

(His one consolation on this trip seems to have been the company of 'the most beautiful woman in the world', the superb soprano

Lina Cavalieri, with gossip of his infatuation for her spreading in spite of Elvira's presence. In later days he was to develop an even keener admiration for the young Moravian star Maria Jeritza, whose Tosca enthralled him above all others.)

And here he is, in January 1906, fretting as ever and unburdening himself over the search for his next libretto which was to be *Fanciulla*:

> I am so utterly depressed by this feverish and disheartening period of searching; not only I, but those who are near me, my publishers and many others, are losing heart.

One of his deepest and most eloquent outpourings of love and appreciation for Sybil came in April of that same year:

> I make the mistake of being too sensitive, and I suffer too when people don't understand me or misjudge me. Even my friends don't know what sort of man I am – it's a punishment that has been visited on me since the first day of my birth. It seems to me that you are the person who has come closest to understanding my nature – and you are so far away from me!! . . . I am sending you a little photograph to remember me by – a thousand affectionate thoughts for that exquisite and beautiful creature who is the *best friend* I have.

And so she continued to be. 'It gave me *immense* pleasure to see you again and to find you exactly the same as ever – young, beautiful, good – and so kind,' he wrote to her after a brief visit to London in 1911, on his way home from the première of *Fanciulla* in New York.

A very rare whiff of tension between them derived from Sybil's adulation of her 'god' Caruso, reportedly a rather shallow and showy man off-stage. While Puccini never failed to acknowledge the tenor's exceptional talent, he found him 'lazy' and 'too pleased with himself'. (Caruso suffered a severe crisis about two years later when his mistress of eleven years, the singer Lina Cavalieri, ran off with his young chauffeur.)

Sybil didn't just provide an ever-ready shoulder for her admirer to cry on. As his London 'scout', she gave him a great deal of practical and informed advice which, even when not taken up, was always worth having. Her responses, in stages during 1906, to his *cris-de-coeur* over the endless problem of finding suitable librettos included the following suggestions: *Anna Karenina*,

Kipling's novel *The Light that Failed* (then running in London as a stage production), Tennyson's *Enoch Arden*, Bulwer-Lytton's *The Last Days of Pompeii* and an unspecified story by Mérimée (the originator of *Carmen*). When these were rejected she came up with more suggestions (during a lightning visit he made to be with her in London in the autumn) one of which roused his enthusiasm though which he didn't in the end use: an unfinished play by Oscar Wilde, *A Florentine Tragedy*. He actually put Sybil to considerable trouble negotiating adaptation rights for it before finally abandoning the project.

He never stopped relying on her. 'Are you going on reading books for me?' he wrote to her after various European premières of *Fanciulla* in 1911. 'Do you know of any grotesque novel or story or play, full of humour and buffoonery? I have a desire to laugh and to make other people laugh.'

One of their most touching exchanges concerns a request he made to her, in the autumn of that same year, from Paris where he was dejectedly facing the prospect of a Madame Butterfly played by an unsuitable 'Madame Pomme de Terre' (Marguérite Carré). 'I see everything through dark coloured spectacles – I'm tired to death of everything, including opera,' he wrote to her before pleading with her to visit him. Failing that, would she send him a magic medicine to raise his spirits? 'Such a medicine must exist in London, and you, who know everything, will find it for me.' To his delight, Sybil promised to join him (and Elvira) in Paris, meanwhile sending him an elixir whose composition remains teasingly unknown. After her short visit he was again dejected:

> I'm not at all well – since the moment you left, I've had nothing but days of discouragement, filled with the usual unhappiness. All I ask is to be allowed to retire into my shell.

In 1907 she arranged to have a translation of Belasco's *The Girl of the Golden West* made for him. They discussed endlessly his plans based on it during a joint Seligman–Puccini holiday at the Puccinis' villa at Abetone that summer, and then corresponded at length during the typically fraught gestation of the opera. It was Sybil who actually suggested the polyglot title he used of *La Fanciulla del West*.

Not surprisingly he had constant need to unburden himself to her during the Doria scandal in successive letters:

I'm only telling you the truth when I say that I have lovingly fingered my revolver.

I only manage to sleep with veronal, and my face is mottled like a Winchester gun.

How can one keep one's brain clear for work and hope to find inspiration? It's impossible, impossible.

I'm still in a state of the greatest unhappiness . . . it's an appalling torment, and I am passing through the saddest time of my life! . . . it's enough to tell you that I don't want to live any longer – certainly not with her.

I can't work any more! I feel so sad and discouraged! My nights are horrible; I cry – and am in despair. Always I have before my eyes the vision of that poor victim . . .
Forgive me if I am always harping on the same subject.

Puccini never stopped dumping on her. If he wasn't doubting the intrinsic worth of a project, then he was questioning his own ability. His letters to her, particularly the despairing ones, are perhaps the single most revealing primary sources for his creative and personal problems, as these further snippets suggest.

Always searching, and finding nothing. I'm in despair – I think it's the most difficult thing in the world.

I am as usual in mid-ocean without any hope of ever reaching harbour.

Turandot languishes. I haven't got the second Act as I want it yet, and I don't feel myself capable any more of composing music . . .

I'm at work on the duet [in *Turandot*]; it's difficult but I shall end by doing it and I hope it will give satisfaction – and then the opera (if God wills) will be finished.

I've done no more work; *Turandot* lies here, unfinished. But I *will* finish it – only just at present I've no desire to work.

He fumed to her over 'the pig of a Toscanini . . . this *God*' who dared to dislike his *Tabarro*: 'When an orchestral conductor thinks poorly of the operas he has to conduct, he can't interpret them properly.' (Unlike Wagner, Strauss, Verdi, Mascagni and Leoncavallo, Puccini was never tempted to conduct.)

Inevitably, he confided to her his rather pathetic plans already mentioned for turning back his biological clock: 'My dear, my life is my own and means the whole world to me – so why not? I have such a fear and such horror of old age!'

Their final meeting was in November 1924 when Sybil, herself by then crippled by sciatica, visited him at the Ledoux clinic in Brussels. She fought back her tears as Puccini rested his head gratefully on a specially soft pillow she had brought him. She grieved deeply over his sudden death and never really recovered from the shock of it. She died in 1935 after succumbing to drug dependency in an effort to relieve the combined blows of both Puccini's death and that of her long-ailing son Esmond. Stanley Jackson describes how she had kept hundreds of letters from Puccini, each bundle tied with a ribbon and stored in chronological order from his first acceptance of an invitation to dinner in 1904 to the last one lamenting his lack of progress with *Turandot*. She also owned copies of each of his scores, all signed bar one. In the flyleaf of *Turandot*, Puccini had written 'To Sybil, our faithful friend, from Elvira and Tonio'.

About a year and a half before his death, Puccini wrote this poem, taken here from Greenfeld's book. Although it is no literary masterpiece, as an expression of his melancholia it is all the more effective for its restraint:

> I am friendless
> And alone
> Even music
> Saddens me.
> When death comes
> To call me
> I shall find happy repose
> Oh, how hard is my life!
> Yet to many I seem happy.
> But my successes?
> They pass . . . and little remains.
> They are ephemeral things:
> Life runs on
> Towards the abyss.
> The young take pleasure in life,

Yet who heeds it all?
Youth is soon past
And the eye scans eternity.

No Peace for the Wicked

As this book goes to press, Puccini's philandering is causing him
a very harassed afterlife which he may nonetheless be chuckling
over. We learn from Nicholas Farrell, writing in the *Spectator* of
31 January 1998, that Puccini's body is to be exhumed for DNA
testing from its final resting place in a small chapel at his beloved
Villa Puccini (now a Puccini museum) at Torre del Lago. His
wife Elvira and the couple's only son Antonio were buried alongside him.

In a nutshell, it now transpires that two people who claim
to be Puccini's illegitimate grandchildren are making competing
claims to the residue of his estate. Although it has been squan-
dered by Antonio's childless wife Rita and her ne'er-do-well
homosexual brother and his butler, the estate still comprises two
flats in Monte Carlo, three villas in Italy including Villa Puccini,
many millions of pounds and some music which will remain in
copyright for a long time to come.

The current battle is between Signora Simonetta Giurumello
and Signor Giacomo Giovannoni, the present caretaker of the
museum at Torre. Signora Giurumello has already, in the days
before DNA testing, made a successful claim to the estate on the
grounds that she is the illegitimate offspring of a liaison between
Antonio Puccini and her mother. In the opposite corner of the
ring, Signor Giacomo Giovannoni swears that his father, Claudio,
the previous caretaker at the museum, was the issue of a liaison
between Puccini and the wife of one of his servants. On looks,
Giacomo Giovannoni seems to have it made, since with his
authentic Puccini moustache, he looks uncommonly like the
maestro, as did his father, the aforementioned Claudio. Giacomo
Giovannoni says he is only pressing his claim, and offering
himself for DNA examination, because Signora Giurumello has
sacked him from his caretaking job at the museum for regaling
visitors with copious details of the composer's love life. In a visit
to the Villa Puccini, Nicholas Farrell did indeed hear the caretaker
waxing lyrically: 'Puccini loved women *molto* and women loved

him *moltissimo*. This great feeling for women he put into his music.'

Bibliography

The author has used information and quotations from the following books with the kind permission, where indicated, of the publishers or author's agents. Both the author and publisher welcome any information regarding errors or omissions so that the necessary corrections can be made in subsequent editions.

Paul Holmes, *Brahms*, Omnibus Press 1987

Malcolm Macdonald, *Brahms*, Dent Master Musicians, The Orion Publishing Group 1990. By permission of Oxford University Press

Robert Schauffler, *The Unknown Brahms*, Greenwood Press, Westport, Connecticut 1933

Ruth Jordan, *Nocturne: A Life of Chopin*, Constable London 1978

Jeffrey Kallberg, *Chopin at the Boundaries*, Harvard University Press 1996

André Maurois, translated by Gerard Hopkins, *Lélia, The Life of George Sand*

Ates Orga, *Chopin*, Omnibus Press 1983

Jim Samson, *Chopin*, Oxford University Press (Master Musicians) 1996. By permission of Oxford University Press

Jeremy Siepmann, *Chopin: The Reluctant Romantic*, Victor Gollancz 1995

G.I.C. de Courcy, *Paganini the Genoese*, Norman: University of Oklahoma Press 1957. By permission of Oklahoma University Press

Alan Kendall, *Paganini: A Biography*, Chappell and Company/Elm Tree Books, London 1982

John Sugden, *Paganini*, Omnibus Press 1986

Mosco Carner, *Puccini*, Duckworth 1974

Howard Greenfeld, *Puccini*, Putnam Berkley Group 1975

Stanley Jackson, *Monsieur Butterfly: The Story of Puccini*, W.H. Allen & Co 1974

Joan Chissell, *Clara Schumann: A Dedicated Spirit*, A Crescendo Book, Taplinger Publishing Company, New York 1983

Nancy B. Reich, *Clara Schumann: The Artist and the Woman*, Cornell University Press 1985. By permission of Cornell University Press

Arthur Jacobs, *Arthur Sullivan: A Victorian Musician*, Second Edition, Scolar Press 1992

David Brown, Tchaikovsky: A Biographical and Critical Study, Victor Gollancz Ltd. 1992

Edward Garden, *Tchaikovsky*, J.M. Dent, 1993

Anthony Holden, *Tchaikovsky*, Bantam Press (a division of Transworld Publishers Ltd) 1995. Copyright © Anthony Holden 1995. Reproduced by permission of the author c/o Rogers, Coleridge and White Ltd, 20 Powis Mews, London W11 1JN

Alexander Poznansky, *Tchaikovsky's Last Days*, Oxford University Press 1996. By permission of Oxford University Press

Alexander Poznansky, *Tchaikovsky: The Quest for the Inner Man*, Schirmer (part of the Macmillan Group, USA) 1991; Lime Tree Books (Reed International Books Ltd, UK) 1991. By permission of Schirmer and Lime Tree Books